AND

75
NIA

UKRAINE

7
IA

GARIA

80

ISRAEL
PALESTINE

EGYPT

SUDAN

SOUTH
SUDAN

UGANDA

DA

GO

IA

MBABWE
IA

RUSSIA

KAZAKHSTAN

UZBEKISTAN

81
GEORGIA

TURKEY

TURKMENISTAN

SYRIA

IRAQ

82

83 JORDAN

SAUDI
ARABIA

UAE

OMAN

ERITREA
87

YEMEN

ETHIOPIA

SOMALIA

89
KENYA

88

TANZANIA

MALAWI

90

MOZAMBIQUE

MADAGASCAR
91

KYRGYZSTAN

94

95

IRAN

AFGHANISTAN

PAKISTAN

97

NEPAL

INDIA

98

SRI
LANKA

MONGOLIA

109

107

CHINA

99

100

BHUTAN

96

BANGLADESH

MYANMAR

108

LAOS

103

THAILAND

VIETNAM

102

CAMBODIA

101

MALAYSIA

SINGAPORE

BRUNEI

NORTH
KOREA

110

SOUTH
KOREA

111

JAPAN

112

106

105

TAIWAN

104

PHILIPPINES

INDONESIA

PAPUA
NEW GUINEA

TIMOR-
LESTE

114

SOLOMON
ISLANDS

VANUATU

FIJI

AUSTRALIA

118

119

113

115

116

117

124

122

120

125

123

NEW
ZEALAND

121

DK EYEWITNESS

HIKE

HIKE

ADVENTURES ON FOOT

CONTENTS

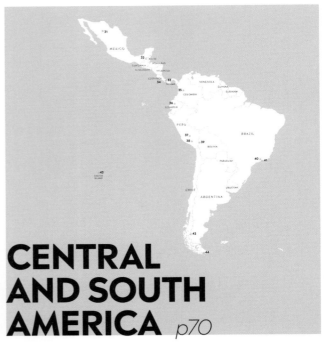

CENTRAL AND SOUTH AMERICA *p70*

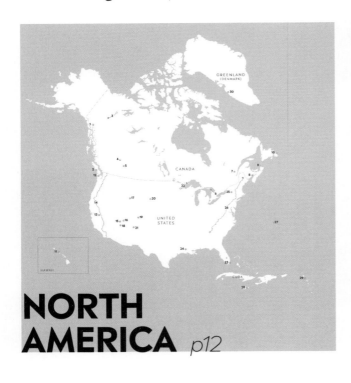

NORTH AMERICA *p12*

EUROPE *p94*

4

Previous page A winter
hike on Cat Bells in
England's Lake District

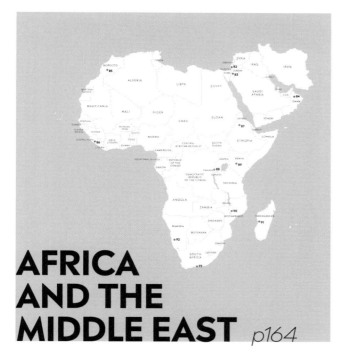

AFRICA
AND THE
MIDDLE EAST *p164*

AUSTRALASIA *p222*

ASIA *p186*

Walking along a
fallen tree trunk on
a hike through an
old-growth rainforest

INTRODUCTION

It's hard to beat the satisfaction of traveling on foot—settling into a steady rhythm, surrounded by incredible scenery, with the freedom to stop wherever takes your fancy. It's an endlessly rewarding—and sustainable—activity, and one that we feel deserves to be celebrated. That's why we've created *Hike*.

Compiled by a team of eager outdoor enthusiasts, this book features a curated selection of 125 spectacular walking trails across the globe. Some have been chosen for their stunning scenery, some for their intriguing history, and others for the inspiring challenge they present. (We say: dream big.) No route has been deemed too short or long, with the options ranging from a half-day boardwalk stroll around a spongy bog in Estonia to an epic six-month trek along the Appalachian Trail in the US. They're not all knee-pounding mountain ascents either, and you'll find plenty of coastal ambles and forest walks alongside more classic backpacking routes.

The book is handily organized by continent, so wherever you're headed you can discover the best trails. Even better, each route has practical information to help you plan your trip, including distance, total ascent, and duration, plus tips on the best sights to see and snacks to devour along the way. We've also included elevation profiles, so you can—quite literally—see the ups and downs of the route. What more do you need to head off on a hiking adventure?

PRACTICAL INFORMATION KEY

 DISTANCE  TOTAL ASCENT DURATION

PREPARING FOR YOUR HIKE

Advance planning is essential before undertaking any hike—especially if you're setting off on a multiday trip or heading out into the backcountry alone. To help you prepare, we've put together some handy pointers on organizing your next hiking adventure.

Planning a Hike

To plan a successful hiking trip, you'll need to consider everything from where you want to go and what kind of distance you'll be able to cover right down to the specific details surrounding equipment, accommodations, and transportation. Most people walk at an average pace of around 3 miles (5 km) an hour, but remember that this will vary depending on the terrain, the conditions, and your level of fitness. Make sure to check the weather in advance (and pack accordingly), and figure out where you'll be sleeping—consider local laws on wild camping and the need to book in advance—and how you'll get to and from the trail's start and end points.

LEAVE NO TRACE
Responsible Hiking

Walking is one of the most sustainable forms of travel. Protect the environment by keeping to the trail, choosing camping spots carefully, and using a stove rather than a fire. Always take your trash with you. Remember not to remove anything from the wild or disturb any animals.

Clothing

The key word here is "layers"—you want to be able to easily add clothes when you're cold and remove them when you're hot. The standard setup is a base layer; a midlayer such as a fleece or, in colder conditions, an insulated puffer jacket; and an outer-layer jacket. Choose a base layer that's made from merino wool, polyester, or nylon, as these materials wick moisture away from your body; avoid cotton as it gets damp quickly and stays damp. Jackets need to be waterproof and breathable—look for something made from GORE-TEX or similar. On your bottom half, choose

Camping surrounded by stunning mountain views on a hike through the Himalayas in Nepal

comfortable pants made from a quick-dry fabric (zip-off styles are especially versatile), and consider packing a pair of (lightweight) waterproof pants.

The kind of hiking boot you choose depends on how long you'll be walking and how much you'll be carrying with you. Key factors include weight, breathability, durability, and water resistance, as well as the level of support you need—we recommend getting fitted by an expert.

Navigation

A paper map and compass are the most reliable and simplest forms of finding your way and won't leave you relying on technology. Still, do bring a smartphone and a GPS watch (if you have one), ensure the relevant apps work offline, and don't forget a power bank—gadgets can quickly eat their way through batteries.

Trail Etiquette

You should stick to marked paths, both to protect the surrounding environment and to avoid any potential legal issues with trespassing. Keep noise to a minimum, avoid bright clothing and equipment where

One of the signposts along the Moselsteig, which winds through western Germany

possible, and make sure to close gates behind you when walking through fields containing livestock. On narrow trails, the usual custom is for hikers walking downhill to give way to hikers coming up.

Further Reading

The following websites are all excellent resources for planning a hike.

alltrails.com
A global database of more than 200,000 trails, with maps and reviews uploaded by hikers.

komoot.com
Intuitive route planner, with plenty of destination-led inspiration.

outdoorgearlab.com
In-depth comparisons of hiking, backpacking, and camping gear.

lnt.org
Pointers for enjoying the outdoors responsibly.

earth.google.com
Useful for viewing interactive 3-D maps and researching unfamiliar terrain.

To download GPX routes for the hikes featured in this book, plus access to other great hiking content, head to dk.com/hike

HIKING SAFETY

Safe Hiking Practice

Don't overestimate distance and make sure you've finished hiking before it gets too dark.

Carry enough water, food, and snacks for the duration of your hike, plus extras in reserve.

Always take a cell phone with you—but don't rely on it for navigation.

Always tell someone where you're going and how long you'll be gone.

In remote areas, try to avoid hiking alone.

ESSENTIAL GEAR

Ready to hit the trail but not quite sure what to take with you? Here's a handy overview of the items you need to consider when heading into the great outdoors. Many of them are essential pieces of gear that you should always have with you, wherever you go; others will be useful if you're hiking across certain types of terrain or in a specific part of the world.

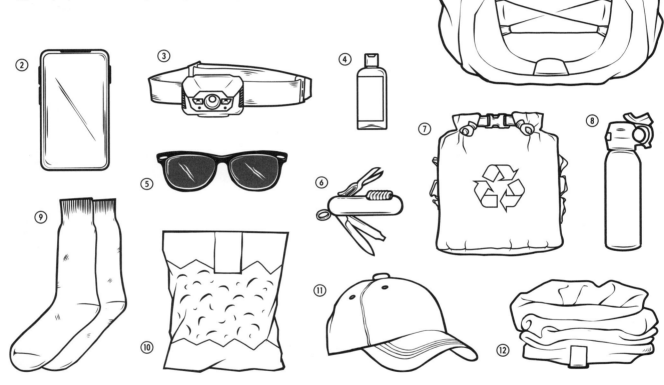

① Backpack Comfort is key: look for padded shoulder straps, a contoured back, and a hip belt.

② Cell phone Serves as a handy backup GPS and is useful for emergency calls (where signal is available).

③ Headlamp Consider beam length and lumens (brightness); 10 lumens is fine around the campsite, but you'll need 300 lumens for navigating at night.

④ Hand sanitizer Useful for cleaning hands when water is scarce.

⑤ Sunglasses Get a light-weight pair with polarized lenses and good UV protection (4 is the best).

⑥ Swiss Army knife This classic multitool comes with all sorts of handy gadgets, such as scissors, a mini saw, and a bottle opener.

⑦ Reusable trash bag As well as being a handy litter store, this can double up as a backpack liner or a storage bag.

⑧ Bear spray Essential in parts of the US. Keep it on you at all times in a readily accessible place.

⑨ Spare socks Look after your feet by regularly changing your socks. Wool is good; merino wool is even better.

⑩ Trail mix The perfect snack for a nutritious on-the-move energy boost.

⑪ Sun hat Guards against sunstroke and can provide warmth if it turns chilly.

⑫ Neck warmer There are few things this small and lightweight that can serve so many purposes—including as a scarf, face mask, bandanna, or headband.

13 Waterproof jacket The best waterproof jackets are also windproof and breathable. Make sure the hood doesn't restrict visibility.

14 Walking poles These protect your knees and help maintain balance in slippery conditions and on hills.

15 Compass Ever reliable for navigating, with no concerns about loss of battery or signal.

16 Water bottle As well as helping to reduce your carbon footprint, a good reusable bottle can be used for other things, such as a cooking aid.

17 Bug spray There are several types of bug sprays, including DEET, Picaridin, and natural insect repellents.

18 Tissues Very lightweight and useful in many situations. Opt for biodegradable ones.

19 GPS watch Uses include tracking your route, location, and elevation and monitoring heart rate and calories burned. Even tells the time, too.

20 Gloves Keep your hands warm and dry and can prevent blisters if you're using walking poles over a long distance.

21 First-aid kit A must-have for any kind of hiking. It should contain a variety of solutions to help treat cuts, wounds, bites, injuries, burns, and blisters.

22 Binoculars The larger the objective lens, the better the resolution (choose 32mm for a compact option). For magnification (how close objects appear compared to the naked eye), 10X is good for all-round viewing.

23 Map Use a topographic map at a scale that suits the distance and terrain being covered.

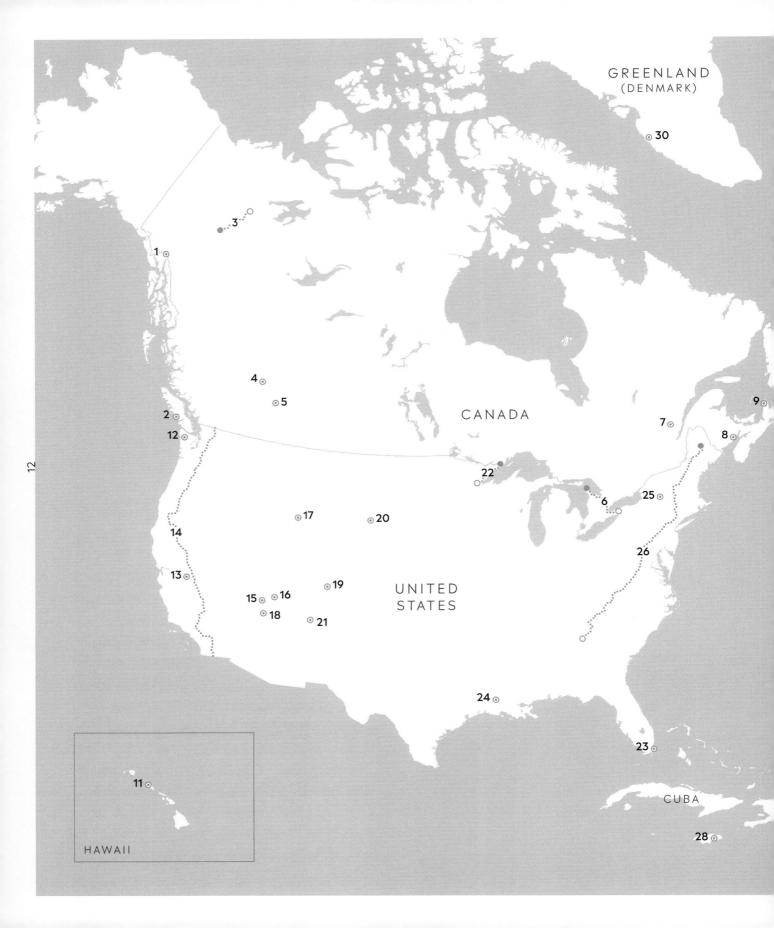

GREENLAND
(DENMARK)

CANADA

UNITED
STATES

HAWAII

CUBA

1
2
3
4
5
6
7
8
9
11
12
13
14
15
16
17
18
19
20
21
22
23
24
25
26
28
30

NORTH AMERICA

The string of glittering glacial lakes, including **CRATER LAKE**, you'll pass on the Canadian leg of the trail tempt a fortifying dip.

CANADA

Bennett

Lindeman

If the weather is on your side, the views from **CHILKOOT PASS** are ample reward for hiking up the 45-degree Golden Staircase.

Happy Camp

Crater Lake

Chilkoot Pass

Sheep Camp

Canyon City Campground

0 ·········· km ·········· 10
0 ·········· miles ·········· 10

UNITED STATES

Finnegan's Point

A short loop trail at **CANYON CITY CAMPGROUND** explores the once-bustling transportation hub of the same name, chock-full of rusting artifacts.

Dyea

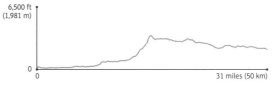

1

Chilkoot Trail

DYEA, ALASKA, US, TO BENNETT, CANADA

Trace the route of 19th-century prospectors on a famous multiday trail linking the Alaskan coast with the goldfields of British Columbia.

When gold was discovered near the Klondike River in Canada's Yukon Territory in 1896, it sparked one of the most frantic gold rushes in history. From 1897 to 1898, a quiet trade route to the interior, used by First Nations peoples for centuries, was transformed into a thronging highway as 100,000 stampeders made the journey from Dyea, Alaska, to Bennett, British Columbia.

Gold fever soon faded here, but in the 1960s, the miners' 31-mile (50 km) Chilkoot Trail transformed once again into a recreational route. Today, it takes eager hikers through lush coastal rainforest and up to the exposed alpine scenery of the formidable Chilkoot Pass, straddling the US–Canada border, before ascending through boreal forests—home to bears and moose—that fringe serene alpine lakes. As you wander along the trail, expect to see plenty of artifacts left behind by gold seekers, from old boot soles to a gas engine winch—each and every one a window into this area's once golden prospecting past.

⊖ 31 MILES (50 KM)

⊗ 5,384 FT (1,641 M)

◷ 3–5 DAYS (ONE-WAY)

ELEVATION PROFILE

6,500 ft (1,981 m)

0

0   31 miles (50 km)

14

Linked to the trail by a damp and misty rainforest path, the driftwood-dotted **SCHOONER COVE** has many starfish living among its shoreline rocks.

Divided into two 0.6-mile (1 km) long paths on either side of the ʔapsčiik ƛaši, the **RAINFOREST TRAIL** is an excellent detour that loops through dense ferns and moss-covered woodland.

Trail end

Radar Hill

Esowista

Green Point Campground

Rainforest Trail

Wickaninnish Bay

Schooner Cove

VANCOUVER ISLAND

Kwisitis Visitor Centre

Florencia Bay

Trailhead

The **KWISITIS VISITOR CENTRE** includes an interesting exhibition on the area's Indigenous peoples, whose fortunes were often bound as much to the sea as to the land.

0 ······ km ······ 4
0 ······ miles ······ 4

2
ʔapsčiik ƛašii

PACIFIC RIM NATIONAL PARK RESERVE, VANCOUVER ISLAND, CANADA

This paved trail provides an insight into First Nations culture while traveling through the verdant forests of the Pacific Rim National Park Reserve.

17 MILES (28 KM)

541 FT (165 M)

1–2 DAYS (ONE-WAY)

Pronounced "ups-cheek ta-shee," ʔapsčiik ƛašii translates as "Going in the right direction on the path." This doesn't just mean literally—although the well-signed and smooth asphalt path makes walking here a breeze—it also relates to being mindful of the life-filled environment around you.

This philosophical point was ensured by building this route in close collaboration with the Yuułuʔiłʔatḥ and Tla-o-qui-aht First Nations communities. All along the trail, Indigenous place names on the signposts help convey respect for their stewardship of this land, and the presence of totem poles and other carvings further reinforces this sense of connection; here, information boards provide cultural insights as well as details on the area's rich flora and fauna. The path itself weaves past fine-sand beaches and through verdant tracts of old-growth rainforest before eventually arriving in the village of Tofino. From here, it's up to you to decide which direction to take next.

ELEVATION PROFILE

300 ft (91 m)

0

0   17 miles (28 km)

Schooner Cove, one of many scenic beaches found along the trail

With a population of around 800, **NORMAN WELLS**, an oil-drilling hub, is the only real community near the trail. You'll need to fly here, then organize a crossing of the adjacent Mackenzie River.

Norman Wells

Mackenzie River

Carcajou River

CANADA

The infamous **TWITYA RIVER** crossing is one of the hardest on the route and can be dangerous. Experience with deep-river crossings is vital.

Devil's Pass

One of the most idyllic stretches of the route follows the **GODLIN RIVER** as it passes between mountain ridges. Here, you can enjoy tranquil riverside camping on sandy beaches.

Twitya River

Godlin River

Godlin Lakes

Ekwi River

Caribou Pass

The raw peaks of the Mackenzie Mountains form the boundary between the Yukon and the Northwest Territories at the western end of the trail. They're served by an aircraft landing strip at **MACMILLAN PASS**.

Macmillan Pass

0 ·········· km ·········· 30
0 ·········· miles ·········· 30

3

Canol Heritage Trail

NORMAN WELLS TO MACMILLAN PASS, CANADA

Arguably Canada's premier wilderness trail, the remote and difficult Canol Heritage Trail follows the subarctic route of an abandoned 1940s pipeline project, which provides quirky industrial archaeology along the way.

234 MILES (377 KM)

25,187 FT (7,677 M)

18 DAYS (ONE-WAY)

Striking a path through the remote Mackenzie Mountains, the Canol Heritage Trail follows the route taken by a World War II oil pipeline. Known as the Canol Project, the line was completed in 1944 but then quickly abandoned only three years later (partly due to maintenance difficulties). Today, evidence of this disused pipeline—including ruined structures like Quonset huts and rusting 1940s army trucks and tractors—is dotted along the trail, which otherwise passes through near-pristine landscapes.

The scale of the land is vast here and the variety of habitats immense. These range from subarctic forests to treeless tundra and include nine spectacular mountain passes, several above the tree line. Snow-dusted mountain peaks bookend pristine waterfalls and awe-inspiring canyons. Wildlife is abundant, too—moose, beavers, caribou, bears, and Dall's sheep call this region home, and

it's no exaggeration to say that many have never set eyes on a human before.

Much of the route follows the old Canol Road, a track unmaintained since the 1970s after its usefulness to loggers and miners ended. This helps make much of the hiking and navigation straightforward, though the route is far from being flat and always easy to follow. Add to this unpredictable and fast-changing weather, swamps, voracious insects, the ever-present threat of grizzly bears and dozens of treacherous river crossings, and it's soon clear that this remote hike is suitable only for experienced, well-equipped hikers. Near-self-reliance is required since help is, at best, a satellite phone call and a flight away.

Logistics and costs add more hurdles; there's the need to organize a flight to a remote airstrip; a boat for trail access; and airdrops of supplies along the way. All of this means only around a dozen hikers complete the entire trail every year; it's far easier to just fly in and out to do a portion of it. For those who do manage to complete it, though, a real sense of accomplishment awaits for having conquered perhaps North America's toughest hiking trail.

ELEVATION PROFILE

6,500 ft
(1,981 m)

0

0   234 miles (377 km)

4

Tonquin Valley Trail

JASPER NATIONAL PARK, CANADA

Phenomenal hikes of all lengths are plentiful in this part of the Canadian Rockies—but for its combination of awe-inspiring scenery and ready accessibility, the Tonquin Valley Trail is hard to beat.

Jasper National Park would figure on any short list of the best places to hike in Canada, and the Tonquin Valley Trail is one of its best. Here, barren peaks draped by ghostly fingers of ice form an endlessly majestic backdrop to the series of wild-flower meadows and mountain lakes that the Tonquin Valley Trail connects. Thanks to careful control by the national park, wildlife thrives, with grazing caribou a common sight, along with moose, elk, deer, and marmots. It's also bear country, with both grizzly and black bears enjoying the berries on the lower mountain slopes.

Yes, the Tonquin Valley Trail has a reputation for mud, mosquitoes, and low nighttime temperatures, but these just help enhance the backcountry experience. And in any case, these hardships are minor; the trail is generally easy to walk and navigate, plus it lies only a 20-minute drive from Jasper, the likable mountain town and National Park hub, where a hearty meal and cozy bed are easily found to celebrate your finish.

⊖ 30 MILES (48 KM)

◯ 4,413 FT (1,345 M)

◯ 3 DAYS (ONE-WAY)

EDITH CAVELL MEADOWS is worth a detour for the views you'll get of Angel Glacier and the craggy Mount Edith Cavell.

ELEVATION PROFILE

10,000 ft
(3,048 m)

0

0   30 miles (48 km)

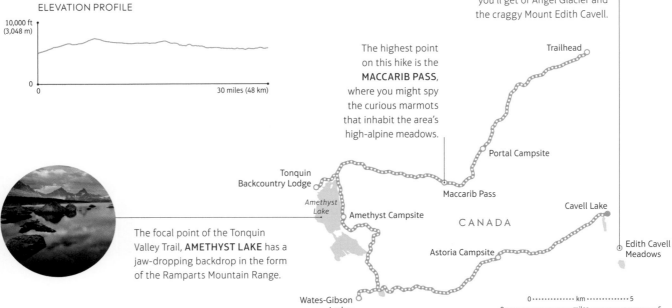

The highest point on this hike is the **MACCARIB PASS**, where you might spy the curious marmots that inhabit the area's high-alpine meadows.

Trailhead

Portal Campsite

Tonquin Backcountry Lodge

Amethyst Lake

Maccarib Pass

Cavell Lake

Amethyst Campsite

CANADA

The focal point of the Tonquin Valley Trail, **AMETHYST LAKE** has a jaw-dropping backdrop in the form of the Ramparts Mountain Range.

Astoria Campsite

Edith Cavell Meadows

Wates-Gibson Lodge

0 ·········· km ·········· 5
0 ·········· miles ·········· 5

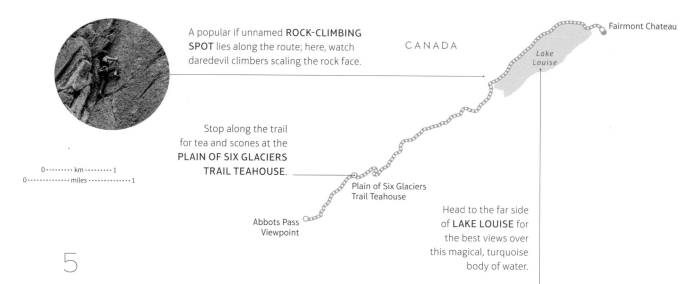

A popular if unnamed **ROCK-CLIMBING SPOT** lies along the route; here, watch daredevil climbers scaling the rock face.

CANADA

Fairmont Chateau

Lake Louise

Stop along the trail for tea and scones at the **PLAIN OF SIX GLACIERS TRAIL TEAHOUSE.**

Plain of Six Glaciers Trail Teahouse

Abbots Pass Viewpoint

Head to the far side of **LAKE LOUISE** for the best views over this magical, turquoise body of water.

0 ·········· km ········· 1
0 ·········· miles ········· 1

5

Plain of Six Glaciers Trail

BANFF NATIONAL PARK, CANADA

Explore the greatest hits of Banff National Park in a memory-making one-day hike into an amphitheater of aquamarine lakes and photogenic glaciers.

9 MILES (14 KM)

1,932 FT (589 M)

1 DAY (RETURN)

Crack. Crack. The sound coming along the trail ahead isn't the noise of hiker boots scuffing over rocks and boulders. No, it's the sound of ever-shifting glaciers, whose crackles and snaps are carried on the wind across bright-blue Lake Louise.

Hikers have long been drawn to this bewitching trail, which takes in the ice tongues, point-perfect peaks, and polar-blue lakes of Canada's most visited national park, Banff. To begin, the out-and-back pathway lulls you into a false sense of achievement—it starts with an easy lakeside stroll—but then it shifts up a gear, ascending past a postcard log-cabin teahouse into a natural mountain amphitheater brimming with undiluted drama. The glacier views are immense, as is the panorama over a landscape of ice and rock from the Abbots Pass Viewpoint.

ELEVATION PROFILE

10,000 ft
(3,048 m)

3,000 ft
(914 m)

0   9 miles (14 km)

Tip

This is a heavily trafficked trail—go at sunrise or as late in the afternoon as the light allows.

NORTH AMERICA

6

Bruce Trail

QUEENSTON TO TOBERMORY, CANADA

*Easily accessible from much of the Greater Toronto Area,
this epic trail follows the Niagara Escarpment, winding its way
along many of Southern Ontario's prettiest trails and byways.*

536 MILES (863 KM)   42,175 FT (12,855 M)   30 DAYS (ONE-WAY)

20

The Niagara Escarpment—a huge geological fault caused by different rates of erosion—famously takes its most dramatic form at the thunderous Niagara Falls. But it actually extends far beyond this famous landmark, forming a crescent that stretches around Lake Michigan in the west to Lake Ontario in the east. The portion that cuts across Southern Ontario is particularly celebrated, providing a haven for nature and an eye-catching contrast to the otherwise rolling landscape. It's this section that forms the backbone of Canada's longest, oldest, and probably busiest marked trail.

The Bruce Trail dates back to the 1960s, when a group of Ontario naturalists were inspired to create a trail that would follow the escarpment from the US border near Niagara Falls to the tip of the Bruce Peninsula, a huge spit of land that almost bisects inky blue Lake Huron. In a painstaking process that involved knitting together thousands of volunteer hours with a medley of conservation authorities,

private landowners, local municipalities, and the Government of Ontario, they eventually forged a route made up of nine contiguous sections. Its subsequent success caught the attention of UNESCO, who designated the escarpment corridor a UNESCO World Biosphere Reserve in 1990.

There's a wonderful range of habitats along the trail, including mature hardwood forests and wetland ecosystems, all of which sustain healthy wildlife populations (including more than 300 species of birds). Yet the trail is by no means all wilderness, and there are significant portions through built-up areas and along minor roads. ▶

ELEVATION PROFILE

3,000 ft
(914 m)

0

0   536 miles (863 km)

Pausing for a rest on the Bruce Trail,
surrounded by fall trees

Tobermory

Bruce Peninsula
National Park

*Lake
Huron*

The lakeside town of **TOBERMORY** provides a hub for boat trips to Flowerpot Island, with its extraordinary rock pillars.

Wiarton

Bayview
Escarpment

Owen Sound

BLUE MOUNTAIN, Ontario's largest ski resort, provides thrills in winter and chairlift rides to views over Collingwood and Georgian Bay in summer.

Blue Mountain

Devil's Glen Provincial Park

CANADA

Mono Cliffs Provincial Park

The otherworldly red-rock formations of the **CHELTENHAM BADLANDS** stand out in an area where escarpment rock formations have largely been smothered by newer glacial deposits.

Caledon Hills

Cheltenham
Badlands

Crawford Lake
Conservation Area

*Lake
Ontario*

Blacks Woods

Hamilton

The biggest city on the Bruce, **HAMILTON** is best known for its many waterfalls—it has over 100 within its city limits, more than any other city in the world.

Grimsby

Queenston

Niagara Falls

Short Hills
Provincial Park

0 ·········· km ·········· 40
0 ·········· miles ·········· 40

The unmissable **NIAGARA FALLS** are the world's largest waterfalls by volume and are awesome in every sense of the word.

REFUEL

Local Produce

Fresh produce grown in the shadow of the Bruce Trail is a real treat for hungry hikers, especially along the southernmost portion of the route. Pick up fresh fruit from one of the many orchards or reward yourself after a long day's hike with a glass of wine—there are a glut of wineries here (*visitniagaracanada.com/taste/wineries*).

This variety is part of the joy of the journey. Each of the trail's nine sections has its own name, as well as a distinct character and landscape. Working south to north, it begins with the Niagara Section, which starts 3 miles (5 km) north of Niagara Falls and winds its way west through fruit orchards and the many vineyards of one of Canada's premier winery regions. The spring blossoms and fall colors are remarkable along the trail's early stages, which, conversely, are the busiest and most urbanized. But the proximity to civilization doesn't detract from the route's charms—especially when it involves passing through places like the city of Hamilton, which is home to more than 100 waterfalls, and the Crawford Lake Conservation Area, where archaeological evidence has inspired the reconstruction of a 15th-century Iroquoian village.

Things begin to take a wilder turn, however, on the Caledon Hills Section, where the Niagara Escarpment has largely been buried by glacial moraine deposits. The rolling landscape here makes the trail particularly challenging, with many stiff climbs and steep descents, though it also gives rise to some of the Bruce's most striking scenery. The otherworldly red-rock terrain of the Cheltenham Badlands—a series of ridged shale formations that once formed the bed of a tropical sea—look like they could be the film location for a movie set on Mars.

Eventually, the escarpment reasserts itself in the high bluffs of Blue Mountain, a popular skiing spot in winter; the slopes here offer expansive views over the town of Collingwood and Lake Huron's Georgian Bay. It's one of the first proper glimpses you'll get of the bay, but it certainly won't be the last—after traversing the gloriously dense woodlands of the mud-prone Beaver Valley, the trail winds back to the shore of Lake Huron and follows it for most of the Sydenham Section. Look out on this stretch for the subtle transition from southern temperate broad-leaf forests to northern boreal needle forests, which occurs around the picturesque Inglis Falls.

The town of Wiarton marks the start of the final Peninsula Section, which opens with a climb up a dramatic spiral staircase. This section is the most challenging and remote part of the Bruce Trail (requiring experience and thorough preparation), but arguably the best has been saved for last—the final 19 miles (30 km) lead across leafy cliffs with unmatched views across the deep blue waters of Georgian Bay.

IN FOCUS
The Trail's Namesake

The Bruce Peninsula, and so the Bruce Trail, is named after James Bruce, the 1847 Governor General of Canada. He is more famously remembered, however, for his role in the Second Opium War with China in 1860, when as special commissioner for Britain, he ordered the sacking of Beijing's Summer Palace, destroying countless priceless treasures.

Hiking along the edge of the shimmering Georgian Bay on the Bruce Peninsula

Home to Canada's deepest canyon east of the Rockies, the **HAUTES-GORGES-DE-LA-RIVIÈRE-MALBAIE NATIONAL PARK** is a perfect spot for a kayak excursion.

Chalet Le Coyote

0 ········· km ········· 5
0 ········· miles ········· 5

Hautes-Gorges-de-la-Rivière-Malbaie National Park

Chalet L'Épervier

Chalet Geai Bleu

Refuge Bihoreau

Take a detour to the **LA NOYÉE LOOKOUT** for broad views of the St. Lawrence River.

CANADA

La Noyée Lookout

Mont Grands-Fonds

Marmotte Hut

The modest ski resort of **MONT GRANDS-FONDS** has some of the best views around from its 2,411 ft (735 m) high belvedere.

L'Ecureil Hut

Saint-Urbain

Sentier des Sommets

Connecting five summits, the **SENTIER DES SOMMETS** trail network overlaps the western end of the Charlevoix Traverse and shouldn't be missed for its classic forest and lake views.

MAKE IT SHORTER
Stop Halfway

The lure of the Hautes-Gorges-de-la-Rivière-Malbaie National Park is such that many opt to do only the first half of the Charlevoix Traverse, then stop to spend a couple of days in the park. A vehicle delivery service offered by La Traversée de Charlevoix (*traverseedecharlevoix.qc.ca*) has your car and camping gear waiting for you in the park.

7

Charlevoix Traverse

SAINT-URBAIN TO MONT GRANDS-FONDS, CANADA

Based on a network of backcountry huts, the Charlevoix Traverse offers the chance to explore near-pristine forests and lakes, dizzying rock walls, and impressive canyons with blissfully minimal luggage.

The Charlevoix Crater was created around 450 million years ago, when an asteroid is thought to have collided with the earth. Much of the crater's 34 mile (54 km) diameter now lies beneath the St. Lawrence River, but a good portion remains on land, forming a huge, relatively flat doorstep between the river and the Laurentian Mountains to the west. It is the loosely defined edges of this crater that guide the Charlevoix Traverse, as it journeys through the heart of the UNESCO-designated Charlevoix Biosphere Reserve.

Tracing a route between two national parks—Grands-Jardins and Hautes-Gorges-de-la-Rivière-Malbaie—the trail is backdropped by vast gray granite rock faces that loom over otherwise gentle lakeland scenery. Birch, ash, maple, and elm trees (which blaze with color in the fall) give way to forests of firs as you venture north into the mountains, where the upper reaches of the Malbaie River scythe a path through giant canyons—forming a natural outdoor playground for canoeists.

Traversing Hautes-Gorges-de-la-Rivière-Malbaie National Park

By largely using a combination of logging and forest roads—the sort that give running shoes the edge over hiking boots—the Charlevoix Traverse is easily one of Canada's most accessible long-distance treks. You don't even need to lug a weighty backpack: there are no campgrounds along the way, with hikers instead sharing a series of sociable cabins ready-stocked with basic mattresses and equipped kitchens. Further services provided by La Traversée de Charlevoix, the nonprofit organization that manages the huts, mean that food and even luggage drops are possible, too. All of this adds up to a rare chance to get deep into the backcountry with only the barest of life's essentials strapped to your grateful shoulders.

ELEVATION PROFILE

3,000 ft (914 m)

0

0   57 miles (91 km)

25

8
Fundy Footpath

POINTE WOLFE TO BIG SALMON RIVER, CANADA

Explore a rare surviving tract of coastal wilderness, around an extraordinary bay fringed with jagged cliffs, steep ravines, amazing tides, and surreal coastal landforms.

Standing on the New Brunswick shore of the Bay of Fundy, looking across to Nova Scotia, your attention is naturally drawn to the bay's tidal drama and odd-shaped ocher-red sandstone formations. It can come as a surprise, then, to learn that these same craggy headlands are also foothills of the Appalachian Mountains.

This fact soon becomes apparent to any hiker embarking on the Fundy Footpath, however. Barely anything is flat along this steep, rooty, and rocky trail, as it negotiates jagged cliffs, outcrops, deep river valleys and potentially treacherous tidal rivers, bays, and mudflats.

The upside to this challenging terrain? Being surrounded by an ancient Acadian Forest that has remained intact for some 10,000 years. Its delicate ecosystem nurtures a rich undergrowth of ferns and lichens, which benefit from the otherworldly fog that often engulfs the footpath in the morning. This atmospheric experience is rounded off with some of the most glorious (albeit primitive) campsites imaginable, at scenic spots beside beaches and streams. They often enjoy complete solitude, too, making the ache in your legs a small price to pay for the serene immersion in nature.

A footbridge through a wooded gorge in Fundy National Park

ELEVATION PROFILE

1,500 ft (457 m)

0

0   30 miles (48 km)

⊖ 30 MILES (48 KM)

◯ 8,409 FT (2,563 M)

◷ 5 DAYS (ONE-WAY)

26

Pointe Wolfe

Fundy National Park

Goose River Campsite

Goose Creek Campsite

CANADA

At low tide, the coastline of **FUNDY NATIONAL PARK** reveals an array of intriguing creatures that inhabit the ocean floor.

The **BIG SALMON RIVER** Suspension Bridge marks the southwestern end of the Fundy Footpath but also leads to a far easier scenic trail that heads up the river valley.

Little Salmon River

Cradle Brook Campsite

Seely Beach Campsite

Big Salmon River

A protected area, **LITTLE SALMON RIVER** contains several remarkable falls as well as the Eye of the Needle—an extraordinary ravine that's well worth a side trip.

0 ·········· km ·········· 5
0 ················ miles ················ 5

The **OBSERVATION DECK** perched upon the side of French Mountain is very exposed—brace yourself for regularly occurring strong winds.

About 1 mile (2 km) in, you arrive at a **FORK**; where you head right to complete the full loop trail.

Observation deck

Fork in route

Wildlife such as moose, bears, and coyotes can be spotted foraging in the densely forested areas that make up Cape Breton's **BOREAL LAND REGION**.

0 ········ km ········ 0.5
0 ········ miles ·········· 0.5

Trailhead

9

Skyline Trail

CAPE BRETON HIGHLANDS NATIONAL PARK, CANADA

The most lauded trail in Cape Breton Highlands National Park, the Skyline Trail traverses corridors of lush wilderness to a jaw-dropping coastal viewpoint.

Setting off from the **TRAILHEAD**, keep an eye out for birds of prey overhead—they can be seen throughout the hike.

6 MILES (9 KM)

669 FT (204 M)

0.5 DAYS (LOOP)

Unyielding beauty greets you at every turn in Nova Scotia's coastal highlands, where breathtaking views stretch end-lessly out to a shimmering blue-sea horizon. Tucked away in that landscape is the Skyline Trail, an easy to moderate loop following established paths and occasionally rocky terrain through the boreal forests and grassy highlands of Cape Breton Highlands National Park. No two experiences on this trail are the same—sometimes coastal winds and dense fog await, while at other times you'll spy spreads of colorful wildflowers. The ultimate highlight, though, is always the observation deck, found on the side of French Mountain, that overlooks the Gulf of St. Lawrence. Here, what you've sacrificed in the way of solitude on the heavily trafficked path is made up for by the spectacular clifftop panorama overlooking the great Atlantic.

MAKE IT SHORTER
Out-and-Back

For a slightly shorter 5-mile (8 km) out-and-back variation of the Skyline Trail, turn left at the first fork rather than right, and follow the path all the way to the main viewpoint overlooking the Gulf of St. Lawrence. Traversing established, level terrain, this route is an easy-breezy option for hikers of all ages, ability, and skills.

ELEVATION PROFILE

3,000 ft (914 m)

0

0   6 miles (9 km)

27

Tip

The East Coast Trail Association (*eastcoast trail.com*) has a lot of useful advice on how to tackle the trail.

10

East Coast Trail

CAPPAHAYDEN TO TOPSAIL, CANADA

This stunning trail on the easternmost edge of North America carves a peaceful path through a varied coastal wilderness.

209 MILES (336 KM)

31,640 FT (9,644 M)

12–16 DAYS (ONE-WAY)

Tracing a line around the eastern shore of Newfoundland and Labrador's Avalon Peninsula, the East Coast Trail leads into the wilderness. The first 16 miles (25 km) of the route opened in 1994, and since then more than 185 miles (300 km) have been added by tireless trail volunteers—many of whom live in the remote coastal communities here.

This dramatic coastal hike is much more challenging than a walk on the beach. The path is usually narrow, is rarely even or easygoing, and is not very well maintained in parts. Accommodation usually takes the form of rough-and-ready camping: there are six official first-come-first-serve campsites with primitive latrines, or you can wild camp in some areas (providing you seek permission from property owners first). But the reward for overcoming these obstacles is the fact that, on the path, you'll often have large swathes of wilderness all to yourself.

From the trail's southern terminus in Cappahayden to its end point at Topsail Beach, you'll pass a huge variety of landscapes: boreal forest, heathlands, and marshes, as well as sandy beaches and towering cliffs that loom over the Atlantic. Interspersed throughout are occasional glimpses of civilization—the odd historic lighthouse or abandoned settlement—but it's nature that dominates, with waterfalls, fjords, and rock formations like Hares Ears providing the main points of interest. ▶

ELEVATION PROFILE

1,500 ft
(457 m)

0

0   209 miles (336 km)

Trekking past Gull Island on the
East Coast Trail in Newfoundland

Cape St Francis
Lighthouse

Pouch Cove

Bauline

Torbay
Point

Torbay

Portugal Cove

St John's

Freshwater
Bay

TOPSAIL BEACH, at the trail's
end, is a popular spot for whale
watching; the peak season is
from mid-July to mid-August.

Topsail

The **FRESHWATER BAY NATURE
RESERVE** is a haven for black-legged
kittiwakes, black guillemots, herring
gulls, and great black-backed gulls.

Cape
Spear

Petty Harbour

N E W F O U N D L A N D

At **CAPE SPEAR**, you'll be
standing on the easternmost
point in North America.

The Spout

The East Coast Trail
Association removed a
3-ton rock from **THE SPOUT**
in 1995, creating an eye-
catching natural fountain
and new tourist favorite.

Bay Bulls

**LOWER LA MANCHE
POND**, sandwiched
between two waterfalls,
is a lovely swimming hole.

Lower La Manche pond

Cape Broyle

Admirals Cove

Ferryland
Lighthouse

Berry Head Arch

REFUEL

Ice Cream Treat

Make up for lost calories at the Tinkers
Ice Cream Shop in Petty Harbour, which
specializes in giant milkshakes topped
with cookies, whipped cream, cheese-
cake, and ice-cream cones. Or how about
an ice cream taco instead? Flavors
include "campfire" and "paradise."

The **BERRY HEAD ARCH** on
the Spurwink Island Path is
so big it can support the
weight of the evergreens
growing on top.

Cappahayden

NORTH AMERICA

Left Cape Spear Lighthouse, standing at the easternmost point in North America

One particularly noticeable feature that recurs along the trail is the stunted, twisted evergreen trees known as tuckamore, kept small—no more than waist-high—and shriveled by the force of the elements on the rough and brutal coastline. (Elsewhere, tuckamore is also known as knieholz, or "knee timber.") You'll see plenty of wild berry bushes lining the path, too; when they're in season, you can enjoy a feast of

> In early summer, icebergs drift off the coast, as they calve off from the frozen Arctic.

cloudberries (also known as bake apples, which dissolve instantly on the tongue), wild strawberries, blueberries, and raspberries as you walk along.

The proximity to the ocean is part and parcel of the trail's appeal. In early summer, icebergs drift off the coast, as they calve off from the frozen Arctic and float all the way down on ocean currents. And throughout the year, there's the chance to glimpse humpback whales—as well as finback and minke whales during their summer migration. Closer to shore, you might spot seals and otters, not to mention thousands of seabirds such as puffins and petrels. (As for landlubber animals, hikers may encounter moose, caribou, foxes, or coyotes.) But the ocean is also one of the more challenging aspects of the hike. In bad weather, you're often exposed to bracing wind and rain

coming off the water, and if walking in low-lying areas, are vulnerable to sudden surges and large waves.

If the weather does take a turn for the worse, you can always hunker down in one of the small communities found along the way, whether that's rugged Admirals Cove or colorful St. John's, known for its brightly painted wooden houses. In these little outposts of civilization, some home to just a dozen or so residents, you'll find food, drink, and a friendly welcome from locals. And if you get tired of camping, there are plenty of cozy guesthouses, B&Bs, and hotels where you can soak your tired limbs in a hot bath and enjoy a night under crisp sheets.

Such moments of homely comfort are only fleeting, however. After all, the real pull of this route is its wild coastal beauty—and it can be found only back out on the trail.

Center Waterside cabins on the Sugarloaf Path section of the trail

Right Looking out from Tors Cove, a village in Newfoundland

MAKE IT SHORTER
The Spout

If you have only a day to spend on the East Coast Trail, make it the 14-mile (23 km) round-trip hike out to The Spout, a spewing, wave-powered geyser. In addition to the geyser, the route features towering sea cliffs, sea stacks, a historic lighthouse, and five waterfalls.

NORTH AMERICA

11

Ka'ena Point Trail

KA'ENA POINT STATE PARK, O'AHU, HAWAII, US

An easy walk to a dramatic promontory dividing O'ahu's northern and leeward coastlines rewards hikers with wave-whipped ocean vistas and spectacular wildlife sightings.

5 MILES (8 KM) · 131 FT (40 M) · 0.5 DAYS (RETURN)

A world apart from Waikīkī's urban glitz, Ka'ena Point—one of the Hawaiian Islands' last intact dune complexes—stands guard on O'ahu's westernmost point. This far-flung promontory had deep cultural significance to the early Hawaiians, who believed this place was a departure point to the afterlife. As you scan the sea from the point's jagged edge, it's easy to understand why this place is sacred: you'll savor sweeping views of ivory-sand beaches to the north and south, the vast Pacific reaching out to the horizon and relentless waves crashing on sharp black rocks.

Two trails lead to Ka'ena Point—one from Yokahama Bay on the west (leeward) side and the other along the Mokuleia coastline on the North Shore. The former is the most scenic of the pair, sticking close to the rugged shoreline for its entire length. The trail, a former dirt road and railroad bed, has almost no elevation gain, but the shrubby terrain offers scant relief

from the sun—Ka'ena means "the heat" in the Hawaiian language.

The area is a haven for birds and marine life, and as you stroll along the shoreline, you'll have an ideal vantage point to spot spinner dolphins hunting for food near the breaking waves or humpback whales blowing spouts out at sea. If you're walking here during spring and summer, keep an eye out on the pearly sand beaches for Hawaiian green sea turtles and the verdant tendrils of the white- and blue-flowered pā'ū o hi'iaka, as well as basking Hawaiian monk seals.

Exploring the rocky shoreline of Ka'ena Point, lapped by the azure Pacific Ocean

ELEVATION PROFILE

300 ft
(91 m)

0

0   5 miles (8 km)

The only sign of civilization at **KA'ENA POINT** is a tall metal pole topped with a solar-powered navigational light.

Pass through the pedestrian gates into the **KA'ENA POINT NATURAL AREA RESERVE**. It's a haven for protected birdlife, thanks to a fence that keeps out feral cats, mongooses, dogs, and other predators.

Ka'ena Point

Ka'ena Point Natural Area Reserve gate

0 ·············· km ·············· 1
0 ·············· miles ·············· 1

O'AHU

33

IN FOCUS

Sacred Spot

Steeped in legend and myth, Ka'ena Point is where early Hawaiians believed their souls would depart the mortal world and leap into the afterlife to join the souls of their ancestors. It's also where the demi-god Maui cast his hook, hoping to snag the neighboring island of Kaua'i and drag it through the ocean to join with O'ahu.

Halfway to Ka'ena Point, you'll pass two **BLOWHOLES** in the volcanic rocks. You'll hear them "breathing" before they spout.

Blowholes

Keawaula Beach

The trail begins at one of O'ahu's most secluded stretches of sand, **KEAWAULA BEACH**. Framed by the Waianae Mountain Range, it's blissfully untouched by development.

Eventually, you'll arrive at the end of the point. Here, pause to take in the beauty of this revered spot as countless birds swoop through the air above you—wedge-tailed shearwaters, red-footed boobys, white-tailed tropicbirds, and the massive Iwa or great frigate bird are just a few of the species you might spot. Look out, in particular, for the Laysan albatross, which nests on the dunes' grasses—these amazing flyers can soar over the ocean for more than a week at a time without stopping.

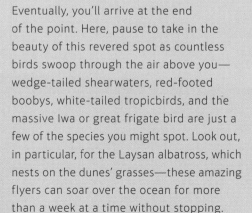

The **HIGH HOH BRIDGE** marks the boundary between temperate rainforest and the subalpine landscape of the Olympic Range.

The campsite at the rustic **OLYMPUS GUARD STATION**, 9 miles (15 km) from the trailhead, is an ideal spot to pitch your tent.

The 60-step, cable-supported **JEMROD GULLY LADDER** provides sturdy footing and handholds, helping you to ascend a near-vertical slope.

12

Hoh River Trail

OLYMPIC NATIONAL PARK, WASHINGTON, US

Admire moss-covered conifers and myriad shades of green in the enchanting Hoh Rainforest, then hike through a glacier-carved valley to the icy shoulder of Mount Olympus.

From its source on Mount Olympus, the milky-colored, glacier-fed Hoh River tumbles 50 miles (80 km) downstream to the Pacific Ocean. This trail tracks the waterway's journey in reverse, starting in the heart of a dripping rainforest—a wet-and-wild place where mosses and ferns flourish on every surface—before meandering upstream through the subalpine meadows and old-growth forest of the glacier-carved Hoh River Valley.

The path offers an extremely gentle grade for the first 12.5 miles (20 km), followed by an abrupt 3,000 ft (914 m) ascent to Glacier Meadows. It's a leg-trembling climb in more ways than one—you'll have to cross a deep, sheer-sided gorge on the High Hoh Bridge and make a wet and slippery ladder ascent. But it's worth it when you reach the top, to be greeted by an otherworldly panorama of blue-tinged crevasses cascading down Mount Olympus.

⊖ 35 MILES (56 KM)

◇ 6,483 FT (1,976 M)

🕐 3 DAYS (RETURN)

Tip

Be prepared for rain. Pack head-to-toe water-proof gear, gaiters, dry sacks, a bag cover, and a tent ground cloth.

ELEVATION PROFILE

6,500 ft (1,981 m)

0

0   35 miles (56 km)

34

Pausing for a rest next to the Hoh River in Olympic National Park

13

Wapama and Rancheria Falls Trail

YOSEMITE NATIONAL PARK, CALIFORNIA, US

Blaze a trail less traveled in California's most popular national park. On this invigorating there-and-back day hike, you'll survey great granite domes and be gently showered by waterfall spray.

12 MILES (20 KM)

2,280 FT (695 M)

1 DAY (RETURN)

Most hikers flock to the well-touristed southern half of Yosemite National Park, but where's the fun in following the crowd? The Wapama and Rancheria Falls Trail takes you far away from the hordes and into the Hetch Hetchy region, a quiet corner in the park's northwest.

This is the least-frequented part of Yosemite, though its monumental geology and multitiered waterfalls are no less impressive than the park's more famous sights. Admire the granite dome of Hetch Hetchy, looming above the glassy reservoir formed by the O'Shaughnessy Dam; listen to the roar of Wapama Falls as it cascades over craggy boulders, christening the air with fine mist; and watch Rancheria Falls, making its splashy 984 ft (300 m) journey along a jagged canyon. You'll be baffled— but glad—that more people haven't caught on.

ELEVATION PROFILE

6,500 ft
(1,981 m)

3,000 ft
(914 m)

0   12 miles (20 km)

RANCHERIA FALLS is a prime picnic spot, where cooling mist hangs in the air and scruffy pine trees frame the foaming cascade.

UNITED STATES

Wapama Falls

Rancheria Falls

Hetch Hetchy Reservoir

WAPAMA FALLS is the largest waterfall in northern Hetch Hetchy Valley and it tumbles year-round.

O'Shaughnessy Dam

Completed in 1923, the **O'SHAUGHNESSY DAM** provides most of San Francisco's drinking water.

0 ·········· km ·········· 1
0 ·········· miles ·········· 1

NORTH AMERICA

Hiking through the
snowy Sierra Nevada
mountains in California

14

Pacific Crest Trail

CAMPO, CALIFORNIA, US, TO E.C. MANNING PROVINCIAL PARK, CANADA

This epic trail forges an unbroken footpath from the Mexican border to Canada, traveling through the most sublime mountain scenery of the western US.

2,555 MILES (4,122 KM)   384,229 FT (117,113 M)   5–6 MONTHS (ONE-WAY)

The jewel in the crown of America's long-distance hiking trails, the Pacific Crest Trail (PCT) follows the pinnacles of the Cascade and Sierra Nevada ranges through some of the most spectacular landscapes in California, Oregon, and Washington.

It's a journey of superlatives and extremes. The PCT crosses barren deserts and tunnels through dense forest canopies, skirts the edge of sapphire lakes and tumbling waterfalls, and traverses the shoulders of conical volcanic peaks and glaciated granite spires. One day you'll hike in the company of spiny barrel cacti in scorching desert heat, and a few days later you'll post-hole through thigh-high snow above 10,000 ft (3,000 m). ▶

ELEVATION PROFILE

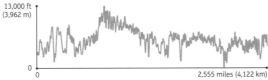

13,000 ft
(3,962 m)

0

0   2,555 miles (4,122 km)

CANADA

E C Manning Provincial Park

North Cascades
National Park

Stehekin

A charming village in the
North Cascades that's
accessible only by plane, by
boat, or on foot, **STEHEKIN**
is the last town you'll see on
your PCT journey.

Glacier Peak Wilderness

Alpine Lakes Wilderness

Snoqualmie Pass

Mount Rainier National Park

Goat Rocks Wilderness

Mount Adams Wilderness

Panther Creek
Bridge of the Gods

Mount Hood Wilderness

Mount Jefferson

BRIDGE OF THE GODS,
a steel-truss cantilever
bridge over the Columbia
River Gorge, marks the
boundary between
Oregon and Washington.

Mount Washington
Wilderness

MOUNT JEFFERSON,
mantled by five sizable
glaciers, has vast subalpine
meadows that explode with
summer wildflowers.

You've never seen water quite as
blue as **CRATER LAKE**, America's
deepest lake at 1,943 ft (592 m). The
lake has no inlet streams—its water
comes only from precipitation.

Crater Lake

Sky Lakes Wilderness

UNITED
STATES

Marble Mountain Wilderness

Burney Falls   Hat Creek Rim

Lassen Volcanic
National Park

**LASSEN VOLCANIC NATIONAL
PARK** is famed for its volcano that
erupted in 1914, but it's also home
to conifer forests, crystal-clear lakes,
and out-of-this-world geothermal
features like steaming sulfur vents
and boiling thermal pools.

Tahoe
National Forest

Yosemite National Park

Ansel Adams Wilderness

Kings Canyon
National Park

Muir Pass

Forester Pass

Mount Whitney

Sequoia
National Park

Kennedy Meadows
General Store

Muir Pass is crowned by
MUIR HUT, a granite
shelter that honors the
conservationist John Muir.
Built by the Sierra Club in
1930, it's the only human-
made structure on top of a
Sierra Nevada pass.

The PCT doesn't touch the 14,505 ft
(4,421 m) summit of **MOUNT
WHITNEY**, but it comes close
enough to necessitate a side trip.
The summit is the highest point
in the contiguous United States.

San Bernardino Mountains

Mount San Jacinto State Park

Campo

MEXICO

0 ·········· km ·········· 200
0 ········· miles ········· 200

State Specials

Each state offers a variety of stops for a dose of comfort food. Call at the Kennedy Meadows General Store *(kennedymeadowsgeneralstore.com)* for hamburgers in California, chow down on salmon chowder at Cascade Locks Ale House *(cascadelocksalehouse.com)* in Oregon, and hit up Stehekin Pastry Company *(stehekinpastry.com)* for cinnamon rolls in Washington.

Completing the trail on a thru-hike in one year requires starting in April or May and finishing by September or October. You'll need to cover an average of 16 to 18 miles (26 to 29 km) daily to allow for the vagaries of weather and your body's need for rest days. Physical strength is critical but so are wilderness smarts and mental toughness. You'll need strong logistics skills to figure out detailed plans for resupply and food drops at remote outposts. You'll also need mental fortitude to withstand hunger and thirst when your best-laid plans don't work out. But if you aren't easily daunted, you can tackle one of the world's greatest hiking challenges—and savor nonstop beauty along the way.

The vast majority of thru-hikers walk the PCT in a northbound direction because it allows for the best weather and trail conditions at the route's widely varying elevations. Northbound hikers start in the small town of Campo near California's border with Mexico. The first 500 miles (805 km) often make or break your PCT dream—you'll face intense heat and sparse water sources in the arid Southern California desert, followed by challenging climbs and descents of some of Southern California's highest mountains. Yet they also inspire with their vast open spaces and remarkably varied terrain.

When you reach the Sierra Nevada's southern tip, you'll join an elite club of PCT hikers high-fiving at the Kennedy Meadows General Store as you refuel with hearty food, cold beer, and a hot shower. A rest break is imperative because in the next trail stretch, there's no easy way out— not a single road crosses the Sierra crest for 185 miles (298 km). This leg requires careful timing—start too early in summer, and trails may still be snow-covered and streams too swollen to safely cross. Amazingly, some of the Sierra's highest passes don't melt out until late July.

Challenges aside, this range offers unparalleled scenery in the form of austere alpine landscapes and dramatically glaciated geology. The PCT ascends up and over a dozen knee-pounding passes, including six that are higher than 11,000 ft (3,350 m): Donahue, Muir, Mather, Pinchot, Glen, and Forester. ▶

Climbing up from Echo Lakes along the Pacific Crest Trail in California

> The biggest highlight is reaching Crater Lake, where an ancient, massive caldera hems in sparkling blue waters. Many thru-hikers opt for the alternative Rim Trail here to get the most eye candy.

Muir Pass is set in a stark landscape of glacial rock and icy blue lakes, while Donahue Pass leads from the Ansel Adams Wilderness—home to some of the Sierra's most photographed destinations, including Banner Peak and Garnet Lake—into the famed Yosemite National Park. Higher and more arduous than them both is Forester Pass, a glacially sculpted landscape often covered in ice and snow—once you've made it up and over, you'll have conquered the highest point along the PCT.

The grades mellow somewhat along the western rim of the Lake Tahoe basin and into the gentler terrain of the Northern Sierra. But the respite is short-lived as you make your way toward the Cascade Range. Gaining access to the Cascades requires trekking through the Hat Creek Rim, a notoriously hot and dry section—this desertlike landscape is almost completely devoid of natural water sources, so make sure you're carrying enough fluid.

The PCT is nothing, however, if not a trail of contrasts, and it soon plunges into the lush green fir groves of Northern California. Here lies the spectacular Burney Falls, where groundwater emerges from springs and pours over a volcanic cliff in shimmering glory. From this point, your trail miles will pass quickly in the lake-dotted Marble Mountain Wilderness, and before you know it, you'll be crossing the border into Oregon.

Southern Oregon appears dry and arid at the start, but the grades are at least much gentler than in California. The section through the Sky Lake Wilderness offers views of the Cascade Range's highest peaks, but the biggest highlight is reaching Crater Lake, where an ancient, massive caldera hems in sparkling blue waters. Many thru-hikers opt for the alternative Rim Trail here to get the most eye candy on this stretch.

Burney Falls, one of the most beautiful cascades in California

One of the meadows in
Goat Rocks Wilderness,
dotted with an array
of colorful blooms

dense ferns, as well as the Goat Rocks Wilderness, a land of rugged peaks and vast valleys filled with pristine lakes and flower-strewn meadows. Here, if the weather cooperates, you can take an optional route above "Old Snowy," an extinct volcano.

Just when you think the views can't get any better, the trail leads you to a glaciated landscape dotted with alpine lakes and lush, green hillsides, all framed by 14,411 ft (4,392 m) Mount Rainier, the king of the Cascades. And if that wasn't enough, the trail then climbs into the Alpine Lakes Wilderness, a vast expanse of jagged peaks, followed by the even more spectacular Glacier Peak Wilderness, an area home to giant conifers and multiple glaciers and snowfields.

For your final leg, you'll tunnel through North Cascades National Park, one of the wettest sections of the PCT. But the rain won't bother you one bit—after all, you have only 80 miles (129 km) remaining before you reach E.C. Manning Provincial Park, just over the Canadian border, and PCT glory.

Pushing northward through Oregon, one of North America's largest volcanoes dominates the horizon. You've made it to Mount Hood (11,250 ft/3,429 m), where skiers and snowboarders ply the slopes year-round. For a trail break, check in to the 1937 Timberline Lodge on Mount Hood's slopes and take a zero day—zero miles added to your tally, but you get to sleep in a comfy and warm bed.

Just before the border with Washington comes a remarkably long descent to the Columbia River crossing at the Bridge of the Gods, the PCT's lowest-elevation point. As you rise back up into the "Evergreen State," your PCT victory is creeping ever closer, and the last 512 miles (824 km) of terrain are nothing short of spectacular. There's a brief foray into temperate rain-forest at Panther Creek, amid the silent awe of massive old-growth trees and

MAKE IT SHORTER
John Muir Trail

One of the PCT's most scenic sections overlaps with 165 miles (266 km) of the famous John Muir Trail (JMT) in California's High Sierra. Hike the JMT section for an epic journey along the Sierra's spine, climbing up and over high-elevation mountain passes through a granite wonderland of glacially sculpted peaks and lake-filled basins.

Peer down into **MYSTERY CANYON**, where you might spy people canyoning in the depths.

Mystery Canyon

0 ·········· km ·········· 0.5
0 ·········· miles ·········· 0.5

East Mesa Trailhead

UNITED STATES

The final section of the outbound journey follows the **OBSERVATION POINT TRAIL**, where you'll be joined by a steady stream of fellow hikers.

Observation Point Trail Junction

Observation Point

At an altitude of 6,507 ft (1,983 m), the views from **OBSERVATION POINT** are spectacular.

42

15

East Mesa Trail to Observation Point

ZION NATIONAL PARK, UTAH, US

Enjoy peace and quiet on a little-known hike across a bronzed plateau to a million-year-old panorama of the American West.

7 MILES (11 KM) 696 FT (212 M) 1 DAY (RETURN)

Observation Point, with its sublime views of horseshoe canyons and sharp big bends, is Zion National Park's bucket-list hike. Most trekkers approach it from the leg-burning East Rim Trailhead in the main canyon (11 miles/17 km), but this out-and-back alternative reveals a far quieter place of liminal beauty.

From the trailhead on the park's upper east plateau, the well-maintained path curves through scattered ponderosa pines, with peekaboo glimpses of the canyon rim and elemental rock formations offering teasers with every stride. Each step brings you closer to one of Utah's most beautiful vistas, which is eventually accessed by linking up with the heavily trafficked Observation Point Trail on the final stretch. Despite the throng of hikers here, the final panorama can't fail to stir your soul as you gawp at all the colored earths of the canyon and miles of layered rock that stretch to the horizon.

ELEVATION PROFILE

8,200 ft (2,499 m)

3,000 ft (914 m)

0

7 miles (11 km)

16

Fairyland Loop Trail

BRYCE CANYON NATIONAL PARK, UTAH, US

Roam a geological wonderland on this uncrowded loop trail through one of Utah's most celebrated national parks, encountering peachy sandstone spires, dramatically striped cliffs, and vivid orange deserts en route.

8 MILES (13 KM) · 1,696 FT (517 M) · 0.5 DAYS (LOOP)

Only on foot can you fully appreciate the beauty of Bryce Canyon's rose-pink rock formations, dwarfed by the scale of its yawning ocher canyons. And there's no better trail for this than the Fairyland Loop, which offers a strenuous but rewarding hike through the park's most memorable areas.

From Fairyland Point, you'll follow the canyon's edge down to the southern side of Boat Mesa, weaving between rocky labyrinths before ascending the southern flank of this hulking desert outcrop. Each vista is more magnificent than the last, with natural rock arches and top-heavy spires of sandstone urging regular photo ops along the meandering pathway.

Late afternoon sunshine in spring and fall illuminates these views with coppery light, but the Fairyland Loop Trail is arguably loveliest in winter—its drama becomes even more pronounced when the apricot-colored rocks are splashed with snow.

ELEVATION PROFILE

10,000 ft (3,048 m)

6,500 ft (1,981 m)

0 — 8 miles (13 km)

0 ·····km····· 0.5
0 ·····miles····· 0.5

UNITED STATES

Fairyland Point

Boat Mesa

Campbell Canyon

Chinese Wall

Tower Bridge

Sunrise Point

CAMPBELL CANYON is dotted with disintegrating hoodoos (curiously shaped rock spires); in the distance you'll see the listing silhouette of the Sinking Ship.

Mammoth hoodoo **TOWER BRIDGE** is off a short side-trail in Campbell Canyon. And yes, if you squint, it looks a little like London's famous bridge.

Over centuries, the series of hoodoos known as the **CHINESE WALL** has been eroded into a curiously even fin of rock—it's nicknamed for its passing resemblance to China's Great Wall.

Jackson Lake

Leigh Lake

Paintbrush Peak

Paintbrush Canyon

Leigh Lake Trailhead

Jenny Lake

Lake Solitude

At **LAKE SOLITUDE**, canyons and streams tumble into serene, reflective waters that mirror views of the mountains and skies above.

As you pass through **PAINTBRUSH CANYON**, keep your eyes peeled for grizzly and black bears, moose, and small wildlife species such as pikas and marmots.

Take in panoramic views of the Three Tetons—Grand, Middle, and South—at **HURRICANE PASS**, while also catching a bird's-eye view of the Schoolroom Glacier feeding into an aquamarine lake.

Hurricane Pass

UNITED STATES

Alaska Basin

Mount Meek Pass

Death Canyon Shelf

Fox Creek Pass

Marvel at the dramatic landscape of **DEATH CANYON SHELF**, a 3-mile (5 km) stretch of the trail set high above sprawling canyons.

Wade through meadows of wildflowers on your way to **MARION LAKE**, a top spot for camping, having lunch, or enjoying a lakeside stroll.

Marion Lake

○ Rendezvous Pass

0 ·········· km ·········· 5
0 ·········· miles ·········· 5

Phillips Pass

IN FOCUS
What's in a Name?

An ever-present focal point along the TCT is a group of mountains dubbed "The Three Tetons" (Middle, Grand, and South). The name originated in the late 1800s, when French trappers visiting the area nicknamed the peaks "Les Trois Tetons," or "The Three Breasts." The Indigenous Shoshone people, however, knew them as "Teewinot," meaning "Many Pinnacles."

Phillips Pass Trailhead

44

Teton Crest Trail

PHILLIPS PASS TRAILHEAD TO LEIGH LAKE
TRAILHEAD, WYOMING, US

If you're a mountain lover seeking hiking heaven in the high alpine zone, you'll find your perfect partner in the Teton Crest Trail.

40 MILES (65 KM)

9,012 FT (2,747 M)

4–5 DAYS (ONE-WAY)

Nestled among the dramatic peaks of the Teton Range, the Teton Crest Trail, or TCT, holds best-of-the-best status among seasoned backpackers. Its rugged landscape will push your body and mind as you navigate ultra-steep trails at elevations above 8,000 ft (2,435 m) for almost the entire journey.

There are several variations of this multiday hike, with both shortcuts and extensions that can help you meet your budget of time. The full 40-mile (65 km) route begins at the Phillips Pass Trailhead and ends at the Leigh Lake Trailhead in Grand Teton National Park. If you want to save some time, you can bypass the first 5 miles (8 km)—and 2,500 ft (762 m) of ascent—by starting at Rendezvous Pass, where you begin your trek with views of the valley floor.

From here, you're perfectly positioned to rub shoulders with soaring, sculpted mountain spires and stumble upon sprawling meadows and turquoise lakes, all while

towering high above expansive vistas of what feels like the whole of Wyoming. Steep upward and downward climbs take you from one awesome campsite to the next, through lush wilderness and to cold creek rivers that flow throughout the range. At rest, you're almost guaranteed to experience at least one immaculate sunrise or sunset, lighting the jewel-toned tundra with a honey-colored glow.

Summer and fall are prime time for this trail—when temperatures are favorable, wildflowers are at peak bloom, wildlife is most active, and forests are at full growth, providing a protective habitat for animals and interesting birdlife. While the hike doesn't require technical climbing equipment, it is without a doubt both difficult and demanding—not least when it comes to planning. Before you set off, you'll need to give careful consideration to timings, prebooking campsites, and negotiating backcountry challenges such as securing water resources, to ensure that you're not inadvertently left stranded.

Your feet will hurt, your muscles will burn, and you will put a substantial amount of mental effort into preparation. But it's a worthy exchange for the unforgettable scenic beauty you'll encounter while exploring the legendary Teton Range.

ELEVATION PROFILE

13,000 ft
(3,962 m)

3,000 ft
(914 m)

0   40 miles (65 km)

45

NORTH AMERICA

18
Rim-to-Rim

GRAND CANYON NATIONAL PARK, ARIZONA, US

Grueling yet astounding, the Rim-to-Rim leads through an erosional masterpiece named one of the Seven Natural Wonders of the World.

Rising in terraced layers and vivid hues above the Colorado River, the sculpted cliffs of the Grand Canyon form the earth's most dazzling scar. This trail takes you from one side of the chasm to the other, starting on the higher, more isolated North Rim. Descending into the canyon on the North Kaibab Trail, each curve of the path delivers heart-squeezing scenery as the world falls away at your feet. On the way, you pass through every ecosystem found between Canada and Mexico, as lush conifer forests drenched with wildflowers morph into a gaunt desert landscape of ancient dark rocks.

After crossing the Colorado on the silver bridge at the bottom, the path switches to the Bright Angel Trail. The dunes above the river here can be a bit of a slog, but from that point on, the canyon seems to fold in around you. Amid such vastness, it's easy to be overwhelmed by the intimacy of this trail, with its splashy creek, shade, and chorus of birdsong. Take a moment to soak it all in at the oasis of Indian Garden, where the Havasupai tribe farmed for centuries, before embarking on the final leg-burning stretch of switchbacks leading up to the top.

Pausing for a moment to enjoy expansive views of the Grand Canyon

⊖ 23 MILES (37 KM)

◯ 6,496 FT (1,980 M)

◷ 2–3 DAYS (ONE-WAY)

ELEVATION PROFILE

10,000 ft (3,048 m)

0

0   23 miles (37 km)

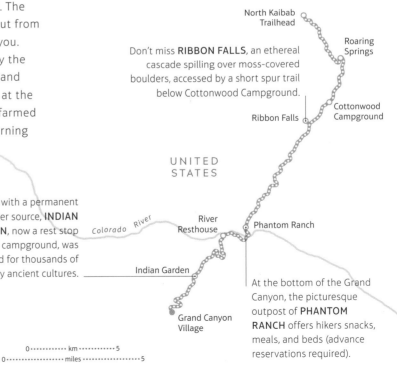

North Kaibab Trailhead

Roaring Springs

Don't miss **RIBBON FALLS**, an ethereal cascade spilling over moss-covered boulders, accessed by a short spur trail below Cottonwood Campground.

Ribbon Falls

Cottonwood Campground

UNITED STATES

Blessed with a permanent water source, **INDIAN GARDEN**, now a rest stop and campground, was farmed for thousands of years by ancient cultures.

Colorado River

River Resthouse

Phantom Ranch

Indian Garden

Grand Canyon Village

At the bottom of the Grand Canyon, the picturesque outpost of **PHANTOM RANCH** offers hikers snacks, meals, and beds (advance reservations required).

0 ·········· km ·········· 5
0 ·········· miles ·········· 5

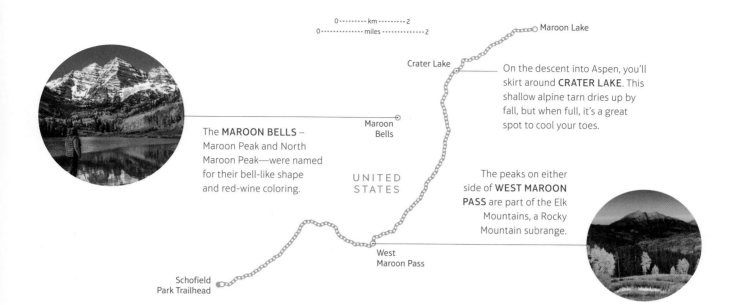

The **MAROON BELLS** – Maroon Peak and North Maroon Peak—were named for their bell-like shape and red-wine coloring.

On the descent into Aspen, you'll skirt around **CRATER LAKE**. This shallow alpine tarn dries up by fall, but when full, it's a great spot to cool your toes.

The peaks on either side of **WEST MAROON PASS** are part of the Elk Mountains, a Rocky Mountain subrange.

Maroon Lake

Crater Lake

Maroon Bells

UNITED STATES

West Maroon Pass

Schofield Park Trailhead

19

West Maroon Pass Trail

CRESTED BUTTE, COLORADO, US

Why drive when you can hike? This beautiful trail through the Elk Mountains links two ski towns at a fraction of the distance they are by road.

22 MILES (36 KM)

5,170 FT (1,576 M)

2 DAYS (RETURN)

It's a circuitous 103-mile (166 km) drive between Crested Butte and Aspen—but on foot, it's a fraction of the distance. Handily, the two ski towns are linked by this scenic trail, lined with snowy peaks, dense aspen groves, emerald meadows, cloud-speckled skies, and—if you time it right—a mesmerizing flower display. Every July, colorful blossoms sweep across the hillsides, turning the landscape into an Impressionist painting. Mother Nature's palette includes the vibrant red petals of Indian paintbrush, blue-and-white Colorado columbine, and deep purple larkspur.

Moderate for the most part, the route leads uphill from the trailhead near Crested Butte to West Maroon Pass, a 12,500 ft (3,810 m) high saddle offering 360-degree views of the Elk Mountains. A long, rocky descent deposits you on the shores of Maroon Lake, whose mirrorlike surface frames a postcard-perfect vista of Maroon and North Maroon peaks. At the trail's end, you can catch a bus into downtown Aspen, where you'll find an array of places to eat and sleep. As your head hits the pillow, you can rest soundly in the knowledge that you'll get to enjoy it all in reverse on the return to Crested Butte tomorrow.

ELEVATION PROFILE

13,000 ft (3,962 m)

6,500 ft (1,981 m)

0

22 miles (36 km)

An old stone tower, once used as a fire lookout tower, is located at the top of **BLACK ELK PEAK**.

0 ·········· km ·········· 1
0 ·········· miles ·········· 1

Black Elk Peak

There are spectacular views from the 6,920 ft (2,109 m) summit of **LITTLE DEVILS TOWER**.

UNITED STATES

Flashers View

Little Devils Tower

Sylvan Lake car park

Cathedral Spires

The **CATHEDRAL SPIRES** are also known as the Needles of the Black Hills of South Dakota.

20

Black Elk Peak Trail

PENNINGTON COUNTY, SOUTH DAKOTA, US

Easily accessible by a popular loop trail, Black Elk Peak is rich in both Native American history and beautiful scenery.

48

7 MILES (12 KM) | 1,624 FT (495 M) | 0.5 DAYS (LOOP)

At 7,244 ft (2,207 m), Black Elk Peak is the highest natural point in South Dakota. It has long been a sacred site for the Lakota people and is historically important as the place where Black Elk, after whom the mountain is named, had the vision that led him to become a famous spiritual leader and healer. Today, the peak is still the focus of an annual pilgrimage to welcome back the Wakinyan Oyate (Thunder Beings) at the spring equinox.

The rest of the year, an ascent of the mountain makes a popular half-day trek with hikers of all ages. There are more than a dozen configurations of routes to the top, but this pleasing loop via trails 4 and 9 is arguably the most scenic. It reaches its literal and figurative apex at the summit of the mountain, where you'll soon realize why the Lakota call Black Elk Peak Hiŋháŋ Káǧa, or "owl maker"—looking out over the landscape, the surrounding rock formations bear an uncanny resemblance to a parliament of owls.

ELEVATION PROFILE

10,000 ft (3,048 m)

3,000 ft (914 m)

0   7 miles (12 km)

IN FOCUS

Black Elk Speaks

The peak is named after the spiritual leader Black Elk, whose story is recounted in the 1932 book *Black Elk Speaks*, by John G. Neihardt. The book has been read widely but has come under scrutiny for inaccurately representing Lakota beliefs, culture, and traditions, either because of a misunderstanding or due to intentional exaggeration to make the book more appealing to white readers.

Pueblo Alto Loop Trail

CHACO CULTURE NATIONAL HISTORICAL PARK, NEW MEXICO, US

Explore the weathered heart of an ancient civilization that thrived for centuries in a remote desert canyon.

Pueblo Bonito, the largest great house in Chaco Culture National Historical Park

Why Chaco Canyon—with its hot summers, cold winters, and scant rainfall—became the cultural center of the Ancestral Puebloan people remains a mystery. What is known, however, is that between 850 and 1150 CE, the community here constructed massive stone buildings, rising four or five stories tall and containing hundreds of rooms. The Pueblo Alto Loop Trail offers an introduction to many of these "great houses," on a journey that proves both scenic and haunting.

The trail scrambles up a rocky slope behind Kin Kletso (Navajo for "yellow house") to the top of a sprawling mesa. Amid the panoramas of this high desert basin, designated overlooks peer down into the remnants of great houses on the valley floor. As the path loops around the edge of the plateau, look for fossilized shrimp burrows, carved basins, and the ghostly outline of ancient roads. You'll also enter two mesa-top ruins, Pueblo Alto and New Alto, walking through rooms where the ancients once stood. Gaze across the quiet expanse broken by canyons and cliffs and, for a few brief moments, feel the centuries fall away.

ELEVATION PROFILE

6,500 ft (1,981 m)

3,000 ft (914 m)

0 — 6 miles (9 km)

⊖ 6 MILES (9 KM)

◇ 623 FT (190 M)

🕐 0.5 DAYS (LOOP)

JACKSON STAIRWAY is a series of steps the Chacoan people cut into a near-vertical rock face, providing access from the canyon to the mesa.

Take a moment to study the complex masonry of **KIN KLETSO**, which has 65 rooms and 5 kivas (underground or partly underground chambers).

A short spur trail leads to an overlook of **PUEBLO BONITO**, a huge complex of more than 600 rooms thought to be the center of society in Chaco Canyon.

New Alto

Pueblo Alto

Jackson Stairway

Kin Kletso

UNITED STATES

Car park

Viewpoint

Pueblo Bonito

0 ·········· km ·········· 0.5
0 ·········· miles ·········· 0.5

49

22

Superior Hiking Trail

MINNESOTA-WISCONSIN BORDER TO
270 DEGREE OVERLOOK, US

Get to know Lake Superior on this footpath across Minnesota,
which provides a beginner-friendly introduction to long-distance
hiking alongside one of the world's largest lakes.

REFUEL
Angry Trout Café

When resupplying in Grand
Marais, stop by the Angry Trout
Café *(angrytroutcafe.com)*, located
in an old commercial fishing
shanty, to get a taste of the bounty
of Lake Superior and its environs,
plus a glass of the house soda.

300 MILES (483 KM)

31,955 FT (9,740 M)

2–4 WEEKS (ONE-WAY)

50

The Superior Hiking Trail is arguably one of
the best long-distance trails in the US for
a first-time thru-hiker. The length and time
requirement (no more than a month) is
manageable, and campsites and resupply
points are, for the most part, abundant.
The one exception to this is the roughly
50-mile (80 km) section through Duluth,
which is open only to day hikers and
prohibits overnight camping.

For this reason, there are two types
of thru-hikes on the Superior Hiking Trail:
"traditional" and "total." The former
traverses only the 260 miles (418 km) of
the route open to backpackers, where
campsites are spaced out roughly every
5 to 10 miles (8 to 16 km); the latter covers
the entire route and involves making
arrangements for transportation between
the trail and nightly lodgings throughout
the Duluth section.

Once you've decided which kind of
thru-hike is right for you, the rest is a
relative breeze. For the most part, the
trail follows the ridges of cliffs skirting
the edge of its namesake lake, along
an undulating path that tops out at just
1,829 ft (557 m). Lake Superior itself is
a body of water so large that it feels
almost like walking alongside an ocean.
And like the ocean, the lake has many
moods, depending on the time of year
and weather. These reveal themselves
day by day, as you hike through a variety

ELEVATION PROFILE

3,000 ft
(914 m)

0

0   300 miles (483 km)

Duluth

Jay Cooke
State Park

The trail starts amid
maple forest at the remote
Minnesota-Wisconsin border
in **JAY COOKE STATE PARK**.

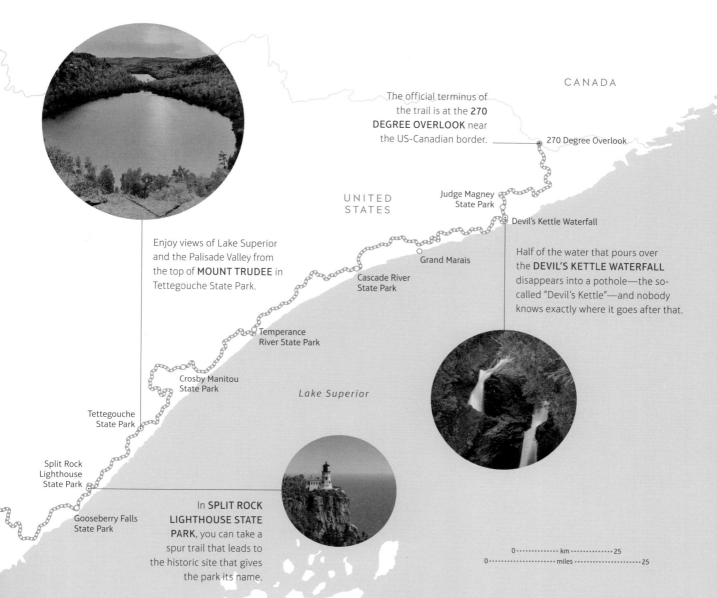

The official terminus of the trail is at the **270 DEGREE OVERLOOK** near the US-Canadian border.

CANADA

270 Degree Overlook

UNITED STATES

Judge Magney State Park

Devil's Kettle Waterfall

Grand Marais

Cascade River State Park

Enjoy views of Lake Superior and the Palisade Valley from the top of **MOUNT TRUDEE** in Tettegouche State Park.

Half of the water that pours over the **DEVIL'S KETTLE WATERFALL** disappears into a pothole—the so-called "Devil's Kettle"—and nobody knows exactly where it goes after that.

Temperance River State Park

Crosby Manitou State Park

Lake Superior

Tettegouche State Park

Split Rock Lighthouse State Park

Gooseberry Falls State Park

In **SPLIT ROCK LIGHTHOUSE STATE PARK**, you can take a spur trail that leads to the historic site that gives the park its name.

0 ········· km ········· 25
0 ········· miles ········· 25

of woodland environments—birch, aspen, pine, fir, and cedar trees—that each lend their own unique smell, look, and feel to the changing landscape.

The seasons play their own special part in the trail experience, too. Spring brings wildflowers and the challenge of muddy conditions (when paths are extra sensitive to erosion and may even be closed), while the warm summer weather sees the arrival of mosquitoes and the appearance of fruit on the wild blueberry and raspberry bushes that line the path (providing handy trail snacks). The fall months, on the other hand, are perhaps the best: trails and campsites start to empty out from September, providing greater solitude, and the forests are dazzling as the leaves change color. As an initiation for your trail legs, it's pretty hard to beat.

23

Spite Highway

ELLIOTT KEY HARBOR, FLORIDA, US

A bitter feud led to the creation of this trail, which traces a route through the tropical forest of Biscayne National Park's Elliott Key.

7 MILES (11 KM)

180 FT (55 M)

1 DAY (RETURN)

In the 1960s, a collection of Florida landowners wanted to develop Elliott Key, a coral reef island just off the coast of Miami, for recreation and tourism. A small group of local conservationists had another idea, however, and began building community support for the creation of a national park that would protect the island and its surrounding waters. By the end of the decade, public favor had swayed their way. In a last-ditch effort to stymie the park plan, the landowners bulldozed a six-lane wide, 7-mile (11 km) stretch of forest down the middle of the island.

It didn't work. President Lyndon B. Johnson signed a bill creating the Biscayne National Park on October 18, 1968, and today visitors can stroll the length of Elliott Key via the landowners' "Spite Highway." Nature has had the last laugh: the foliage around the edges of the highway now forms a pleasantly shaded tunnel, and the surrounding mangrove forests are home to a number of endangered species. Keep an eye out for the large yellow-brown patterned Schaus' swallowtail butterfly, once endemic to southern Florida but now found only on several small islands in Biscayne National Park.

Elliott Key, one of the collection of islands that form Biscayne National Park

The northern terminus of the trail is just past **SEA GRAPE POINT**, which looks out to Fowey Rocks Light, a cast-iron lighthouse built in 1878.

Northern terminus

Alongside the trail are clusters of **POISONWOOD**, a tree native to the Florida Keys and identifiable by the black splotches of toxic sap on its mottled bark.

ELLIOTT KEY HARBOR is the main gateway to the island. There's a camping area here if you fancy staying the night.

Elliott Key Harbor

ELLIOTT KEY

ELEVATION PROFILE

300 ft (91 m)

0

0   7 miles (11 km)

0 ········· km ········· 1
0 ··········· miles ··········· 1

Tip

October to April offers the best weather; avoid hiking in the sticky summer months (June to August).

A **BRIDGE** that stretches for 1,312 ft (400 m) provides expansive views over the lake. Pause here to watch for waterbirds winging across the surface.

Around 9 miles (14 km) in, you'll leave the water behind and enter bottomland **HARDWOOD FOREST**.

Lake Chicot

Bridge

Hardwood forest

South Landing Trailhead

UNITED STATES

Cypress forest

0 ·········· km ·········· 2
0 ·········· miles ·········· 2

24

Lake Chicot Loop

VILLE PLATTE, LOUISIANA, US

Get a taste for the wonders of the wetlands, with a two-day walk amid wildlife-filled swamps and leafy hardwood forest inside Louisiana's biggest state park.

One of only a handful of long-distance trails in Louisiana, the Lake Chicot Loop immerses you in majestic wetlands that are bursting with life. Towering tupelo and bald cypress trees rise above the shimmering water. Along the banks, alligators and turtles sun on logs, while great blue herons stalk the shoreline, patiently waiting for breakfast to swim past. In early spring and fall, the skies fill with migratory birds, including eye-catching species like the

roseate spoonbill—sometimes called the "Cajun flamingo" on account of its bright pink plumage.

Although it's possible to hike the loop in one (long) day, it's far more rewarding to stop at one of the backcountry sites along the way. That way you can enjoy the auburn light shimmering off the water as the sun sets over the forest, followed by the nightly insect chorus as the sky fills with stars.

Boardwalk paths lead you into the watery epicenter of a sun-dappled bald **CYPRESS FOREST**. It feels like treading through a primeval landscape.

ELEVATION PROFILE

300 ft (91 m)

0

0   18 miles (29 km)

⊖ 18 MILES (29 KM)

⊘ 889 FT (271 M)

🕐 2 DAYS (LOOP)

Uncover **LAKE PLACID**'s proud Olympic history—the town has twice hosted the Winter Games and many of the venues are open to visitors.

Lake Placid

High Peaks Wilderness

Long Lake

You're likely to see float planes coming and going from **LONG LAKE**, which is dotted with vacation homes.

Tirrell Pond

Blue Ridge Wilderness

The north end of **TIRRELL POND** has a long sandy beach where you can lie and warm up in the sun after a dip in the deep, cold waters.

West Canada Lake Wilderness

UNITED STATES

0 ········· km ········· 20
0 ········· miles ········· 20

Piseco

Piseco Lake

Silver Lake Wilderness

West Stony Creek

Northville

Depending on the time of year, **WEST STONY CREEK** can be a challenging water crossing that requires wading.

Great Sacandaga Lake

REFUEL

Lake Placid

Most thru-hikers will mail resupply boxes to post offices in Piseco, Blue Mountain Lake, or Long Lake, as opportunities to gorge on town food are limited. Until you get to Lake Placid, that is. There are plenty of sandwich shops, pubs, and restaurants to placate your hiker hunger—check out the in-house smoked barbecue at Smoke Signals *(smokesignalsq.com)*, with an order of fried pickle spears to start.

54

25

Northville–Placid Trail

NORTHVILLE TO LAKE PLACID, NEW YORK, US

The Northville-Placid Trail is as much about water as it is about the woods, linking a series of lower-elevation lakes and ponds in New York's Adirondack Park.

138 MILES (222 KM)

15,128 FT (4,611 M)

8–10 DAYS (ONE-WAY)

Traversing some of the most remote areas of the Adirondack Park, the Northville-Placid Trail was created in the early 20th century, before the car became the primary mode of transportation in the US. It was the first project by the Adirondack Mountain Club and the route's start and end points—Northville and Lake Placid—were chosen because both towns had train stations, enabling city dwellers to access the trail with ease. Unfortunately, neither station is still in use, but the footpath endures—albeit with some changes over the years. More than once, beaver dams have flooded the trail, forcing the path to be rerouted.

Beaver interventions aside, you won't find a great deal of drama on this trail. The route keeps mostly to lower elevations—the high point is a mere 3,008 ft (917 m) above sea level—in contrast to most other multiday trails in the US. Instead, the focus here is on the beauty of the forest and the lakeland landscapes—the section of trail

Gentle lakeland scenery in New York's beautiful Adirondack Park

that goes by Spruce, West Canada, and Cedar lakes is some of the most secluded and peaceful wilderness in the northeast. And if you like swimming as much as hiking, you'll find plenty of tent sites and shelters near pristine lakes. There's nothing as refreshing as a quick dip in shockingly cold water after a long day walking.

Fall is the best time of year to hike the Northville-Placid Trail—the Adirondacks are a renowned leaf-peeping destination, and the splendor of the changing foliage is at its peak in September and October. No matter the season, though, the sorbet-colored sunsets at the end of each day will stay with you long after the hike is over.

ELEVATION PROFILE

3,000 ft (914 m)

0

0   138 miles (222 km)

Hikers descending
Mount Katahdin at the
northern terminus of
the Appalachian Trail

26

Appalachian Trail

SPRINGER MOUNTAIN, GEORGIA, TO
MOUNT KATAHDIN, MAINE, US

One of the world's oldest trails, the Appalachian Trail traces the narrative of a nation and is the ultimate long-distance challenge.

2,193 MILES (3,529 KM)

385,450 FT (117,485 M)

5–7 MONTHS (ONE-WAY)

Few long-distance trails set the imagination ablaze like the Appalachian. Snaking 2,193 miles (3,529 km) from Springer Mountain in Georgia to Mount Katahdin in Maine and traversing 14 states, it traces the spine of the Appalachian Mountains.

These peaks are steeped in American history. They were originally inhabited by the Cherokee, Iroquois, Powhatan, and Shawnee people, who were forcibly displaced from the 1700s onward by waves of European settlers. The communities established by these immigrants grew with a distinctly Appalachian character, via the trade of foodstuffs, musical influences, and campfire stories of the dreaded Boojum (Bigfoot) and Bell Witch. ▶

ELEVATION PROFILE

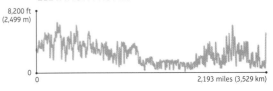

8,200 ft
(2,499 m)

0

0   2,193 miles (3,529 km)

Tip

Pick up a copy of the *Appalachian Trail Thru-Hiker's Companion* guide from the Appalachian Trail Conservancy.

Later, however, the area's abundant natural resources came to the attention of the ever-growing coal-mining and logging industries, and by the early 20th century, they threatened to wipe out this beloved swathe of green. The mountains' rescue came in the form of forester and conservationist Benton MacKaye, who was struck by the idea of an Appalachian Trail while atop Stratton Mountain in Vermont in 1921. Forged from a mixture of Native American foot trails and settler wagon routes, the route was envisioned, not just as a means of protecting the environment, but as the "solution to the problem of living," by providing relief from the incessant noise and stress of industrialization and offering the chance to gain some perspective on life.

So if you're in need of a fresh outlook, then the Appalachian Trail calls. But before you heed its cry, bear in mind that this is no walk in the park. To become a thru-hiker and complete the whole route usually takes between five and seven months. It requires training, preparation, a kitty of around $3,000, high-quality camping equipment, and a bottomless supply of inner grit. Indeed, the trail receives around 3 million walkers annually, and of the roughly 3,000 of those who attempt the "thru," only one in four make it. (The record for the fastest completion of the route is held by ultra-marathon runner Scott Jurek, who covered the 2,000-plus miles/3,000-plus km in a staggering 46 days, 8 hours, and 7 minutes.) Astonishingly for such a famous trail, only around 21,500 people have completed it since the final stage was mapped in 1936.

The trail can be hiked in either direction; there are pros and cons to both options ,and the one you choose will affect when you begin. Starting in Georgia and following the northbound route is the most popular. It requires setting off in late March or early April to ensure enough warm weather for the steep mountain passes in the colder northern states toward the finish—a short window that tends to result in a busy trail and crowded campsites. ▶

Backpacking along the trail through Grayson Highlands State Park, Virginia

The **SETTLERS MUSEUM** in Virginia tells the story of the Scottish, Irish, and German settlers who made a home here in the mid-1700s.

Settlers Museum

Cherokee National Forest

Big Creek Country Store

Great Smoky Mountains National Park

Springer Mountain

Time travel back to the 1920s at the **BIG CREEK COUNTRY STORE**, an old-fashioned general store just north of Waynesville.

Across the White Mountains in New Hampshire, the trail merges with the 23-mile (37 km) **PRESIDENTIAL TRAVERSE**, passing seven peaks named after former presidents.

Summon all your wits for the **100-MILE WILDERNESS** in Maine, a remote section of the trail with several bridge-free river crossings.

Mount Katahdin

100-Mile Wilderness

Presidential Traverse

White Mountain National Forest

Green Mountains

Mount Greylock

UNITED STATES

Dover Oak

High Point State Park

Delaware Water Gap

The scene of John Brown's failed abolitionist uprising in 1859, **HARPERS FERRY NATIONAL HISTORICAL PARK** marks the midpoint of the trail.

Duncannon

Michaux State Forest

Harpers Ferry National Historical Park

Shenandoah National Park

The largest tree on the entire Appalachian Trail, the mammoth **DOVER OAK** in New York State is 20 ft (6 m) wide and believed to be more than 300 years old.

McAfee Knob

Jefferson National Forest

MCAFEE KNOB—a slab of rock suspended 1,740 ft (530 m) above the Catawba Valley in Virginia—is a must-not-miss photo opportunity.

REFUEL

Village Farmer and Bakery

Don't miss the Village Farmer and Bakery (*villagefarmerbakery.com*) near Delaware Water Gap in Pennsylvania. Run by Susan and Charles Cooper since 1976, it's famous for its "True Love" lunch deal comprising a hot dog and slice of homemade pie for less than $3.

0 ·········· km ·········· 150
0 ·········· miles ·········· 150

59

NORTH AMERICA

Following the southbound route from Maine, on the other hand, means facing the most difficult terrain of the trail right away, coupled with the added challenge of an extra-heavy backpack due to limited resupply points. This choice does bring the benefit of a later start in May or June, as the southern states are flatter and less affected by inclement weather, but is really best tackled by very fit hikers only.

As an alternative, however, you can flip-flop. This means starting the hike in the middle of the trail—say at Harpers Ferry in West Virginia—heading north and then returning to your starting point and completing the southbound section. This option is often the best: you start walking on manageable terrain, have a longer time frame to complete the trail, enjoy better weather throughout, and, most importantly, help conserve the trail by reducing overcrowding. All routes still

allow you to gain certification as a "2,000-miler"—just be sure to register with the Appalachian Trail Conservancy before you set off.

Whichever route you choose, one thing's for sure: this is a life-changing pilgrimage that will strip your world back to basics, with each day bringing new highs and lows. The changing landscapes offer as many scenes of sublime beauty— the fog-shrouded Great Smoky Mountains of North Carolina and Tennessee, the gentle farmland and rolling hills of Virginia, and the maples of Vermont ablaze with fall color—as they do strenuous tests of your physical and mental resolve. Famously tough sections include boulder-strewn Pennsylvania—aka "Rocksylvania"—the rough, wind-bitten mountains of New Hampshire, and the giant obstacle course of rocks at Mahoosuc Notch in Maine, but even the relatively easy terrain can prove

Taking photos of Harpers Ferry National Historical Park in West Virginia

Top Great Smokey
Mountains National
Park, Tennessee

Bottom The summit
of Mount Katahdin,
in Maine

challenging, as the repetitive daily routine
and seemingly endless tally of miles ahead
combine to take their toll.

Yet it is the very repetitiveness of life
on the trail—placing one foot after the
other, day after day, week after week, and
month after month—that opens up the
new perspective envisaged by MacKaye.
The lack of everyday distraction allows
time to think, and the focus of working
toward a single goal provides purpose—
not to mention a huge amount of satisfaction as each obstacle is overcome and
the miles begin to gradually tick down.

It's helped, massively, by the support
of those you meet on the trail. The mantra
of thru-hiking is "Hike Your Own Hike," but
those embarking on the challenge none-
theless form their own special community,
swapping tales from the trail at the
campsites and on supply visits to towns.
And it's this camaraderie that will leave
lasting memories long after the mud has
been washed from your boots and your
backpack has been stowed in the depths
of your closet.

Completing the trail is a phenomenal
accomplishment, and it can take a while
for its full enormity to sink in. But as the
aches in your muscles slowly subside, a
profound sense of achievement begins
to settle—after all, many people dream
of walking the Appalachian Trail, and to
have actually realized that ambition is
something very special indeed.

MAKE IT SHORTER
Roan Highlands

Thru-hiking isn't the only option.
Travelers with only a few days to
spare should head straight for the Roan
Highlands, a 19-mile (31-km) ridgetop
section in Tennessee with the largest
natural rhododendron garden in the
world. It's ideal for hikers wanting a
scenic but strenuous sample of the trail.

The coastal stretch from Coney Island to **HAMILTON PARISH** starts with a 740 ft (226 m) long footbridge that spans Bailey's Bay.

Entering the **SANDYS PARISH** section, you'll wander through deep limestone cuts now covered in rubber tree roots and tropical foliage.

SOUTHAMPTON's stretch of trail meanders through thick spice-tree groves before cutting through Gibb's Hill Lighthouse.

St George's
Coney Island
Bailey's Bay
Hamilton Parish
Flatts
Somerset
BERMUDA
Paget Parish
Sandys Parish
Warwick Parish
Southampton

0 ·········· km ·········· 4
0 ·········· miles ·········· 4

27

The Bermuda Railway Trail

ST. GEORGE'S TO SOMERSET, BERMUDA

Look beyond Bermuda's famous pink-sand beaches and colorful knee-length shorts, and you'll discover a wonderful coastal hiking trail that was once home to a working railroad.

23 MILES (37 KM)
1,066 FT (325 M)
1–2 DAYS (ONE-WAY)

Stretching from the town of St. George's in the east to the village of Somerset in the west, this 23-mile (37 km) pedestrian and bicycle path was once where Bermuda's first and only commuter train rumbled across the island. Dubbed the "Old Rattle and Shake," the train operated from 1931 to 1948. While the railroad itself folded with the arrival of the automobile, its track is now the path for this tranquil amble through fragrant fiddlewood forests next to the turquoise Atlantic Ocean.

The route is formed of nine noncontiguous sections of hiking trails. Some are connected by overwater footbridges that were built upon the old train line's cement pylons, while others have been carved straight through Bermuda's bedrock. The entire trail can be conquered in a full day of walking, but it's arguably more satisfying to tackle individual sections one or two at a time, allowing the island's tropical beauty to slowly unfold.

ELEVATION PROFILE

300 ft (91 m)

0

0   23 miles (37 km)

28
Blue Mountain Peak Trail

PENLYNE CASTLE, JAMAICA

Stand on the roof of Jamaica on a vigorous hike in the heart of the nation's lush Blue Mountains—where some of the finest coffee in the Caribbean is grown.

11 MILES (17 KM) | 3,957 FT (1,206 M) | 1 DAY (RETURN)

If you'd climb a mountain for a great coffee, then this challenging trail in the cool rainforests of the Blue and John Crow Mountains National Park has your name on it. The classic hike to Blue Mountain Peak, Jamaica's highest point at 7,402 ft (2,256 m), begins in the misty mountain village of Penlyne Castle. It's surrounded by coffee plantations like Whitfield Hall, which is also a rustic hiking lodge where you can sample Jamaica's famed Blue Mountain

The slopes of Blue Mountain, covered in tropical montane rainforest

coffee from the source. You'll certainly need the caffeine hit for this hike—most walkers set off shortly after midnight, to reach the summit in time to watch the sunrise.

If you huffed and puffed up the steep trail in the dark, you can take your time to admire the national park's incredible biodiversity on the descent. Look out for the endangered yellow-and-black Homerus swallowtail, the largest butterfly in the Americas, on your way back to Penlyne Castle for a celebratory cup of Joe.

ELEVATION PROFILE

10,000 ft (3,048 m)

0

0   11 miles (17 km)

Enjoy a much-deserved rest at **PORTLAND GAP**, where you can refill your water bottle and use the bathroom facilities.

Watch the sun rise above the Caribbean Sea from **BLUE MOUNTAIN PEAK**. On a clear day, you can see Kingston to the south and maybe even the hazy form of Cuba to the north.

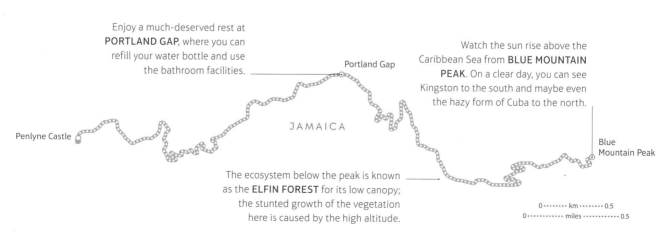

Portland Gap

Penlyne Castle

JAMAICA

Blue Mountain Peak

The ecosystem below the peak is known as the **ELFIN FOREST** for its low canopy; the stunted growth of the vegetation here is caused by the high altitude.

0 ········· km ········· 0.5
0 ········· miles ········· 0.5

29

Waitukubuli National Trail

SCOTTS HEAD TO FORT SHIRLEY, DOMINICA

Trek from one end of Dominica to the other on this long-distance rainforest trail through the island's mountainous interior.

96 MILES (155 KM)

25,548 FT (7,787 M)

2 WEEKS (ONE-WAY)

64

There can't be too many trails that span both the length and breadth of an entire country. Dominica's Waitukubuli Trail, the longest in the Caribbean, does exactly that, starting on the Scotts Head peninsula in the far south of the island and finishing, via the east and north coasts, near the Officer's Quarters at western Fort Shirley.

The trail is split into 14 segments, many of them individual trails in their own right. Between them, they take in virgin rainforest and wave-washed beaches, botanical gardens and coffee estates, and the magnificent Morne Trois Pitons National Park. The latter is the country's only UNESCO World Heritage Site, whose volcanic attractions include Boiling Lake and the Valley of Desolation. Its "Three Peaks" are just some of the dozen or so mountains that rear up across the island, including more than half of the region's active volcanoes, making the country feel much more rugged and wild than most of

Hiking between the villages of Capuchin and Pennesville at the north of the island

its Caribbean counterparts—"Waitukubuli" is actually the Indigenous name for Dominica itself and means, suitably enough, "tall is her body."

Tackling the trail from start to finish will take around two weeks, and you'll certainly have earned your stripes by the end of it—Segment 1 out of Scotts Head to the Soufriere Estate involves rope-climbing in parts, and many of the trails are slow-going jungle slogs. It can be tough, but for an insight into the island, Waitukubuli is difficult to beat. Not only does the hike offer a good overview of agricultural life in Dominica, as it moves

ELEVATION PROFILE

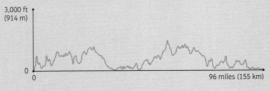

3,000 ft (914 m)

0

0   96 miles (155 km)

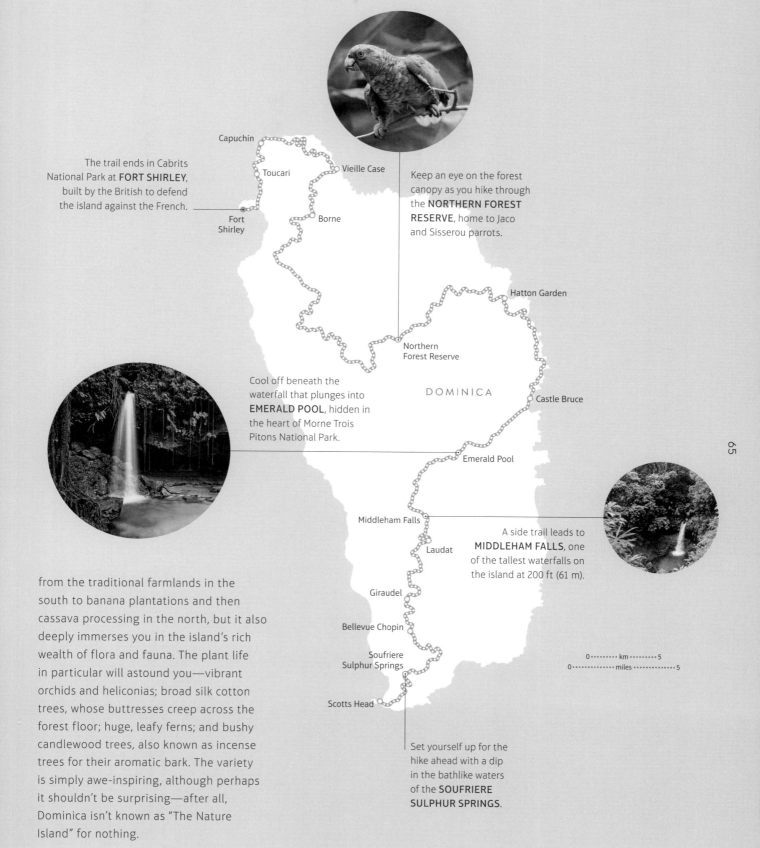

The trail ends in Cabrits National Park at **FORT SHIRLEY**, built by the British to defend the island against the French.

Capuchin

Toucari

Vieille Case

Borne

Fort Shirley

Keep an eye on the forest canopy as you hike through the **NORTHERN FOREST RESERVE**, home to Jaco and Sisserou parrots.

Hatton Garden

Northern Forest Reserve

DOMINICA

Castle Bruce

Cool off beneath the waterfall that plunges into **EMERALD POOL**, hidden in the heart of Morne Trois Pitons National Park.

Emerald Pool

Middleham Falls

A side trail leads to **MIDDLEHAM FALLS**, one of the tallest waterfalls on the island at 200 ft (61 m).

Laudat

Giraudel

Bellevue Chopin

Soufriere Sulphur Springs

Scotts Head

0 ········· km ········· 5
0 ············· miles ············· 5

from the traditional farmlands in the south to banana plantations and then cassava processing in the north, but it also deeply immerses you in the island's rich wealth of flora and fauna. The plant life in particular will astound you—vibrant orchids and heliconias; broad silk cotton trees, whose buttresses creep across the forest floor; huge, leafy ferns; and bushy candlewood trees, also known as incense trees for their aromatic bark. The variety is simply awe-inspiring, although perhaps it shouldn't be surprising—after all, Dominica isn't known as "The Nature Island" for nothing.

Set yourself up for the hike ahead with a dip in the bathlike waters of the **SOUFRIERE SULPHUR SPRINGS**.

Passing through
swamps and meadows
on the Arctic Circle Trail

30

Arctic Circle Trail

KANGERLUSSUAQ TO SISIMIUT, GREENLAND

Leave civilization behind and march into the steep glacial valleys and sweeping Arctic tundra of Greenland's interior, on a soundless pilgrimage through wilderness at its purest.

102 MILES (165 KM)

10,453 FT (3,186 M)

7-10 DAYS (ONE-WAY)

Located entirely within the Arctic Circle, the Arctic Circle Trail (ACT) is Greenland's longest waymarked trail and runs from the Arctic desert at Kangerlussuaq to the western seaboard at Sisimiut. While over 80 percent of the nation's landmass is covered in ice and mostly inaccessible, the ACT crosses one of the largest ice-free areas in Greenland—taking trekkers far away from the material world and deep into a land of silence, peace, and isolation. The route does not pass through or close to any settlements, so you must be experienced and entirely self-sufficient throughout; at the halfway point, you'll find yourself more than 50 miles (80 km) away from the nearest outpost.

From Kangerlussuaq, Greenland's main air transport hub, the trail initially follows a dusty road running adjacent to

Kangerlussuaq fjord. But it soon branches off into the untamed Arctic tundra that quickly becomes the standard: lush glacial lakes, boulder-strewn moraine, and tall cairns adorned with reindeer antlers. Once onto the tundra, the isolation hits you. Only around 1,500 people complete the ACT every year, so if you're hiking solo, then you need to be comfortable with your own company. The skies are big, the landscapes wide, and the silence deafening. Other than some hard-to-spot reindeer, muskox, Arctic foxes, and hares, you're all on your own. Take a deep breath and feel the emptiness wash over you; it will be your companion for the remainder of the journey.

Even though the trail is waymarked, route finding can still be a challenge, particularly in foggy conditions. Red-marked cairns and boulders help to sign the way, but careful navigation is continually required. (The ACT is essentially a summer trail, with the vast majority of hikers completing it between June and September when the weather is more favorable and the days longer—even never-ending during high summer.) ▶

ELEVATION PROFILE

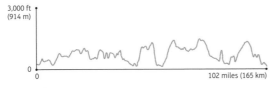

3,000 ft
(914 m)

0

0   102 miles (165 km)

Tip

Mosquitoes and flies can descend in plague-like proportions. Pack a mosquito head net and insect repellent.

NORTH AMERICA

Despite the endless domed mountains, steep ascents are mercifully short, with the trail tending to follow the contours of terrain instead of traversing high passes or peaks. Eight basic, free-to-use huts are spread along the route for accommodations, although most people wild camp as it allows greater flexibility. Invariably, you'll walk to your own agenda, but if nothing else, you'll be glad of the huts for pit stops or as shelter from bad weather as you trace a path across the lonely landscape.

Gradually gaining elevation from east to west, the trail slips from one wide valley to the next, undulating along rocky lakeshores and climbing into a rugged mountain range buffeted by winds before descending into a sheltered valley where only the trickle of a stream disturbs the stillness. This area of Greenland is mottled with hundreds of lakes, so water is never

far away. Large parts of the trail are spent hiking along the shores of these magnificent lakes or hopping over winding creeks, while the more mountainous stretches are peppered with countless highland tarns—there are a handful of rivers to cross, too.

As the route nears the seaboard, the terrain grows steeper and even more

MAKE IT LONGER
Icy Add-on

Opt to start your trek inland at the edge of the Greenland ice sheet, 23 miles (37 km) east of Kangerlussuaq. This extension takes in the awesome Russell Glacier and a UNESCO-listed ancient Inuit hunting ground.

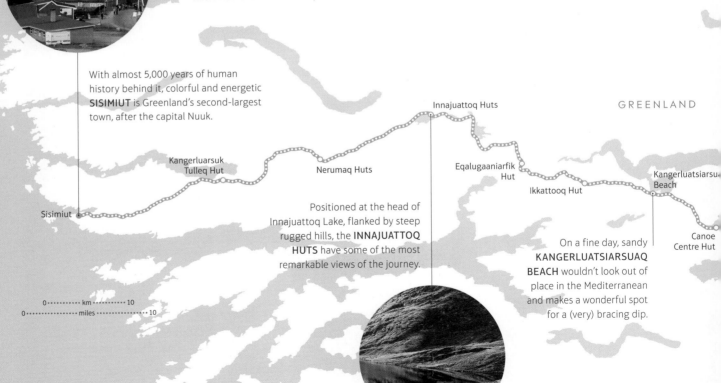

With almost 5,000 years of human history behind it, colorful and energetic **SISIMIUT** is Greenland's second-largest town, after the capital Nuuk.

GREENLAND

Innajuattoq Huts

Kangerluarsuk
Tulleq Hut

Nerumaq Huts

Eqalugaaniarfik
Hut

Kangerluatsiarsu
Beach

Ikkattooq Hut

Sisimiut

Positioned at the head of Innajuattoq Lake, flanked by steep rugged hills, the **INNAJUATTOQ HUTS** have some of the most remarkable views of the journey.

Canoe
Centre Hut

On a fine day, sandy **KANGERLUATSIARSUAQ BEACH** wouldn't look out of place in the Mediterranean and makes a wonderful spot for a (very) bracing dip.

0 ······· km ······· 10
0 ··········· miles ··········· 10

The aurora borealis shimmering over Kangerlussuaq Fjord

the day, preoccupied with thoughts of soft beds and fresh food. But it's worth savoring these final few miles. Sisimiut is hardly a sprawling metropolis, but after spending so long in the pristine and silent wilderness, pavements of pedestrians and the hum of traffic will come as a shock.

The Arctic Circle Trail is a special place. It roams Greenland's hinterland, a land for pioneers. A land of a hundred lakes on the fringes of the known world. An unsullied and uncorrupted land that is hard to find anywhere else on earth. Its silence is a wondrous thing, and you'll miss it when it's gone.

scenic as glaciated peaks rise and plunge dramatically into the ocean. By now, backpacks are lightened as supplies have been eaten and hikers, who have walked into their fitness, tend to romp through

AMITSORSUAQ LAKE
makes for a straightforward but magnificent shore walk, with views extending all the way to the glaciated peak of Aqqutikitsoq, north of Sisimiut.

Amitsorsuaq Lake

Katiffik Hut

Hundesø Hut

Kangerlussuaq

The lonely settlement of **KANGERLUSSUAQ** might not seem much to look at, but it is a gateway to spectacular scenery and activities such as ice camping.

The tiny, crimson **KATIFFIK HUT** contains a sleeping platform large enough for 3 people plus a small cooking area.

⊙ 31

MEXICO

32 ⊙
BELIZE

GUATEMALA
HONDURAS

EL SALVADOR
NICARAGUA

COSTA RICA
34 ⊙ ⊙ 33
PANAMA

VENEZUELA

GUYANA

35 ⊙
SURINAM

COLOMBIA

36 ⊙
ECUADOR

PERU

BRAZIL

37 ⊙

38 ⊙ ⊙ 39

BOLIVIA

40 ⊙ ⊙ 41

⊙ 43
EASTER
ISLAND

PARAGUAY

URUGUAY

CHILE

ARGENTINA

⊙ 42

⊙ 44

CENTRAL AND SOUTH AMERICA

31

Tararecua Canyon

REKOWATA HOT SPRINGS TO
PAMACHI, MEXICO

*Walk in the footsteps of the Indigenous Rarámuri on this difficult
and thrilling trek through Mexico's magnificent canyon country.*

23 MILES (37 KM) · 4,446 FT (1,355 M) · 5 DAYS (ONE-WAY)

72

Tucked in the highlands of northern Mexico is one of the largest canyon systems on Earth. Though the Grand Canyon in Arizona remains better known, this slice of the Sierra Madre Occidental mountain range is deeper, greener, and four times larger than its US counterpart. The Copper Canyon region is also home to the Indigenous Rarámuri (Tarahumara), a people famed for their long-distance running abilities. This challenging multiday trek through Tararecua Canyon goes past several of their astonishingly remote settlements— many Rarámuri live traditional lifestyles little changed for centuries.

The first part of the hike follows the Rio San Ignacio, ensuring you're never far from a drinking source until the very final leg of the journey (as elsewhere in the wild, be sure to treat or filter water before consuming). The scenery is breathtaking as you make your way through the steep

wooded canyons, but it's no walk in the park. This trackless wilderness presents constant challenges as you follow the rugged riverbanks. Sometimes the sheer canyon walls descend right to the water's edge, requiring you to hop from rock to rock and wade to get across; at other times, the overgrown banks require a bit of bushwhacking. Thankfully, crystalline pools along the way provide the perfect setting to refresh after hours of trudging beneath the hot sun. And at nighttime, you can camp on whatever flat spots

ELEVATION PROFILE

6,500 ft
(1,981 m)

0

0   23 miles (37 km)

Gazing out over the Copper Canyon region
in the northern Mexican state of Chihuahua

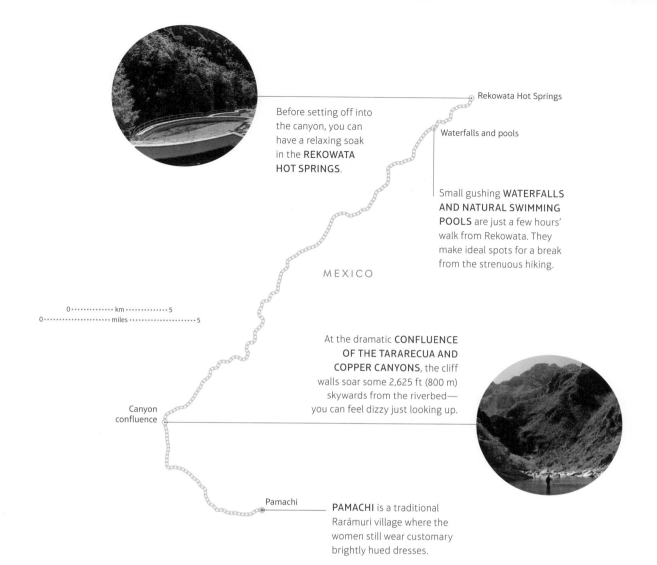

Before setting off into the canyon, you can have a relaxing soak in the **REKOWATA HOT SPRINGS**.

Rekowata Hot Springs

Waterfalls and pools

Small gushing **WATERFALLS AND NATURAL SWIMMING POOLS** are just a few hours' walk from Rekowata. They make ideal spots for a break from the strenuous hiking.

MEXICO

0 ·········· km ·········· 5
0 ·········· miles ·········· 5

At the dramatic **CONFLUENCE OF THE TARARECUA AND COPPER CANYONS**, the cliff walls soar some 2,625 ft (800 m) skywards from the riverbed—you can feel dizzy just looking up.

Canyon confluence

Pamachi

PAMACHI is a traditional Rarámuri village where the women still wear customary brightly hued dresses.

you can find along the gurgling flume and drift off to sleep beneath the clear, star-filled skies.

After days of negotiating your way along the San Ignacio, you'll find your way onto the Arroyo Pamachi, a stream that sometimes dries up outside of the rainy season. The faint trail eventually intersects with a rock saddle that leads you up and out of the canyon. It's a tough climb to the top (being comfortable with heights is a minimum requirement), but when you reach the summit, the vast canyon stretches out before you in all its grandeur, and you'll enjoy a view that few but the local Rarámuri have ever experienced.

IN FOCUS
The Rarámuri

In spite of incursions by conquistadors, railroads, missionaries, tourists, and drug cartels, the Rarámuri have maintained their deep-rooted traditions (and language). Many still migrate during the year, residing in the cooler highlands in the summer and the warmer canyons in the winter. One of the cornerstones of Rarámuri society is *korima*, the tradition of selfless sharing with others.

Watch the sunset over the Maya Biosphere Reserve from the top of **LA DANTA**, the largest building in El Mirador at 253 ft (77 m).

Spend your first night on the trail at the atmospheric Mayan ruins of **EL TINTAL**. After El Mirador, it's the area's second-largest Mayan site.

El Mirador

La Danta

Nakbé

Wakná

El Tintal

GUATEMALA

0 ········· km ········· 5
0 ········· miles ········· 5

La Florida

Carmelita

The final stop on the trail is the photogenic ruins of the Mayan village of **LA FLORIDA**, which feature an ancient Mayan building you can walk through.

32

El Mirador

CARMELITA, GUATEMALA

Feel like an intrepid adventurer on a jungle trek to ancient Mayan ruins in northeastern Guatemala.

60 MILES (96 KM)   6,900 FT (2,103 M)   6 DAYS (LOOP)

74

Built half a millennia before Guatemala's famed Mayan city of Tikal, the archaeological wonder of El Mirador is thought to have flourished from around the 6th century BCE to the 1st century CE. This former great city can be reached only via a sweaty six-day hike along a crude, lowland jungle track. For most visitors, that's half the fun.

The route begins in the village of Carmelita, north of the tourist hub of Flores. From here, your guide from the community-run Carmelita Cooperative will lead you deep into the jungle along relatively flat dirt paths lined by trees and laced with roots. With camping supplies typically carried by mules, you can focus on spotting bright-billed toucans and howler monkeys— perhaps even a jaguar's paw print.

The loop trek also takes in the El Mirador "suburbs" of El Tintal, Nakbé, Wakna, and La Florida. But these partly excavated Mayan ruins pale in size and splendor to the sprawling remains of El Mirador. The impressive stone structures here—including La Danta, one of the largest pyramids in the world—loom suddenly out of the trees, rising up from a jungle that seems determined to engulf them once again.

ELEVATION PROFILE

1,500 ft (457 m)

0

0   60 miles (96 km)

Looking toward the deep-green cloud forests of Volcán Barú National Park

ELEVATION PROFILE

- 6 MILES (10 KM)
- 2,598 FT (792 M)
- 1 DAY (ONE-WAY)

33
The Quetzal Trail

ALTO CHIQUERO TO BAJO GRANDE, PANAMA

Hike a forested mountain trail in search of the elusive quetzal in western Panama's lush Chiriquí Province.

The verdant cloud forests of Volcán Barú National Park form the backdrop to this spectacular hike in Panama's Talamanca Mountains. The trail is named after one of Central America's most striking birds—but even if you don't see the resplendent quetzal, with its iridescent green body and dramatic tail plumes, you're sure to stumble upon other avian wonders (some 250 bird species are found here).

As you make your way through dense forest, along a steep, undulating trail, the air is noisy with birdsong, plus the occasional roar of a howler monkey, and sun-dappled butterflies wing past. You'll also make several stream and river crossings—some via bouncy suspension bridges; others by rock hopping or wading through knee-high water. Toward the trail's end, you'll enjoy magnificent views atop Alto Respingo, the perfect perch for spying ornate hawk-eagles soaring above the biologically rich forests you've just traversed.

Amid the **BOSQUE DE LAS LIANAS** ("forest of the vines"), you'll see some towering old-growth species—look out here for the resplendent quetzal.

The **SUSPENSION BRIDGE** over an offshoot of the Rio Caldera makes a fine backdrop to jungle photos.

PANAMA

Bajo Grande

Mirador Las Rocas

Bosque de las Lianas

Suspension Bridge

Alto Chiquero

Mirador de Alto Respingo

Near the halfway point, a side trail leads to the **MIRADOR LAS ROCAS**; when clear, it has fabulous views over the rolling, forest-covered horizon.

0 ·········· km ·········· 1
0 ·········· miles ·········· 1

Sirena

Cross the waters of the **RÍO CLARO**, keeping an eye out for small (and harmless) caiman.

Río Claro

Playa Sirena

0 ·············· km ·············· 2
0 ·············· miles ·············· 2

COSTA
RICA

La Leona

Madrigal

At the headland at **PUNTA SALSIPUEDES**, leave the beach and follow the trail through the forest behind the cliffs.

Punta Salsipuedes

Punta La Chancha

The ranger station at **LA LEONA** marks the entrance to Corcovado; the flock of scarlet macaws that live near here provide a colorful introduction to the wildlife within.

34

Corcovado National Park

LA LEONA TO SIRENA, COSTA RICA

Shadow the Pacific Ocean on a river-crossing beach hike that runs alongside Central America's wildest rainforest.

It's a jungle out there. Rugged and remote, the lush Corcovado National Park stretches across the southern section of the Osa Peninsula, in southeast Costa Rica. *National Geographic* called it "the most biologically intense place on earth," and the numbers are mind-boggling: more than 100 types of butterflies, over 375 species of birds, and at least 8,000 types of creepy-crawly (pack your insect repellent).

See how many you can spy on this hike between the ranger stations at La Leona,

on the park's eastern boundary, and Sirena, 10 miles (16 km) further along the coast. It's hot, and much of the trail is on energy-sapping sand, but there's a good chance of spotting some of Costa Rica's most hard-to-see inhabitants here—scarlet macaws, squirrel monkeys, Baird's tapirs, and maybe even a jaguar, if you're lucky. This cornucopia of wildlife swoops, swings, and stalks its way through the park's dense rainforest and along its black-sand beaches, where palm trees laden with coconuts reach out from the forest fringes for the frothy surf.

ELEVATION PROFILE

300 ft
(91 m)

0

0   10 miles (16 km)

⊖ 10 MILES (16 KM)

⊗ 932 FT (284 M)

🕐 1 DAY (ONE-WAY)

35

Valle de Cocora

PARQUE NACIONAL NATURAL LOS
NEVADOS, COLOMBIA

*Trek through the Valle de Cocora, a protected area in the heart
of Colombia's Zona Cafetera, to walk beneath the graceful
forms of the lofty* palma de cera.

Tip

Leave Salento, the
nearest town, early
(no later than 7:30 a.m.)
to explore the valley
in near solitude.

7 MILES (11 KM)

2,350 FT (716 M)

1 DAY (LOOP)

Creeping up the lower sections of the
Parque Nacional Natural Los Nevados,
the Valle de Cocora is threaded with well-
trodden trails, along which lie lush expanses of grassland and dense cloud forest.
While these do their part to demand your
attention, it's the limber skyscrapers of the
palma de cera that really steal the show.

    Standing at an average of 148 ft (45 m)
tall, these wax palms (Colombia's national

tree) are the tallest palm trees
in the world. But it's not just their lofty
height that draws the eye—they're
rendered all the more striking for their
dramatic spacing. Hundreds of trees
line the valley at the route's finale, positioned perfectly apart like candles on
a birthday cake.

    As you gaze skyward, you may
spot a variety of birdlife—toucans, condors, and eagles—nestled in the branches
of the palms, or spy larger wildlife, such as
the spectacled bear, wandering between
their elongated trunks. It's not a problem
if you don't, though: the elegantly swaying
palms are more than beguiling enough
on their own.

77

ELEVATION PROFILE

10,000 ft
(3,048 m)

6,500 ft
(1,981 m)

0   7 miles (11 km)

0 ········ km ········ 0.5

0 ········ miles ········ 0.5

Cocora

Valle de
Cocora

COLOMBIA

Finca La
Montaña

Acaime

The last section of the hike
passes through the **VALLE
DE COCORA**, where you can
truly appreciate the scale of
the giant wax palms.

The opening section of the trail
passes through **CLOUD FOREST**,
with several creek crossings via
suspension bridges.

Detour to **ACAIME**, a bird
sanctuary, to glimpse 18
species of hummingbirds.

36

Quilotoa Loop

SIGCHOS TO LAGUNA QUILOTOA, ECUADOR

Explore a dramatic stretch of central Ecuador on this challenging but rewarding high-altitude hike. The scenery is mesmerizing— glistening lakes, sleepy villages, and, of course, soaring mountains.

22 MILES (36 KM)

7,775 FT (2,370 M)

3 DAYS (ONE-WAY)

Tip

It can take a few days to acclimatize to the altitude—avoid alcohol, get some rest, and drink lots of water.

Found at the northern end of the Avenue of the Volcanoes—a chain of towering peaks running along the Andean spine of Ecuador—the Quilotoa Loop combines epic scenery with cultural insights and a physical challenge. The route (which, slightly confusingly, is actually a one-way hike rather than a loop) showcases the best of the region and shouldn't be taken lightly. Much of it is uphill, and all of it takes place at altitudes ranging from 9,186 to 12,795 ft (2,800 to 3,900 m). Needless to say, taking the time to properly acclimatize before setting off is essential.

But with these physical efforts come plenty of rewards. The starting point of the trail is the pretty town of Sigchos, from where you'll hike for three days through a rugged landscape of patchwork fields, precipitous cliffs, and plunging canyons. Isolated villages and hamlets provide an insight into rural life seemingly unchanged

for centuries, as well as the chance to admire local arts and crafts. (Isinlivi, where you spend your first night, produces beautiful wooden carvings, while Chugchilán, the second-night stop, is famous for its woolen goods.) These communities also offer the welcome balm of friendly guesthouses, perfect to rest your weary body at the end of the day (and save you the hassle of bringing camping gear).

Eventually, tired but elated, you'll reach your final destination: Laguna Quilotoa. Hidden from view until the

ELEVATION PROFILE

13,000 ft
(3,962 m)

3,000 ft
(914 m)

0   22 miles (36 km)

Hiking along the Quilotoa Loop through the Ecuadorian Andes

The small, rural town of **SIGCHOS** is the capital of a canton known as the "hanging garden of the Andes" on account of its array of beautiful flora.

Sigchos

0 ········· km ········· 2
0 ········· miles ········· 2

Cochalo

After completing a steep uphill section of the trail, you'll be ready for a breather at the **MIRADOR CAÑÓN DEL TOACHI** in Chinalo, which offers panoramic views of the Toachi canyon.

Isinlivi

At 9,416 ft (2,870 m), the tranqui village of **ISINLIVI** has a great guesthouse, offers spectacular mountain views, and is within striking distance of a ruined Inca fortress.

Set at 10,498 ft (3,200 m) above sea level, the welcoming village of **CHUGCHILÁN** has an artisanal cheese factory.

Chinalo

Chugchilán

MAKE IT SHORTER

A Different Town

If time is tight or you're after a less strenuous hike, start the route in either Isinlivi or Chugchilán, rather than Sigchos. This will shorten the hike by one or two days, respectively.

ECUADOR

Guayama Grande

last moment, this turquoise-green crater lake is the product of a mighty volcanic eruption 800 years ago, with its distinctive color due to the presence of dissolved minerals in the water. After a tough three-day trek, your legs will be aching, but be sure to summon up a final burst of energy to walk around the crater rim—during which you can admire some of the finest views in Ecuador.

According to local legend, the **LAGUNA QUILOTOA** crater lake is bottomless, but this is a slight exaggeration—it's actually 820 ft (250 m) deep.

Laguna Quilotoa

Quilotoa

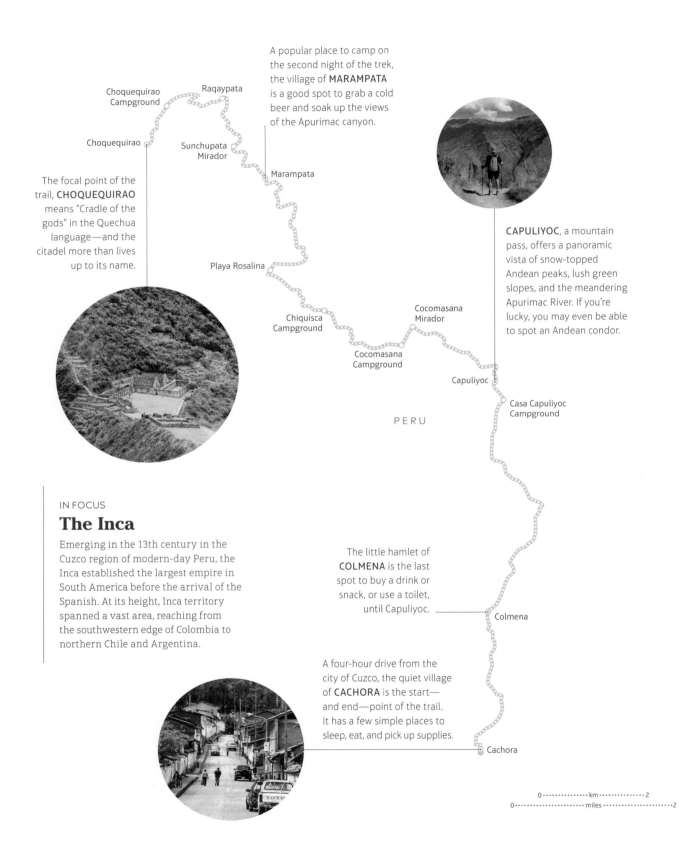

Choquequirao
Campground

Raqaypata

A popular place to camp on the second night of the trek, the village of **MARAMPATA** is a good spot to grab a cold beer and soak up the views of the Apurimac canyon.

Choquequirao

Sunchupata
Mirador

Marampata

The focal point of the trail, **CHOQUEQUIRAO** means "Cradle of the gods" in the Quechua language—and the citadel more than lives up to its name.

CAPULIYOC, a mountain pass, offers a panoramic vista of snow-topped Andean peaks, lush green slopes, and the meandering Apurimac River. If you're lucky, you may even be able to spot an Andean condor.

Playa Rosalina

Cocomasana
Mirador

Chiquisca
Campground

Cocomasana
Campground

Capuliyoc

Casa Capuliyoc
Campground

PERU

IN FOCUS

The Inca

Emerging in the 13th century in the Cuzco region of modern-day Peru, the Inca established the largest empire in South America before the arrival of the Spanish. At its height, Inca territory spanned a vast area, reaching from the southwestern edge of Colombia to northern Chile and Argentina.

The little hamlet of **COLMENA** is the last spot to buy a drink or snack, or use a toilet, until Capuliyoc.

Colmena

A four-hour drive from the city of Cuzco, the quiet village of **CACHORA** is the start— and end—point of the trail. It has a few simple places to sleep, eat, and pick up supplies.

Cachora

0 ·············· km ·············· 2
0 ·············· miles ·············· 2

37

Choquequirao

CACHORA, PERU

*Skip the heaving mass of tourists at Machu Picchu and strike out along
a far quieter ancient trail through the Peruvian Andes to the awe-inspiring
—and little-visited—Inca citadel of Choquequirao.*

Tip
Guided tours usually
include camping
equipment, so there's
no need to bring your
own gear.

38 MILES (62 KM)

13,809 FT (4,209 M)

4 DAYS (RETURN)

The Inca Trail, a four-day route that leads to the spectacular ruins of Machu Picchu, is one of the most legendary treks in the world. But in recent years, it has suffered from overtourism, with the trail and archaeological site becoming increasingly crowded. Fortunately, the surrounding region is crisscrossed with many other centuries-old Inca trails and ruins that offer a similarly rewarding experience—and with far fewer fellow hikers.

At the head of the pack is the epic Choquequirao trail, which leads to a remote citadel that has been described as the "sister" of Machu Picchu. The classic route takes four days there and back, but shorter and longer variations are also possible. Although you can do it independently, this is a challenging hike at altitude, so a guide is highly recommended.

Starting from the quiet town of Cachora, the trail takes you through a seemingly untouched section of the Peruvian Andes. It follows paths laid down by the Inca and their forerunners and crosses high mountain passes shrouded in clouds. Along the way, you'll make thigh-aching ascents and descents, camp out overnight, and encounter the occasional isolated settlement, whose residents are often on hand to provide flagging travelers with energy-boosting meals and snacks. There are also innumerable viewpoints offering sweeping vistas of the Apurimac River, which winds its way through the eponymous canyon below.

Needless to say, the highlight of the trek is the ruins of Choquequirao, which are spread across a series of mountain slopes, around 10,010 ft (3,050 m) above sea level. With its stunning array of houses, temples, plazas, ritual baths, aqueducts, and terraces, the site resembles Machu Picchu in its architecture–not surprising, given that it was occupied during a similar period in the 15th and 16th centuries. But Choquequirao is larger and immeasurably quieter than its more famous counterpart and, intriguingly, less than half of the site has been excavated—so there's still plenty more to be discovered.

ELEVATION PROFILE

13,000 ft
(3,962 m)

0

0   38 miles (62 km)

Tip

After the hike, head to the hot springs at the nearby town of Chivay for a well-earned soak.

The **RÍO COLCA** journeys through the canyon, before eventually becoming the Río Majes, which flows straight into the Milky Way according to Inca mythology.

38

Colca Canyon

CABANACONDE, PERU

Keep your eyes peeled for giant Andean condors circling high in the sky as you descend to the base of one of the deepest canyons on earth.

Encircled by towering cliffs, the oasis village of **SANGALLE** is dotted with natural swimming pools.

A long, jagged slash through the flanks of southern Peru, the Colca Canyon is around 11,155 ft (3,400 m) at its deepest point, dwarfing counterparts such as the famed Grand Canyon. Stretching for 43 miles (70 km), it is scattered with pretty villages, ribboned with agricultural terraces, flanked by a rugged Andean range, and patrolled by herds of llamas and their wild vicuña cousins.

This popular, self-guided trail runs from Cabanaconde, high on the canyon's cliff-top, down to Sangalle, an oasis at the base where you spend the night, before retracing your route the following day. Despite the remarkable landscapes, the biggest draw of the hike is the chance to spot an Andean condor. Riding warm air currents like fighter pilots, scanning constantly for their next meal, these majestic creatures—with a wingspan of up to 11 ft (3.3 m)—are the largest birds of prey in the world.

ELEVATION PROFILE

13,000 ft (3,962 m)

6,500 ft (1,981 m)

0

7 miles (11 km)

⊖ 7 MILES (11 KM)

⊗ 3,475 FT (1,059 M)

🕓 2 DAYS (RETURN)

In an elevated location, the village of **CABANACONDE** offers views of the canyon and the mountains beyond.

Rio Colca

Sangalle

0 ········· km ········· 0.5
0 ········· miles ········· 0.5

Viewpoint

Viewpoint

PERU

Viewpoint

Cabanaconde

The **SANTUARIO**, a clifftop ceremonial complex, is home to the sacred Titikala rock, from where the name "Titicaca" derives.

La Chincana

Santuario

Kasapata

Challapampa

The first significant set of ruins on the trail, **KASAPATA** was once a *tambo* (waystation) for tired pilgrims.

ISLA DEL SOL

0 ·············· km ·············· 2
0 ·············· miles ·············· 2

Lake Titicaca

Yumani

YUMANI has terraced fields and a "magic" spring that is said to give drinkers the ability to speak Spanish, Quechua, and Aymara.

ANOTHER WAY
Isla de la Luna

Just west of Isla del Sol, tiny Isla de la Luna ("Island of the Moon") was closely associated with the Inca moon goddess, Mama Killa. A 2-mile (3 km) hiking trail runs around the island, which has several ancient ruins.

39

Isla del Sol

CHALLAPAMPA TO YUMANI, BOLIVIA

Retrace an ancient pilgrim trail on Isla del Sol ("Island of the Sun") in the middle of Lake Titicaca, one of the most important religious sites in the Inca world.

9 MILES (14 KM)
1,591 FT (485 M)
1 DAY (ONE-WAY)

Long venerated by people from across the Andes, Isla del Sol became a major pilgrimage destination under the Inca. They considered it the birthplace of sun god Inti, father of Manco Cápac, the founder of the Inca dynasty.

Almost 500 years on from the fall of the empire, boats sail to the rocky island from the lakeside town of Copacabana, dropping travelers off at the hamlet of

Challapampa on the northeast coast. From here a gentle trail—the Sacred Route of the Eternal Sun—loops around the edge of Isla del Sol, passing the ruins of Inca and pre-Inca temples, shrines, homes, and waystations, notably Titikala, the sacred rock from which the sun allegedly first rose. It finishes in the village of Yumani, from where boats depart for Copacabana.

As you follow this historic path, the sun watches over your progress, arcing overhead before drifting down toward Lake Titicaca. Its golden rays are a constant reminder of why devotees flocked to Isla del Sol from far and wide for hundreds of years.

ELEVATION PROFILE

16,000 ft
(4,876 m)

10,000 ft
(3,048 m)

0

9 miles (14 km)

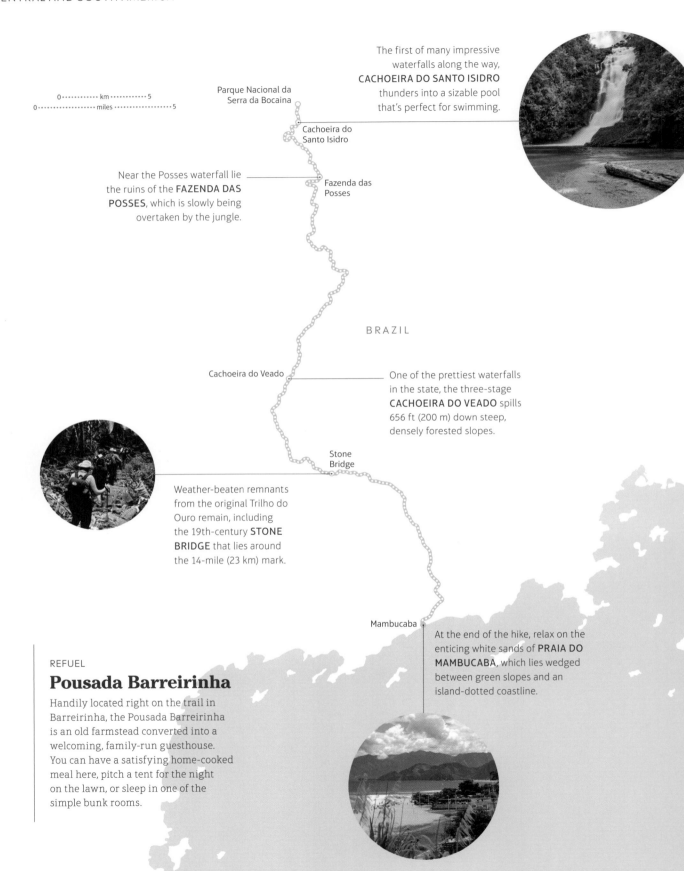

0 ·········· km ·········· 5
0 ·········· miles ·········· 5

The first of many impressive waterfalls along the way, **CACHOEIRA DO SANTO ISIDRO** thunders into a sizable pool that's perfect for swimming.

Parque Nacional da Serra da Bocaina

Cachoeira do Santo Isidro

Near the Posses waterfall lie the ruins of the **FAZENDA DAS POSSES**, which is slowly being overtaken by the jungle.

Fazenda das Posses

BRAZIL

Cachoeira do Veado

One of the prettiest waterfalls in the state, the three-stage **CACHOEIRA DO VEADO** spills 656 ft (200 m) down steep, densely forested slopes.

Stone Bridge

Weather-beaten remnants from the original Trilho do Ouro remain, including the 19th-century **STONE BRIDGE** that lies around the 14-mile (23 km) mark.

Mambucaba

At the end of the hike, relax on the enticing white sands of **PRAIA DO MAMBUCABA**, which lies wedged between green slopes and an island-dotted coastline.

REFUEL

Pousada Barreirinha

Handily located right on the trail in Barreirinha, the Pousada Barreirinha is an old farmstead converted into a welcoming, family-run guesthouse. You can have a satisfying home-cooked meal here, pitch a tent for the night on the lawn, or sleep in one of the simple bunk rooms.

84

40

Trilho do Ouro

PARQUE NACIONAL DA SERRA DA BOCAINA
TO MAMBUCABA, BRAZIL

Listen to the cry of howler monkeys while hiking a centuries-old trail through the jungle-clad mountains of southeast Brazil.

33 MILES (53 KM)

2,743 FT (836 M)

3 DAYS (ONE-WAY)

In the 1690s, fortune hunters stumbled upon staggering sums of gold in the mountains north of Rio de Janeiro (present-day Minas Gerais). The momentous discovery would cause an upheaval on two continents as Europeans flocked to the new settlement, chasing dreams of striking it rich. Tiny settlements in Brazil exploded into boom cities overnight, and new roads were laid to transport the gold to port and on to Portugal. Vestiges of these old routes survive today, including a forest-lined track through the coastal mountains north of Paraty.

Called the Trilho do Ouro (Gold Trail), the path takes you from the heights of the protected Serra da Bocaina, at an elevation of 5,249 ft (1,600 m), down to the edge of a seaside town overlooking the Baía da Ilha Grande. Much of the trail passes through the original Mata Atlântica, lush Atlantic rainforest that harbors a dazzling variety of plants and animals. Mata Atlântica once covered vast swathes of Brazil's east coast – over 386,102 sq miles (1 million sq km), in fact. Today, only 7 percent remains, and

A path through Mata Atlântica rainforest on the Trilho do Ouro

hiking the Trilho do Ouro is one of the best ways to experience this endangered neotropical wilderness.

As soon as you step through the northern entrance gate of the Parque Nacional da Serra da Bocaina, you enter a verdant forest seething with life. On a day's walk, you might encounter a troop of spider monkeys swinging through the trees, spy shimmering butterflies winging along the riverbanks, or hear the primordial cry of a howler monkey as night descends. Some hikers wake to find large paw prints in the mud near their encampment—signs of big cats (including jaguars) that prowl by night amid the dense jungle canopy. ▶

ELEVATION PROFILE

6,500 ft (1,981 m)

0

0   33 miles (53 km)

CENTRAL AND SOUTH AMERICA

Although ostensibly downhill, there are plenty of taxing uphill stretches, along with steep knee-destroying descents. The slippery terrain adds to the challenge. Even if you hike outside of the rainy season, you'll contend with slick wet tree roots along the path, slippery moss-covered boulders, and unavoidable mud patches. The occasional fall is almost a rite of passage on the Trilho do Ouro, and those who've hiked it before all agree on three essentials: reliable shoes, a walking stick, and an unhurried pace.

The crossing of creeks and rivers is another constant; at some points, you can wade or rock-hop over narrow gurgling stretches, at others, bouncy suspension bridges or more rustic *pinguelas* (narrow log and rope bridges) take you across the rushing waters. There's even a small metal one-person gondola (not always in service) that travels along an overhead cable on one final stretch of the Rio Mambucaba.

Much of the forest feels pristine and untouched, though humans have left their mark on the landscape. You'll pass the ruins of old *fazendas* (farms from the days of European settlement) and homesteads, some of which date back to the 19th century. A handful of working farms still dot the trail, some set in bucolic locales fronting mirror-like lakes and rolling pastures dotted with the odd araucária (a towering evergreen that can live for hundreds of years).

The last day of the hike is also the hardest, with steep and mucky terrain. You'll find yourself slip-sliding over the original paving stones (known as *pé de moleque*), which were laboriously laid by enslaved workers during the 18th century, and used by mules to carry first gold then later coffee down to the coast. It is thought that the trail was plotted over existing routes blazed by the Guaianazes Indigenous people long before the Portuguese arrived.

The finish is pure exhilaration—after myriad river crossings and soggy ups and downs through forests and valleys, you emerge with breathtaking views back to the lush mountain slopes you've just traversed. From there, you can treat yourself to some well-deserved R&R on the shores of the Costa Verde (green coast)—home to some of Brazil's most beautiful beaches.

Right Cachoeira do Veado, one of numerous cascades found along the Trilho do Ouro

Below The river and beach near the trail's end in the village of Mambucaba

MAKE IT LONGER
Pico do Gavião

A rewarding detour is the ascent up Pico do Gavião. Well signposted about halfway along the trail, this 3-mile (4.5 km) return trail takes you to a 5,249 ft (1,600 m) summit where you'll have views over the surrounding peaks and south to the island-studded coastline.

41

Ilha Grande Circuit

VILA DO ABRAÃO, BRAZIL

Escape the bustle of civilization to discover pristine beaches, virgin Atlantic rainforest, and sleepy fishing villages on this multiday hike around the periphery of Ilha Grande.

41 MILES (66 KM)

9,875 FT (3,010 M)

5 DAYS (LOOP)

Looking at Ilha Grande on a map, you'd be forgiven for assuming that any island so close to civilization would have long succumbed to its influence. Not so. Although just over 62 miles (100 km) by road and boat from Rio de Janeiro, the isle harbors one of the world's richest ecosystems—expect pure stretches of untouched rainforest and unspoiled beaches. This is not a hike that brims with the promise of wildly different views every day but rather one that celebrates discovering this perfectly preserved microcosm of Brazil's natural bounty at your own unhurried pace.

The hike begins with a half-day jaunt that winds past an aqueduct and waterfall within easy distance of the island's main port of Vila do Abraão. You can expect to be in company for this first stage, as it's popular with visitors—but few venture further along the trail. Leaving the crowds behind, days weave into a single tapestry, the threads joined together by your footsteps as the trail takes its meandering path in and out of the jungle-clad hills, cutting through vine canopies before forging into patches of sky-high bamboo.

It's no accident this stretch of Brazil's coastline is called the Costa Verde: fecund to the point of excess, its lush greenness is punctuated by sparkling lagoons and tangled mangroves. Wildlife flourishes here, too. The ominous shriek of the howler monkey rises above the call of the bare-throated bellbird, or "araponga" as the locals call it, each one distinctly discernible above the cacophony of the forest fauna.

There's gold amid the green, though—the island's 102 beaches are never far away. No sooner does the heat and humidity reach an unbearable peak than the trail intuitively emerges onto a beach, the sea water an irresistible lure to help you cool off. It's almost a shame to return to Vila do Abraão—though, to console you, there's always the promise of a boat trip back to your favorite of the island's beaches.

The mangrove-fringed shore of Pouso, one of over a hundred beaches on Ilha Grande

ELEVATION PROFILE

1,500 ft
(457 m)

0

0   41 miles (66 km)

At the **PRAIA DO SUL BIOLOGICAL RESERVE**, spy armadillos, howler monkeys, and parrots.

Praia Japariz

Praia do Bananal

Praia de Fora

One of the isle's few human-made attractions, the **AQUEDUCT** was built in 1893 to provide water to the island's hospital.

Ubatuba

Praia Longa

Aqueduct

Vila do Abraão

Palmas

Praia de Araçatiba

ILHA GRANDE

Praia do Sul Biological Reserve

Provetá

Dos Rios

Praia do Aventureiro

Parnaioca

At **PRAIA DO AVENTUREIRO**, see the "broken" coconut palm—the tree's trunk grows horizontally, skirting over the water before turning 90-degrees to grow skyward.

Even on a hike littered with stunning beaches, **PARNAIOCA** stands out. Vying for the title of the most beautiful beach in Brazil, this long stretch of yellow sand is one not to miss.

MAKE IT LONGER
Parrot Peak

Allow an extra day at the end of the route to tackle the 7-mile (11 km) round-trip trail to the top of Parrot Peak from Vila do Abraão. This tough hike to the island's second-highest point requires a bit of scrambling in the final stages. Do so and you'll enjoy spectacular views of the island and beyond—on a clear day, you can see Rio de Janeiro.

0 ·········· km ·········· 3
0 ·········· miles ·········· 3

42

Laguna de los Tres

EL CHALTÉN, ARGENTINA

Immerse yourself in the awe-inspiring terrain of Patagonia on a trail through Parque Nacional Los Glaciares, one of South America's trekking hot spots.

14 MILES (22 KM)

3,435 FT (1,047 M)

1 DAY (RETURN)

90

Admiring Monte Fitz Roy reflected in the waters of the Laguna de los Tres

Ragged granite mountains blanketed with snow. Creaking glaciers reaching out into lakes dotted with icebergs. Expanses of wild steppe and dense subpolar forests. Parque Nacional Los Glaciares is home to some of Patagonia's most spectacular landscapes. Even better, the reserve—a UNESCO World Heritage Site—is easy to explore independently thanks to a network of well-marked trails and well-maintained campsites.

The popular "Lagoon of the Three" trek runs from the village of El Chaltén—gateway to the northern Fitz Roy sector of the park—to Laguna de los Tres, and back again. This lagoon sits at the base of

Monte Fitz Roy, the centerpiece of a jagged, snow-covered massif. The peak is known to the Indigenous Tehuelche people as El Chaltén ("the mountain that smokes") on account of the clouds that swirl around its summit. On a clear, sunny day, Fitz Roy and its neighbors are perfectly reflected in the lake's blue-green waters, an image of heart-stopping beauty.

Laguna de los Tres

Laguna Sucia

A crystal-clear, ice-cold lake, **LAGUNA DE LOS TRES** takes its name from the three mountains that loom above it.

ARGENTINA

Laguna Madre

Laguna Capri

The **MIRADOR RÍO DE LAS VUELTAS** is a viewpoint that offers superlative vistas of the mountain-fringed valley of the meandering Río de las Vueltas.

Mirador Fitz Roy

Mirador Río de las Vueltas

El Chaltén

ELEVATION PROFILE

6,500 ft (1,981 m)

0

0   14 miles (22 km)

0 ·········· km ········· 1
0 ············· miles ············· 1

A welcoming village that sits inside the boundaries of Parque Nacional Los Glaciares, **EL CHALTÉN** is the trekking capital of Argentina.

Easter Island's only town, **HANGA ROA** has several notable sights, including the Tautira *moai*, which stands proudly on its own platform close to the harbor.

Hanga Roa

A dormant 1,063 ft (324m) volcano on the southwestern edge of the island, **RANO KAU** has a large chunk missing from its crater rim—this gap provides a perfect frame for the Pacific Ocean beyond.

EASTER ISLAND

Rano Kau

Orongo

ORONGO, a windswept archaeological site, contains the ruins of a series of oval-shaped ceremonial buildings, some of which are covered by petroglyphs.

43
Birdman Trail

HANGA ROA, EASTER ISLAND, CHILE

Follow in the footsteps of the young men who took part in an epic annual contest of courage, daring, and endurance on the remotest inhabited island on earth.

Easter Island—known to locals as Rapa Nui—is renowned for its *moai*, inscrutable monolithic statues sculpted from volcanic rock. But they are only one aspect of the island's rich cultural heritage. This easy-to-follow trail retraces a route once used during the Birdman contest, an annual competition that ran for more than 150 years in the 18th and 19th centuries. The winner's patron would be named "Tangata Manu" (Birdman) at a ceremony at the ceremonial village of Orongo and gain authority over the island for the next 12 months.

The route starts in the town of Hanga Roa, climbs up to the crater rim of the Rano Kau volcano, and finishes in Orongo, whose ruins sit on a clifftop above the Pacific. At this point, Birdman contestants would scale the 984 ft (300 m) cliffs, swim through shark-infested waters, scale the nearby islet of Motu Nui, and compete to claim the first egg laid by a sooty tern that season. Fortunately, your only responsibility once you're finished is to kick back and enjoy the views.

ELEVATION PROFILE

1,500 ft (457 m)

0

0   6 miles (9 km)

⊖ 6 MILES (9 KM)

⊘ 1,237 FT (377 M)

◷ 1 DAY (RETURN)

44

Dientes de Navarino Circuit

PUERTO WILLIAMS TO RUTA Y-905, CHILE

Journey to the southernmost tip of South America for an adventurous hike through the remote, challenging, and starkly beautiful region of Tierra del Fuego.

REFUEL

Centolla

Try the delicious local speciality: *centolla* (king crab). These monster-sized crustaceans have spiny shells and can measure up to 3 ft (1 m) from the tip of one leg to another. Restaurants in Puerto Williams serve a range of *centolla* dishes.

23 MILES (37 KM)
6,900 FT (2,103 M)
4–7 DAYS (ONE-WAY)

For travelers seeking a genuine taste of the wilderness, few places can compare with Tierra del Fuego ("Land of Fire"). Divided between Chile and Argentina, this rugged, sparsely populated archipelago is the most southerly section of the South American continent. Often referred to as "el fin del mundo" (the end of the world), the region is barely 620 miles (1,000 km) north of Antarctica.

On the Chilean side of Tierra del Fuego, Navarino Island is home to Puerto Williams, the southernmost city on earth. Located on the shores of the Beagle Channel—which bisects the region and takes its name from the HMS *Beagle*, the ship that took naturalist Charles Darwin on his ground-breaking voyage around South America—it is the starting point for one of the continent's great treks: the Dientes de Navarino circuit.

Looming above Puerto Williams are the Dientes ("Teeth") in question, a range of fanglike mountains that stretches across the island. From the city, a woodland trail leads up to the summit of Cerro Bandera ("Flag Hill"). Here you get your first real glimpse of the landscape of the circuit, a varied mix of subpolar tundra, dark-green moorland, crystalline lakes, forests of lofty lenga beech trees, and fearsome snow-streaked peaks. Over the next four to seven days—depending on the precise route you take and how fast you cover the ground—you'll experience a world seemingly untouched by human hands.

ELEVATION PROFILE

3,000 ft (914 m)

0

0   23 miles (37 km)

Enjoying the view over Puerto Williams and the Beagle Channel from the trail

Reaching the top of the steep **PASO VIRGINA** can be exhausting, but you're treated to superb views of Laguna de los Guanacos and the Beagle Channel.

The Museo Antropológico Martín Gusinde in **PUERTO WILLIAMS** provides an insight into the history of the region and the cultures of its Indigenous peoples.

Puerto Williams

Ruta Y-905

Laguna de los Guanacos

Paso Virgina

CHILE

Laguna Róbalo

Cerro Bandera

One of several lakes on the trek, **EL SALTO** is nestled on the far side of Cerro Bandera.

Laguna El Salto

Laguna Martillo

Laguna del Paso

Laguna Escondida

93

0 ········· km ········· 2
0 ········· miles ········· 2

Paso Ventarron

Laguna de los Dientes

LAGUNA DE LOS DIENTES is the southernmost point of the trek and a good spot to camp. The surrounding woodlands have been devastated by beavers that were misguidedly introduced to the region in the 1940s.

As will quickly become clear, this is a tough trek that, apart from the opening section, is not well marked. There are no facilities and the weather is notoriously temperamental—expect ferocious winds, swirling mist, snow storms and plunging temperatures, as well as flashes of sunshine. Although it's possible to hike independently, going with a local guide who knows the terrain well is highly recommended.

There's an immense sense of satisfaction when you reach the end of the trail at the shore of the Beagle Channel. It can be difficult to leave the dramatic landscapes of the Dientes behind, but the lure of a hearty meal, hot shower, and cozy bed in Puerto Williams helps soften the blow.

ICELAND

⊙ 45

FAROE
ISLANDS
⊙ 46

SWEDEN

NORWAY
⊙ 47

FINLAND

⊙ 75
ESTONIA

LATVIA

DENMARK
⊙ 48
⊙ 49

LITHUANIA

BELARUS

56
○
● 57

53
○

50
○

UNITED
KINGDOM

55
○

52
○

IRELAND

54
○

51

NETHER-
LANDS
58

62 ⊙

POLAND

BELGIUM
59 ⊙

LUX.

60 ⊙

GERMANY

61 ⊙

CZECH
REPUBLIC
76 ⊙

SLOVAKIA

⊙ 68

FRANCE

SWITZ.
64 ⊙
66 ⊙

63 ⊙

AUSTRIA

HUNGARY

77 ⊙

MOLDOVA

67 ⊙

65 ⊙

SLOVENIA

ROMANIA

CROATIA

BOSNIA-
HERZ.

SERBIA

BULGARIA

69 ⊙

ITALY

MONTE-
NEGRO

78 ⊙

KOSOVO

70 ⊙

72

ALBANIA

N. MAC.

PORTUGAL

SPAIN

GREECE

80 ⊙

74 ⊙

79 ⊙

73 ⊙
MADEIRA

71 ⊙
CANARY
ISLANDS

94

RUSSIA

UKRAINE

GEORGIA

⊙ 81

TURKEY

CYPRUS

EUROPE

45

Laugavegurinn Trail

LANDMANNALAUGAR TO THÓRSMÖRK, ICELAND

Iceland's most famous hiking trail, Laugavegurinn combines jaw-dropping volcanic landscapes with the comfort of welcoming mountain huts at the end of each day's adventures.

Tip
Before heading out each day, check safetravel.is for the latest weather conditions and volcanic activity.

32 MILES (52 KM)

4,587 FT (1,398 M)

4 DAYS (ONE-WAY)

96

If you were wondering why Iceland is known as the "Land of Fire and Ice," a few days' walk through the mind-bending geology of the Laugavegurinn Trail should clear things up. This four-day hike traverses lands forged by volcanism—obsidian lava fields, sputtering geothermal springs, and rainbow-hued ravines—as well as serving up views of some of Iceland's most famous glaciers.

In a place where nature's majesty is so plain to see, it's important to respect it. The trail is open only from June to September, and that's for good reason: fog and snow smother the ice fields for the rest of the year, making hiking an inadvisable, indeed potentially lethal, pursuit. Even in summer, adverse weather can easily roll in, and you'll be fording a couple of rivers whatever the conditions, so this isn't one for total beginners. That said, if you're

reasonably fit, willing to get your feet wet, and don't mind sacrificing a few creature comforts, hiking Laugavegurinn promises to be one of life's great adventures.

Running for 32 miles (52 km), the trail's natural beauty is ratcheted up to the extreme from the start, with the rhyolite mountains of Landmannalaugar catching the light in hues of red, orange, and icy blue. Laugavegurinn translates as "hot springs route," and it certainly lives up to its name, with steam from bubbling pools shrouding the lava-strewn canyons between Hrafntinnusker and Álftavatn. Perhaps the most striking landscape, though, belongs to Mælifellssandur, where a vivid green volcano rises like a little elfin hat from a desert of pure black sand. Amid such desolate beauty, the basic mountain huts you'll call home are oases of comfort and warmth, providing a dose of normality amid this strange and unforgettable plane.

As you descend to the trail's end in the glacier-sandwiched Thórsmörk (Valley of Thor), it feels like returning to earth from another world. But you'll be left with no doubt in your mind that this is truly a land of the gods.

ELEVATION PROFILE

6,500 ft
(1,981 m)

0

0   32 miles (52 km)

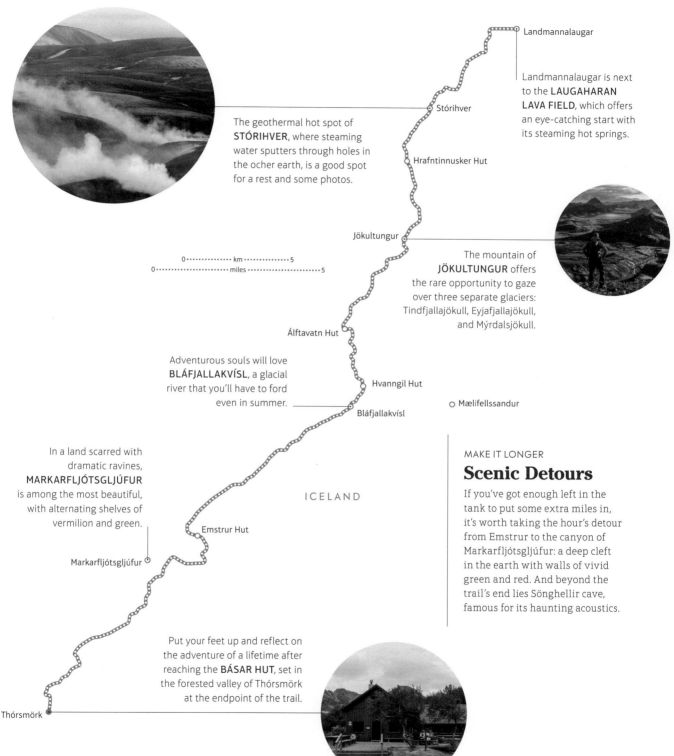

Landmannalaugar

Landmannalaugar is next to the **LAUGAHARAN LAVA FIELD**, which offers an eye-catching start with its steaming hot springs.

Stórihver

The geothermal hot spot of **STÓRIHVER**, where steaming water sputters through holes in the ocher earth, is a good spot for a rest and some photos.

Hrafntinnusker Hut

Jökultungur

0 ·········· km ·········· 5
0 ·········· miles ·········· 5

The mountain of **JÖKULTUNGUR** offers the rare opportunity to gaze over three separate glaciers: Tindfjallajökull, Eyjafjallajökull, and Mýrdalsjökull.

Álftavatn Hut

Adventurous souls will love **BLÁFJALLAKVÍSL**, a glacial river that you'll have to ford even in summer.

Hvanngil Hut

Bláfjallakvísl

Mælifellssandur

In a land scarred with dramatic ravines, **MARKARFLJÓTSGLJÚFUR** is among the most beautiful, with alternating shelves of vermilion and green.

Markarfljótsgljúfur

ICELAND

MAKE IT LONGER
Scenic Detours

If you've got enough left in the tank to put some extra miles in, it's worth taking the hour's detour from Emstrur to the canyon of Markarfljótsgljúfur: a deep cleft in the earth with walls of vivid green and red. And beyond the trail's end lies Sönghellir cave, famous for its haunting acoustics.

Emstrur Hut

Put your feet up and reflect on the adventure of a lifetime after reaching the **BÁSAR HUT**, set in the forested valley of Thórsmörk at the endpoint of the trail.

Thórsmörk

46
The Postman's Path

BØUR TO GÁSADALUR, FAROE ISLANDS, DENMARK

Rugged seascapes abound on this age-old trail that was once trodden by the island's hardy postie.

2.5 MILES (4 KM)

1,427 FT (435 M)

0.5 DAYS (ONE-WAY)

As commutes go, the hike from Bøur to Gásadalur on the Faroese island of Vágar is a real humdinger—austere mountains on one side, the vast expanse of the steely Atlantic on the other, and a sloping pathway that leads down to a cluster of turf-topped houses. But until 2004, when a tunnel finally connected the two villages by road, this was the only way in and out for the local postman, who used to hike along the path three times a week to deliver mail to Gásadalur's dozen or so inhabitants. Follow in his footsteps to what was once one of the most isolated settlements in the Faroes, its houses still huddled a mere gust of wind away from the clifftop edge.

Just before you stride into Gásadalur, take the short detour to the impossibly photogenic **MÚLAFOSSUR** waterfall, which tumbles off a cliff ledge 492 ft (150 m) into the sea below.

98

Gásadalur

Múlafossur

ELEVATION PROFILE

3,000 ft (914 m)

0

0   2.5 miles (4 km)

IN FOCUS

The Corpse Stone

Until Gásadalur got its own cemetery in 1873, the villagers had to carry their deceased over the mountain to bury them in Bøur. It's for this reason that the large, flat rock next to the path near Gásadalsbrekkan is known as the Corpse Stone—it was the only place on the trail where a coffin could be rested.

Risasporið

VÁGAR

According to local legend, the imprint in the rock at **RISASPORIÐ** is actually a huge footprint, made when a giant leapt from here to Mykines.

Trailhead

Pause at **GÁSADALSBREKKAN** to take in the stellar views across to the island of Mykines, which swarms with puffins in summer.

Gásadalsbrekkan

0 ········· km ········· 0.5
0 ········· miles ········· 0.5

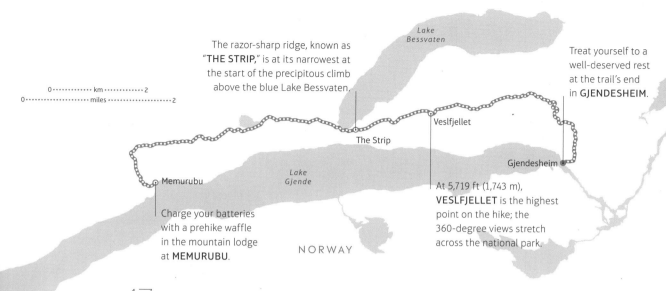

The razor-sharp ridge, known as **"THE STRIP,"** is at its narrowest at the start of the precipitous climb above the blue Lake Bessvaten.

Treat yourself to a well-deserved rest at the trail's end in **GJENDESHEIM**.

Lake Bessvaten

0 ·········· km ·········· 2
0 ·········· miles ·········· 2

Veslfjellet

The Strip

Memurubu

Lake Gjende

Charge your batteries with a prehike waffle in the mountain lodge at **MEMURUBU**.

NORWAY

At 5,719 ft (1,743 m), **VESLFJELLET** is the highest point on the hike; the 360-degree views stretch across the national park.

Gjendesheim

47

The Besseggen Ridge

MEMURUBU TO GJENDESHEIM, NORWAY

Steel your nerves for a challenging mountain hike along a razor-thin ridge in Norway's Jotunheimen National Park.

9 MILES (14 KM)
3,615 FT (1,102 M)
1 DAY (ONE-WAY)

The Besseggen Ridge is something of a celebrity in Scandinavia. Norway's best-known day hike, in the country's most illustrious national park, its jagged spine is believed by some to have been forged by Thor's mighty hammer. The hike involves a boat trip along Lake Gjende, a long climb and an even longer descent, but it's the ridge itself—a threadline precipice that'll turn even the toughest mountaineer's legs to jelly—that is the star attraction. It's incredibly steep and exposed to high winds (you'll need a head for heights, as the rock just drops away into thin air in

places), but the views are some of the finest in Norway: a wide sweep of craggy peaks and rolling glaciers, and, far, far below, the glinting green waters of Gjende.

Preparing to cross the ridge between Lake Gjende and Lake Bessvaten

ELEVATION PROFILE

6,500 ft
(1,981 m)

0

0   9 miles (14 km)

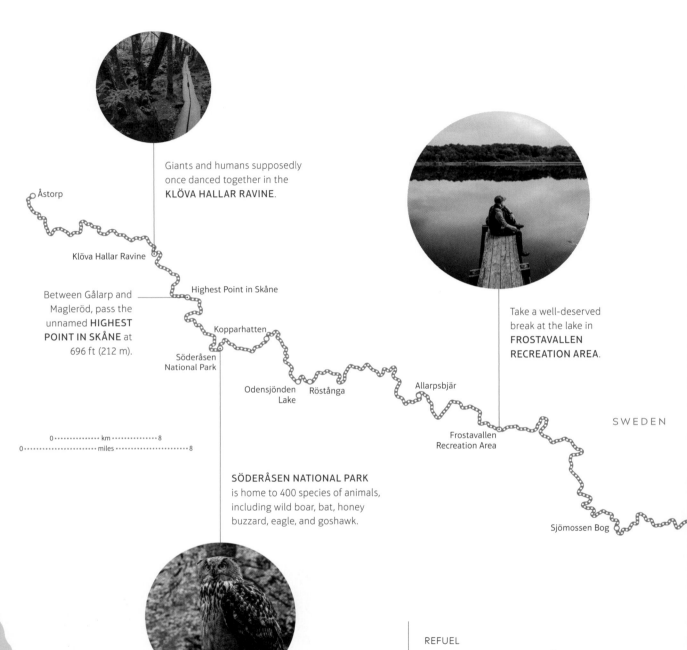

Giants and humans supposedly once danced together in the **KLÖVA HALLAR RAVINE**.

Åstorp

Klöva Hallar Ravine

Between Gålarp and Magleröd, pass the unnamed **HIGHEST POINT IN SKÅNE** at 696 ft (212 m).

Highest Point in Skåne

Kopparhatten

Söderåsen National Park

Odensjönden Lake   Röstånga

Allarpsbjär

Take a well-deserved break at the lake in **FROSTAVALLEN RECREATION AREA**.

Frostavallen Recreation Area

SWEDEN

0 ·········· km ·········· 8
0 ·········· miles ·········· 8

SÖDERÅSEN NATIONAL PARK is home to 400 species of animals, including wild boar, bat, honey buzzard, eagle, and goshawk.

Sjömossen Bog

REFUEL

Stationen Röstånga

Should you fancy a night away from the wind shelters, you'll pass through Röstånga, a honeypot of hotels, restaurants, and cafés. Stationen Röstånga (*stationshusetrostanga.se*) serves tapas, *smörrebröd* (open sandwiches), and hearty main courses for hungry hikers.

48

Skåneleden

ÅSTORP TO BRÖSARP, SWEDEN

Moving from deep ravines and volcanic viewpoints to knifelike ridges and forgotten boglands, this epic cross-country trail in southern Sweden is an immersive journey into nature and myth.

100 MILES (160 KM)

7,379 FT (2,249 M)

14 DAYS (ONE-WAY)

If there's one thing you learn when hiking in Skåne County, Sweden's southernmost region, it's that there's always more than one route to choose—and none is like the other. Somewhat confusingly, Skåneleden, the country's most comprehensive long-distance hike, is made up of six separate subsections labeled SL1 to SL6, a puzzle of crisscrossing trails that each offer fresh perspectives on some of the country's most bewitching national parks and coastlines. Seen on a trail map, it looks like an unwound ball of twine.

That means the hardest part, before even packing your bag or lacing up your boots, is deciding which one to tackle. Hike 229 miles (370 km) east to west from Sölvesborg to Ängelholm along SL1, or stride 201 miles (325 km) right through the middle of the region, north to south, from Hårsjö to Trelleborg on SL2—where do you begin?

Fall foliage beside a stream in Söderåsen National Park

For lovers of nature and myths, there's no route better than the relatively flat SL3, Skåneleden's third subtrail, which delves deep into spectacular national parks and wanders high above tumbling ravines. At 100 miles (160 km), it's also the second-shortest route and can be divided into 14 manageable sections that wend from Åstorp at the foot of Söderåsen ridge, north of Helsingborg, to the Hills of Brösarp nature reserve. ▶

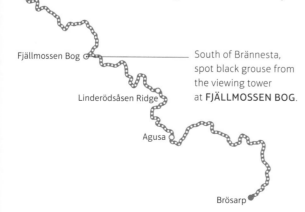

Fjällmossen Bog

Linderödsåsen Ridge

Agusa

Brösarp

South of Brännesta, spot black grouse from the viewing tower at **FJÄLLMOSSEN BOG**.

ELEVATION PROFILE

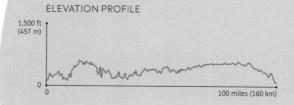

1,500 ft (457 m)

0

0

100 miles (160 km)

101

Golden beech
trees in Söderåsen
National Park

Myth and legend are
deeply intertwined with
the landscape in this
part of Sweden.

That Sweden is a fantasy land of deciduous forests is clear from the very start, as you wind east across the northern slope of the Söderåsen ridge. Here, among the beech trees and lichen-covered boulders, you'll find rock formations reputedly made by giants and a cave said to have been inhabited by a girl with magical powers.

Myth and legend are deeply intertwined with the landscape in this part of Sweden, and that's especially true in Skåne's largest protected area, Söderåsen National Park. The path here leads through wildlife-rich forest to the perfectly circular Odensjönden Lake, named after Odin, the Norse god of wisdom and death; it's fabled to be bottomless, and perhaps also an entrance to Odin's home. Such tales are easy to believe atop

Kopparhatten, the park's best-known viewpoint (located right on the trail), from where the steep-sloped ravines of Skåne's Grand Canyon look as though they were cleft by Odin's axe.

But fable turns to fact as you approach the route's halfway mark, traversing what was once a shallow sea where dinosaurs swam. This whole area brims with exquisite geography and geology, the fault lines marked by volcanic activity that took place between 200 million and 80 million years ago. Highlights include fossil fields, bedrock lakes, and Allarpsbjär, a wooded hillock formed from prehistoric lava flow, where you can spy basalt pillars and the remains of crater vents. Good navigation skills are essential here: the iron content is so high in the surrounding landscape that you can't trust your compass.

It's hard to escape the fairy-tale feel of the forest for long, however, and you're soon lured deep into its spell along the Linderödsåsen Ridge. Carnivorous sundew plants blanket the boggy ground and decaying trees draped in moss and fungi stand alongside the path—little wonder that stories of goblins and trolls abound in this area.

The transition back into the real world on the final section comes as something of a dramatic shock, although there are lingering traces of storybook Sweden in the medieval villages, Bronze Age burial mounds, and half-timbered, thatched cottages you pass. But there's nothing that says your journey into the Swedish wilderness has to stop at Brösarp—after all, the Skåneleden has five more routes to discover. Which one will you choose next?

MAKE IT LONGER
Join the SL4

One section of Skåneleden not enough for you? From Brösarp, you can immediately hook up with the 117-mile (188 km) SL4. This route unravels around southeast Skåne, focusing on coastal hiking, a shoreline of fudge-colored beaches, and shifting dunes.

A misty morning in the Hills of Brösarp nature reserve

Explore the subterranean passage grave at **KONG ASGERS HØJ**—one of Denmark's best examples of this style of burial ground.

Dating from 1852, the quaint structure of **BOGØ MILL** offers far-reaching views over the shimmering Grønsund strait.

Stretching over 4 miles (6 km), the **MØNS KLINT** are over 70 million years old and protected as a nature reserve.

Nyord

Nyord

DENMARK

Stege

Møn

Råbylille Strand

Møns Klint

Klintholm Havn

Kong Asgers Høj

Bogø

Bogø By

Damsholte

Hårbølle Strand

49

Camønoen

MØN, DENMARK

Nicknamed "Denmark's friendliest hiking trail," the Camønoen winds across the islands of Møn, Bogø, and Nyord, skirting along spectacular coastlines, through wooded glades, and over sloping grassland as it goes.

108 MILES (174 KM)   4,196 FT (1,279 M)   7 DAYS (LOOP)

Established in 2016, the Camønoen is a relatively new hiking trail. But that hasn't stopped it from quickly becoming one of Denmark's most alluring long-distance hikes. Marked by a wide and accessible path, the trail's relative ease (a deliberate choice by its creators) is the reason for its popularity—and for its nickname. It's wheelchair friendly and family friendly, and there are Camøno benches dotted frequently along the route, providing ample opportunity to pause for a break and chat with your fellow walkers.

Woven between stretches of leafy woodland and undulating grasslands, the Danish coastline reveals itself as you amble along. In the glow of the sun, the calm azure waters could be mistaken for the Caribbean—though the limestone cliffs of the Møns Klint reveal your location more accurately. Keep your pace gentle and savor the unhurried bliss of quiet nature all around.

Tip

Visit the Møns Museum (*museerne.dk/mons-museum*) near the trail's start for maps and other useful information.

ELEVATION PROFILE

650 ft (198 m)

0

0   108 miles (174 km)

The looming limestone cliffs of the Møns Klint, overlooking the Baltic Sea

104

50
National Famine Way

STROKESTOWN TO DUBLIN, IRELAND

Follow in the footsteps of the ill-fated emigrants known as the "Missing 1490" as you journey through some of the most bitter days of Ireland's past.

104 MILES (168 KM) · 2,700 FT (823 M) · 6 DAYS (ONE-WAY)

At the height of the Great Famine in 1847, 1,490 Irish tenants were evicted from their properties in Roscommon and forced to make an arduous journey on foot to Dublin, from where ships would take them to the Americas. It was a harrowing ordeal: the travelers had no money, food, or shelter. Many wouldn't survive to the end, with some dying during the walk and even more passing away on the so-called "coffin ships" that sailed from their homeland.

The National Famine Way sets out to unravel the history of these "Missing 1490." As you walk along the self-guided route, which runs through countryside beside the Royal Canal, the trail's downloadable audio guide recounts the harrowing trek through the eyes of 12-year-old Daniel Tighe, one of the missing who survived the ordeal. His words wind their way into the landmarks that punctuate a sea of green landscape, each bearing the shadow of the emigrants' story.

ELEVATION PROFILE

650 ft (198 m)

0

0 — 104 miles (168 km)

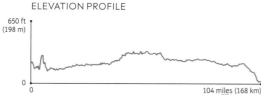

Strokestown · Termonbarry · Abbeyshrule · Coolnahay Harbour · Mullingar · IRELAND · Enfield · Maynooth · Blanchardstown · Dublin

Strokestown Park House, in **STROKESTOWN**, was the home of Major Denis Mahon, who forced the emigration of the "Missing 1490." Today, it houses the National Famine Museum.

Near Mullingar's **KILPATRICK BRIDGE**, spy a pair of bronze bound shoes—it's one of dozens of such sculptures that line the route, symbolizing the hope and pain of the emigrants' journey.

The **FAMINE MEMORIAL**, created by Irish sculptor Rowan Gillespie, is found at Custom House Quay at the end of the trail.

0 ·········· km ·········· 20
0 ·········· miles ·········· 20

Looking out over the
striking gold, green, and
gray cliffs of Golden
Gap in Dorset

51

South West Coast Path

MINEHEAD TO SOUTH HAVEN POINT, ENGLAND

Conquer England's longest and best-loved National Trail, encompassing the country's most dramatic coastal scenery, chocolate-box fishing harbors, and golden-sand beaches.

630 MILES (1,014 KM)

75,295 FT (22,950 M)

6–8 WEEKS (ONE-WAY)

Postcards of England's comely left limb showcase the gleaming sand, the thatched cottages and promenades, the sun, surf, and sea. But inspect them more closely and you'll spot another telling trait: a coast that soars and plunges like a stegosaurus spine, concealing countless secret coves. These made the region a magnet for smugglers—which is why a footpath hugging the shore's edge was created, so coastguards could spy ne'er-do-wells pulling into remote inlets and bays. Today, though, these tracks have been combined to form England's longest National Trail, tracing over 600 miles (1,000 km) of the country's most spectacular coastline. ▶

ELEVATION PROFILE

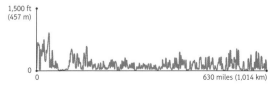

1,500 ft
(457 m)

0

0   630 miles (1,014 km)

106

Stretching between Minehead in west Somerset and South Haven Point near Poole in Dorset, the path traverses the entire mainland seaboards of Devon and Cornwall. Some hike the whole trail in one burst, dashing around in as little as 30 days, though most allow seven or eight weeks to absorb the varied scenery. It's also easy to split the trek into shorter stages, as many settlements are well served by transport links.

There's food and accommodations to suit every budget and taste, from beachside fish and chips and campsites to Michelin-starred seafood and stylish boutique hotels. Indulgent cream teas and pasties are justified regardless, with ascents and descents totalling some 114,829 ft (35,000 m)—equivalent to climbing Mount Everest nearly four times.

Though the route here is described from Minehead, you can tackle it in either direction. High summer (July and August) brings the sunniest, warmest days, with basking sharks cruising near-shore waters, but also crowds of vacationers. Spring—when wildflowers spangle clifftops, and temperatures and rainfall are moderate—is a fine compromise, though fall has its appeal, with blazing colors in deciduous woodland and purpled heath. In winter,

you can expect short days and unpredictable weather, offset by empty paths and particularly dramatic skies and seas.

Whenever you walk, you'll discover that each stretch of this route has a unique character. The first section, heading west along the coast of Exmoor National Park, is arguably the wildest, craggiest, and most romantic. Here, the clifftop path seems to weave through time, passing by prehistoric hut circles and barrows, Roman fortlets and medieval field systems, in between charming fishing villages such as Porlock Weir and Lynmouth. There are climbs aplenty here, too, including the trail's highest point at Great Hangman (1,043 ft/318 m). ▶

REFUEL
Ann's Pasties

A deceptively simple but tasty and tummy-lining filled pastry, the Cornish pasty is the quintessential feast-to-go. It's also the subject of heated debate: who bakes the best? Our pick is Ann's Pasties (*annspasties.co.uk*), with shops in Lizard, Porthleven and Helston.

Tucked into a rocky cleft, the pretty village of **BOSCASTLE** houses a fascinating Museum of Witchcraft and Magic.

Boscastle
Tintagel
Newquay
Fowey
St Ives
Gurnard's Head
Falmouth
St Michael's Mount
Land's End
Kynance Cove

The roller-coaster trail between St. Ives and Land's End provides spectacular vistas, notably from **GURNARD'S HEAD** (with its enticing pub).

Make time to cross the tidal causeway to **ST. MICHAEL'S MOUNT**, the intriguing priory-turned-castle perched on an inshore rock opposite Marazion.

Stride along the vertiginous cliff-hanging path from Lynton to reach the **VALLEY OF ROCKS**, watching for wild goats grazing among the crags once dubbed "Little Switzerland."

Delve into magical **CULBONE WOOD** above Porlock to discover the beautiful medieval St. Beuno's Church.

Valley of Rocks

Culbone Wood

Minehead

Woolacombe

Barnstaple

Clovelly

Bude

ENGLAND

Arguably the loveliest village on the Jurassic Coast, **ABBOTSBURY** retains evocative reminders of its long history, including the ruined abbey and St. Catherine's Chapel.

Lyme Regis

South Haven Point

Abbotsbury

Swanage

Exmouth

Weymouth

0 ·········· km ·········· 25
0 ·········· miles ·········· 25

Torquay

Plymouth

Dartmouth

Salcombe

A winsome haven on the Dart river, guarded by twin castles, **DARTMOUTH** is a favorite with vacationers and yachties.

From the national park, the trail emerges onto a rather easier and more populated stretch of north Devon. Several attractive seaside resorts stud this rocky patch, their glistening sands luring families and surfers alike. The going gets positively flat around the dual estuaries of the Taw and Torridge rivers—but the trail soon bucks again as it turns west toward the Atlantic. Clovelly—Devon's most photogenic coastal hamlet, tumbling down the hillside to its historic harbor—offers a brief respite before the challenge resumes as you continue on to Hartland Point. If the West Country is England's leg, this wild headland is the kneecap—the point where the path veers sharply south onto arguably the most testing portion of the trail. You'll barely have time to catch your breath between the end of each long descent and the start of the sheer climb that follows; in return, you'll enjoy spectacular views along the rocky cliffs and, for the most part, glorious solitude until the perky resort of Bude.

From here, watch for signs you're in Kernow (Cornwall): the white-on-black

> If the West Country is England's leg, this wild headland is the kneecap—the point where the path veers sharply south onto arguably the most testing portion of the trail.

cross of St. Piran's Flag, and place names beginning Porth- (meaning bay or harbor in old Cornish), Pol- (lake or pool), Pen- (headland), and Tre- (homestead). The path is no less demanding, albeit studded with some of the trail's loveliest fishing villages, golden sands, and the rock-top bastion of Tintagel. These castle ruins were forever linked to the legendary King Arthur by 12th-century writer Geoffrey of Monmouth, several hundred years after his putative reign—and well before the construction of the castle itself.

Tracking the edge of the Cornish coast, the path leads on to the colorful artist hub of St. Ives and the Penwith Peninsula, the farthest-flung quarter of this wildest west. Beyond the throngs at Land's End, the path veers east again, onto Cornwall's southern coast. This region has a flavor subtly different but no less alluring than its rockier northern seaboard, with quaint fishing harbors and scenic highlights, including the Lizard Peninsula, mainland England's southernmost point, and the trail's loveliest beach at Kynance Cove.

Surfers on the beach at Croyde in north Devon

Left The Minack Theatre in Cornwall, found on the stretch near Land's End

Right A cobbled street in the fishing village of Clovelly, north Devon

A short ferry ride from Cremyll Point brings you into south Devon at Plymouth, the only city on the trail. The coastline on this stretch is peppered with beach resorts, notably the "English Riviera" around Torbay—a 22-mile (35 km) stretch famed for its craggy coves, subtropical plants, and balmy climate.

Beyond Exmouth, switchbacks return in the geological wonderland dubbed the Jurassic Coast—over 93 miles (150 km) of scarps and summits up to 250 million years old. Red sandstone cliffs segue from east Devon into Dorset, where fossil-hunters scour the shingle. Watch your feet: the path bucks on a final stretch that rivals north Cornwall for leg-burning climbs. There's just time to sink those weary feet into the soft sands of Studland Bay at the route's terminus, South Haven Point— though you might find yourself tempted to turn around and tackle it all again.

MAKE IT SHORTER
Land's End Circuit

Many hikers tackle the path in stages, and everyone has their favorite patch. For a satisfying three- or four-day taster, traversing some of the most dramatic clifftop stretches, circumnavigate the 52-mile (84 km) Penwith Peninsula from St. Ives to Marazion, returning along the St. Michael's Way.

EUROPE

The distinctive streaky bacon stripes of the **HUNSTANTON CLIFFS** are one of Norfolk's best-known attractions.

The **CLEY MARSHES** are Norfolk's oldest nature reserve and an important bird breeding sanctuary.

Brancaster

Cley Marshes

Hunstanton Cliffs

Wells-next-the-Sea

Sheringham

Cromer

Take a short detour to marvel at the impressive 11th-century paintings at **HOUGHTON ON THE HILL**'s St. Mary's Church.

Castle Acre

ENGLAND

Houghton on the Hill

Great Yarmouth

Hopton-on-Sea

Knettishall Heath Country Park

0 ·········· km ·········· 20
0 ·········· miles ·········· 20

52

Peddars Way and Norfolk Coast Path

KNETTISHALL HEATH COUNTRY PARK TO
HOPTON-ON-SEA, ENGLAND

Trace Norfolk's changing geology on a peaceful trail that takes in glorious landscapes of low valleys, heath, and windswept coastline.

128 MILES (206 KM)

4,940 FT (1,506 M)

8 DAYS (ONE-WAY)

Combining two stand-alone routes to form a single National Trail, the Peddars Way and Norfolk Coast Path winds from past to present. Some signs of days gone by are obscure, like the shallow Pingo Ponds left by glaciers in the last Ice Age. Others are less so: look out for the Songline sculptures on the Peddars Way section, etched with poetry and images to evoke the geology and history of the land. And on the Norfolk Coast Path, marvel at the red-and-white stripes of the Hunstanton Cliffs, each band formed by the slow passage of years. But many of the trail's delights are simply timeless. Salt marshes teem with birds, seals frolic on the shore, and the wind whips along long stretches of golden sand in a natural cycle that has played, and will continue to play, for millennia.

ELEVATION PROFILE

650 ft
(198 m)

0

0

128 miles (206 km)

53
Cat Bells

HAWSE END, ENGLAND

The perfect introduction to hiking in the Lake District, this short but sweet trail takes in pretty meadowland and a cheeky scramble up a wee fell, as well as panoramic views of classic Lakeland landscapes.

Believed to be a distortion of "Cat's Bield"—meaning "refuge of the wildcat," from a time when wildcats were widespread in Britain—Cat Bells is one of the smallest fells (mountains) in the Lake District. But despite its modest stature, this "family fell" makes up in spectacle what it lacks in height.

Richly rewarding views unfold one step at a time during the easygoing climb: idyllic Derwentwater sits serenely to your left, while majestic green-and-gold hills roll away to your right. Near the top, a brief scramble leads onto a rocky plateau where a neat cairn marks the summit. From here, a spectacular panorama unfolds over the verdant valley of Borrowdale and the island-studded surface of Derwentwater, with the market town of Keswick at its helm. A gentle descent leads down to this tranquil body of water, the edge of which you'll trace back toward your beginning. The only way to make this hike better? Ending with a pint at a cozy pub in Keswick.

◯ 4 MILES (6 KM)

◯ 1,184 FT (361 M)

◯ 0.5 DAYS (LOOP)

ELEVATION PROFILE

1,500 ft
(457 m)

0

0   4 miles (6 km)

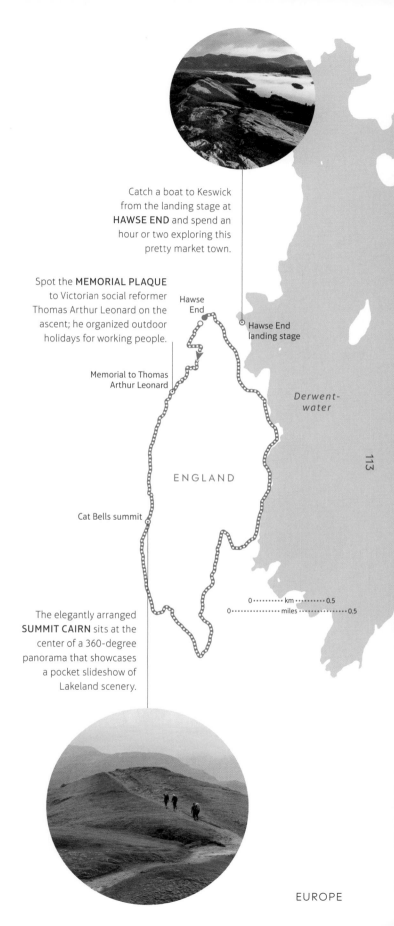

Catch a boat to Keswick from the landing stage at **HAWSE END** and spend an hour or two exploring this pretty market town.

Spot the **MEMORIAL PLAQUE** to Victorian social reformer Thomas Arthur Leonard on the ascent; he organized outdoor holidays for working people.

Hawse End

Hawse End landing stage

Memorial to Thomas Arthur Leonard

Derwent-water

ENGLAND

Cat Bells summit

0 ·········· km ·········· 0.5
0 ·········· miles ·········· 0.5

The elegantly arranged **SUMMIT CAIRN** sits at the center of a 360-degree panorama that showcases a pocket slideshow of Lakeland scenery.

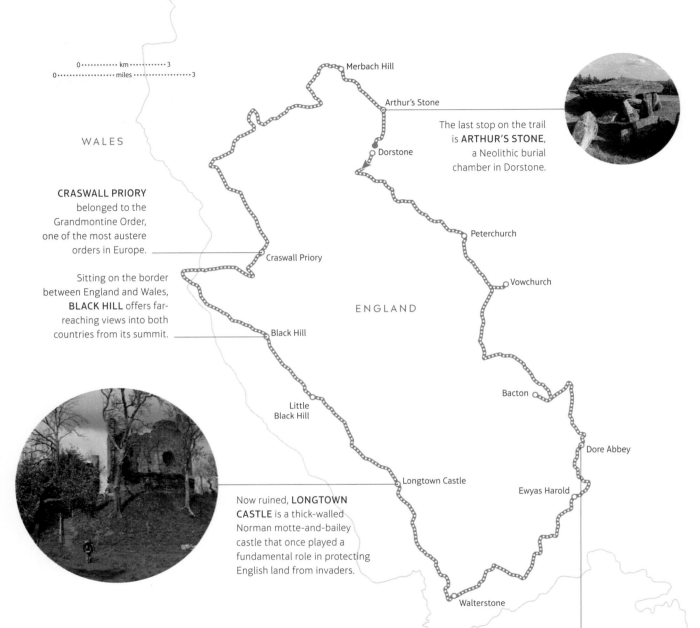

0 ·········· km ·········· 3
0 ·········· miles ·········· 3

Merbach Hill

Arthur's Stone

The last stop on the trail
is **ARTHUR'S STONE**,
a Neolithic burial
chamber in Dorstone.

Dorstone

WALES

CRASWALL PRIORY
belonged to the
Grandmontine Order,
one of the most austere
orders in Europe.

Craswall Priory

Peterchurch

Sitting on the border
between England and Wales,
BLACK HILL offers far-
reaching views into both
countries from its summit.

Black Hill

Vowchurch

ENGLAND

Little
Black Hill

Bacton

Dore Abbey

Longtown Castle

Ewyas Harold

Now ruined, **LONGTOWN
CASTLE** is a thick-walled
Norman motte-and-bailey
castle that once played a
fundamental role in protecting
English land from invaders.

Walterstone

IN FOCUS
Ley Lines

Although Alfred Watkins himself did not
attribute mystical properties to the ley
lines, there have been many theories
about their supernatural powers. Some
believe that ley lines are a source of
psychic energy, which may influence
other paranormal phenomena such
as UFOs and crop circles.

DORE ABBEY was one of the country's
great medieval Cistercian monasteries.
The buildings seen today are a fraction
of the former abbey but still stand
resplendent in their glory.

54
Twin Valley Ley Line Trail

DORSTONE, ENGLAND

Follow ancient ley lines through the wildest parts of Herefordshire, on an intriguing route complete with historical sites and spiritual spaces of days gone by.

43 MILES (69 KM) 5,890 FT (1,795 M) 3 DAYS (LOOP)

In 1921, antiquarian Alfred Watkins was struck by the revelation that Herefordshire's ancient sites were connected by straight lines. Dubbing these alignments "ley lines," he surmised that Neolithic people used them to navigate across Britain—and possibly the globe. Although discredited by archaeologists, the theory captured the public imagination, with some claiming that ley lines hold supernatural powers.

The idea still fascinates today—as proved by this loop trail, established in 2021 to celebrate the centenary of Watkins' epiphany. The route follows the lines through open fields, along ocher footpaths and over wooden bridges across streams, with the wind-whipped grass pointing you toward a glut of historic landmarks. Revel in the sight of saintly churches secreted in the bosom of rolling hills, along with the ancient abbey at Dore—once one of Britain's most important monasteries—and the shadowy ruins of Longtown Castle.

Where the lines may sometimes not be clear, the tangible routes carved by two rivers step in to guide your path. The Dore streaks through the aptly named Golden Valley, while the Monnow twists its way under the stark silhouette of the Black Mountains. As the trail weaves up to their peaks, becoming ever more challenging, there's little to disturb the rural tranquility other than the slow crunch of progress. Your reward for the climb? Seemingly everlasting views across England and Wales. Savor the sight, magnificent enough to inspire a burst of spirituality in even the most doubtful, before you make your way back to Dorstone and the fabled ruins of Arthur's Stone.

ELEVATION PROFILE

3,000 ft
(914 m)

0

0   43 miles (69 km)

Taking in the view from atop Black Hill, one of the peaks in the Black Mountains

55
Cwm Idwal

SNOWDONIA NATIONAL
PARK, WALES

*Hike to a stunning glacial valley carved
out by ice—and around the beautiful
lake that sits in its center.*

The steep-sided bowl of Cwm Idwal is
littered with remnants of the great sheet
of ice that once weighed down these
hillsides—slopes of scree, boulder fields,
and moraines that were all left behind
by a glacier as it retreated up the cliffs
millennia ago. As you circuit Llyn Idwal
lake, walking amid a landscape that feels
barely changed in 10,000 years, you'll see
pockets of rare plants more commonly
found in the Arctic and high Alps (Snowdon
lily, mountain avens, and purple saxifrage)
clinging to the rocky ledges. It's the rocks
that steal the show, though: Darwin's
Boulders, named after the naturalist,
who carried out fieldwork here; the
climbers' playground that is the Idwal
Slabs; and Twll Du, the Devil's Kitchen,
named for the mists that swirl up through
a cleft in the cliff face, giving the landscape
a truly primordial appearance.

ELEVATION PROFILE

3,000 ft
(914 m)

0

0   3 miles (5 km)

⊖ 3 MILES (5 KM)

⊗ 689 FT (210 M)

◷ 0.5 DAYS (RETURN)

IN FOCUS
The Legend of Idwal

According to Welsh folklore, Llyn Idwal
is named after the son of a 12th-century
prince. Handsome and clever, Idwal was
drowned in the lake by his jealous uncle.
Legend has it that the birds here were so
filled with grief that they vowed never to
fly over the lake again, a promise they
(allegedly) still keep today.

0 ········· km ········· 0.25
0 ········· miles ············· 0.25

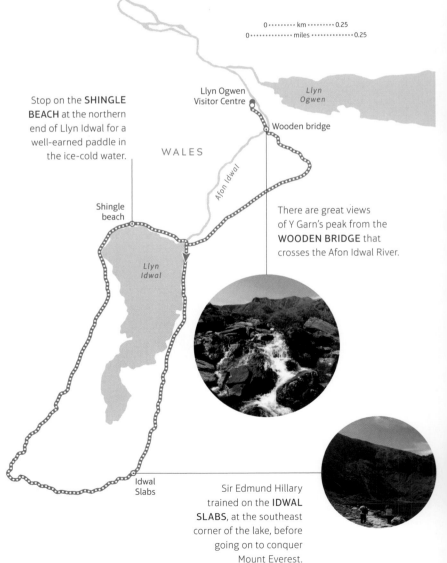

Llyn Ogwen
Visitor Centre

*Llyn
Ogwen*

Stop on the **SHINGLE
BEACH** at the northern
end of Llyn Idwal for a
well-earned paddle in
the ice-cold water.

Wooden bridge

WALES

Afon Idwal

Shingle
beach

There are great views
of Y Garn's peak from the
WOODEN BRIDGE that
crosses the Afon Idwal River.

*Llyn
Idwal*

Idwal
Slabs

Twll Du ○

Sir Edmund Hillary
trained on the **IDWAL
SLABS**, at the southeast
corner of the lake, before
going on to conquer
Mount Everest.

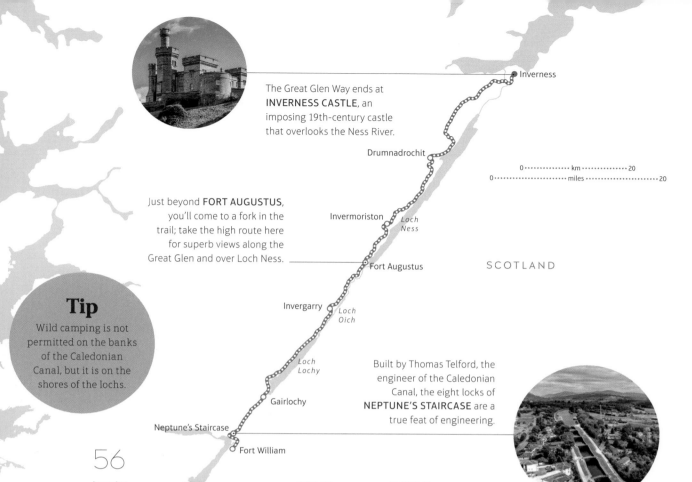

The Great Glen Way ends at **INVERNESS CASTLE**, an imposing 19th-century castle that overlooks the Ness River.

Inverness

Drumnadrochit

Just beyond **FORT AUGUSTUS**, you'll come to a fork in the trail; take the high route here for superb views along the Great Glen and over Loch Ness.

Invermoriston

Loch Ness

Fort Augustus

SCOTLAND

Tip
Wild camping is not permitted on the banks of the Caledonian Canal, but it is on the shores of the lochs.

Invergarry

Loch Oich

Loch Lochy

Built by Thomas Telford, the engineer of the Caledonian Canal, the eight locks of **NEPTUNE'S STAIRCASE** are a true feat of engineering.

Gairlochy

Neptune's Staircase

Fort William

0 ·········· km ·········· 20
0 ·········· miles ·········· 20

56
The Great Glen Way
FORT WILLIAM TO INVERNESS, SCOTLAND

Walk from one side of Scotland to the other via a famous glen, passing through quintessential Highlands scenery on the way.

75 MILES (121 KM)

7,972 FT (2,430 M)

6 DAYS (ONE-WAY)

The Great Glen Way packs the best of the Scottish Highlands into six scenic days. Rambling from Fort William on the southwest coast to Inverness on the northeast, it travels the entire length of Scotland's longest glen, skirting the shores of tranquil lochs, tip-toeing beneath towering mountains, and dipping in and out of forests that are home to pine martens and red deer. It's a tremendous introduction to long-distance walking, with the prevailing wind behind you and an easy-to-follow path that utilizes woodland tracks, old drove roads, and the towpath that runs alongside the historic Caledonian Canal—constructed in the 1800s to bypass the often treacherous boat journey by sea. Keep an eye out for ospreys and golden eagles along the way—and the looping silhouette of the Loch Ness Monster, of course.

ELEVATION PROFILE

1,500 ft (457 m)

0

0   75 miles (121 km)

57
Fife Coastal Path

KINCARDINE TO NEWBURGH, SCOTLAND

Follow Fife's diverse coastline from the Firth of Forth to the Firth of Tay, on this clearly waymarked route via long sandy beaches, picturesque fishing villages, historic castles, and serene nature reserves.

115 MILES (185 KM)

6,847 FT (2,087 M)

8–10 DAYS (ONE-WAY)

The peninsular region of Fife juts out into the wild North Sea, bounded at its top and bottom by the great estuaries, or firths, of the Tay and the Forth. This walk along the coastline here is full of variety, from rugged rocky remoteness to bustling towns and villages. Navigation is easy thanks to a cornucopia of signs, and, with few hills, the going never really gets too tough, so you can just settle in and enjoy the scenery.

Setting off from Kincardine, the trail wends its way along the edge of the Firth of Forth, via industrial sites, naval bases, tumbledown churches and castles, and nature reserves such as Torry Bay. At the latter, large flocks of wading birds can be seen on the artificial lagoons, built using ash from the nearby Longannet Power Station. But this busy backdrop soon gives way to a smattering of rustic fishing villages such as St. Monans, a justly popular spot with a clifftop castle and disused windmill, once used to extract salt from the seawater.

The wild ruggedness only increases as you approach Fife's easternmost point, where rough, narrow paths will challenge

The remains of St. Andrews Cathedral, built during the medieval era

your footwork and make you thankful for sturdy boots. At low tide, you can walk along the rocky shoreline here, looking out to sea for pods of dolphins (don't worry if you arrive at high tide, as there are alternative routes to follow).

Things ease off as you head north along glorious golden beaches, passing puzzling geological formations, such as the pink sandstone Buddo Rock and the conglomerate tower Rock and Spindle, as well as pretty St. Andrews, the home of golf. On the final stretch, you'll pass through fields and pine woods, with the Tay narrowing westward to no more than a river, before arriving at the ancient town of Newburgh. The distillery here is known as "the spiritual home of Scotch whisky"—so why not put your feet up and relax with a wee dram?

ELEVATION PROFILE

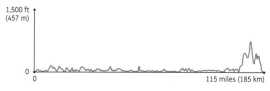

1,500 ft
(457 m)

0

0   115 miles (185 km)

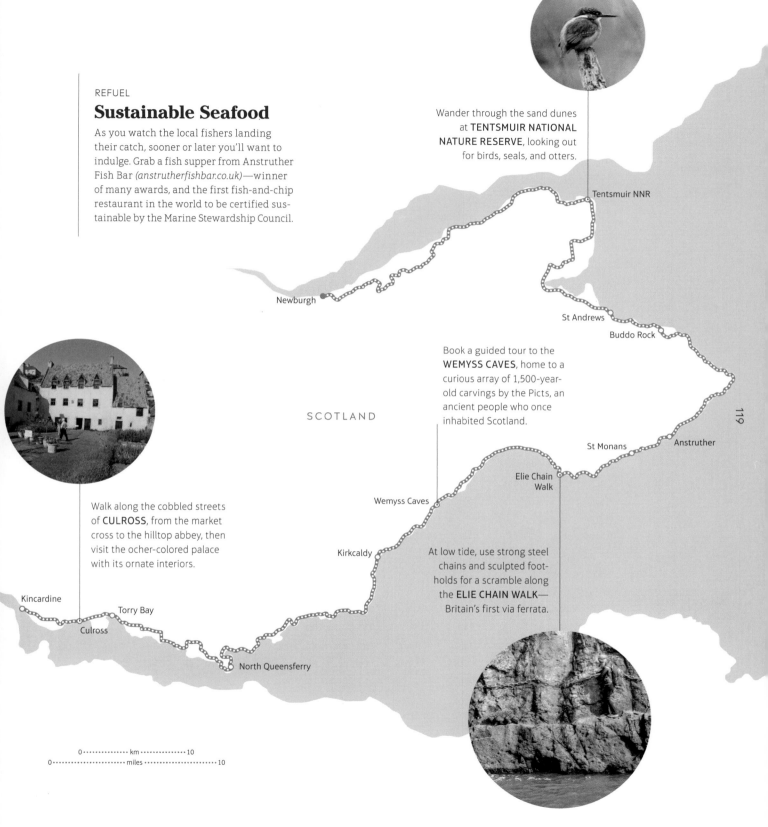

REFUEL

Sustainable Seafood

As you watch the local fishers landing their catch, sooner or later you'll want to indulge. Grab a fish supper from Anstruther Fish Bar (*anstrutherfishbar.co.uk*)—winner of many awards, and the first fish-and-chip restaurant in the world to be certified sustainable by the Marine Stewardship Council.

Wander through the sand dunes at **TENTSMUIR NATIONAL NATURE RESERVE**, looking out for birds, seals, and otters.

Book a guided tour to the **WEMYSS CAVES**, home to a curious array of 1,500-year-old carvings by the Picts, an ancient people who once inhabited Scotland.

SCOTLAND

Walk along the cobbled streets of **CULROSS**, from the market cross to the hilltop abbey, then visit the ocher-colored palace with its ornate interiors.

At low tide, use strong steel chains and sculpted footholds for a scramble along the **ELIE CHAIN WALK**— Britain's first via ferrata.

Tentsmuir NNR

Newburgh

St Andrews

Buddo Rock

St Monans

Anstruther

Elie Chain Walk

Wemyss Caves

Kirkcaldy

Kincardine

Torry Bay

Culross

North Queensferry

0 ·········· km ·········· 10
0 ·········· miles ·········· 10

58
Pieterpad

PIETERBUREN TO SINT-PIETERSBERG,
THE NETHERLANDS

*Explore the Netherlands' most famous long-distance path,
a modern pilgrimage that highlights a lesser-known side
of the country's fascinating past.*

310 MILES (495 KM)

8,999 FT (2,743 M)

26 DAYS (ONE-WAY)

120

Winding across the near pancake-flat Netherlands, the Pieterpad takes you from the country's northernmost point on the mainland to its southern tip beside Belgium. You might imagine that this is a journey of quintessential Dutch scenes—windmill-framed canals, colorful tulip fields, and centuries-old cheese farms—but this life-affirming trail of unpaved paths and forgotten roads reveals another side to the country. Running along the tourist-free borderlands with western Germany, the route meanders from the beaches of the salt-licked Wadden Sea coast across the clay paths of Groningen to the sandy soils of Drenthe. On the way, it takes in the medieval cities of Groningen, Nijmegen, and Maastricht, with evocative historical sights filling the spaces in between.

Unlike many of Europe's flagship multiday trails, the Pieterpad comes with a particularly intriguing and organic back-story. It wasn't conceived by good-willed conservationists or a government-financed tourism agency but by two friends who lived at opposite ends of the country. As the story goes, Bertje Jens, who lived in Groningen, and her great friend Toos Goorhuis-Tjalsma, who lived in Tilburg, felt impassioned to create a rambling route between their hometowns. So inspired were they by a similar long-distance trail in Germany's Black Forest, that the pair walked the length of the Netherlands between 1978 and 1983, mapping and detailing as they went, before eventually stretching the trail across the whole country. ▶

ELEVATION PROFILE

1,500 ft
(457 m)

0

0   310 miles (495 km)

Walking along the Pieterpad through peaceful
countryside near Oudemolen

Tip

The Pieterpad website (*pieterpad.nl*) has a wealth of maps and information about the route.

Medieval **GRONINGEN** is often described as the most beautiful city in the Netherlands that visitors overlook. Don't make the same mistake.

Pieterburen

Groningen

Consider how Neolithic people once lived along parts of the **DE HUNEBED HIGHWAY** in little-known Drenthe.

De Hunebed Highway

NETHERLANDS

Coevorden

Ommen

REFUEL

Hotel De Kroon

Recharge with a night at the Hotel De Kroon (*hoteldekroon.com*), a wonderfully atmospheric hotel and restaurant in Gennep. Right on the trail, the building overlooks the historic market square and has a lovely terrace where you can sip the hotel's own cellar-brewed beers.

Sallandse Heuvelrug National Park

Ascend the **ARCHEMERBERG** in Sallandse Heuvelrug National Park—on a clear day you can see Germany from this 256 ft (78 m) hill.

Vorden

Groesbeek War Cemetery

Pause to remember the soldiers of World War II in the former battlegrounds outside **NIJMEGEN**.

Gennep

GERMANY

Venlo

Dutch wine? It's better than you might think. Toast the end (or start) of your hike on a white-wine estate in **LIMBURG**.

BELGIUM

Sittard

Maastricht

Sint-Pietersberg

0 ·········· km ·········· 40
0 ·········· miles ·········· 40

EUROPE

A tree-lined stretch of the Pieterpad in the province of Drenthe

Understandably, most trekkers opt to tackle the trail over a series of shorter 9–14 mile (15–22 km) stages, starting and ending in the route's more easily accessible cities and towns. This can be handy if you're strapped for time and only want to absorb the Pieterpad's highlights (of which there are many), and is helped by a wide range of accommodation options from beginning to end. But the trail can be hiked in any season and in any direction, so it's up to you

> If history is your thing, then the Pieterpad is momentous even by the standards of the Netherlands' rich past.

to follow the tracks to see where they lead. If history is your thing, then the Pieterpad is momentous even by the standards of the Netherlands' rich past. Those of a prehistoric persuasion will be keen to wind back to Neolithic times at the megalithic tombs of Drenthe, the oldest monuments in the country. Arch-shaped and set with heavy stone, these colossal graves south of Groningen are so distinctive that Dutch folklore claims they were hand-built by giants, or *huynen*. That association helps explain the local name for the burial sites – *hunebeds* – and their unique archaeological history has given birth to the De Hunebed Highway, a sort of macabre variation on Route 66.

This is not just a hike about the ancient mists of time, though – farther south the path crosses the Rhine and

Meuse rivers, strategic battlegrounds on the frontline of World War II. In particular, the riverlands outside Nijmegen and Groesbeek on the German border provided the backdrop for the heroics and human sacrifice of Operation Market Garden, the largest airborne operation in history. Here, you can stop off at museums and memorials to learn stories of Nazi sieges, Allied paratroop landings and the disastrous "A Bridge Too Far" offensive. Back on the trail, the silence of the surrounding forest paths allows for quiet reflection on these poignant tales.

By the time you reach the end of the route, the Pieterpad will have revealed a side to the Netherlands that you never even knew existed. And one that very few travellers get to see.

MAKE IT LONGER

Cross-border Trails

Both of the trail's gateways link up with other long-distance routes. At Pieterburen, you can join the E9, a path between Cabo de São Vicente in Portugal and Narva-Jõesuu in Estonia. And from Sint-Pietersberg, you can take the GR5 into Belgium, Luxembourg and France.

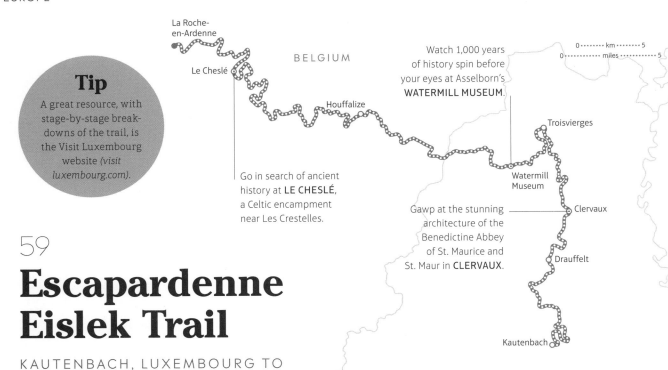

Tip

A great resource, with stage-by-stage breakdowns of the trail, is the Visit Luxembourg website (*visit luxembourg.com*).

La Roche-en-Ardenne

Le Cheslé

BELGIUM

Houffalize

Watch 1,000 years of history spin before your eyes at Asselborn's **WATERMILL MUSEUM.**

Troisvierges

Watermill Museum

Clervaux

Drauffelt

Kautenbach

LUXEMBOURG

Go in search of ancient history at **LE CHESLÉ,** a Celtic encampment near Les Crestelles.

Gawp at the stunning architecture of the Benedictine Abbey of St. Maurice and St. Maur in **CLERVAUX.**

59

Escapardenne Eislek Trail

KAUTENBACH, LUXEMBOURG TO
LA ROCHE-EN-ARDENNE, BELGIUM

A tale of two countries, this classic long-distance route meanders slowly past historic sights and along snaking waterways.

The pace of life can be slow in Europe's Low Countries, especially so when tackling this grand itinerary, which weaves from fairy-tale Luxembourg to storied Ardennes in Belgium. This quiet corner of the continent is often overlooked by visitors but is rich in history and natural beauty—a fact recognized by the European Ramblers Association, which has named the Escapardenne Eislek Trail one of its "Leading Quality Trails—Best of Europe."

The Luxembourg half weaves through lush valleys and along winding riverbanks, calling at time-stopped medieval villages such as Munshausen, with its witch's hat-topped church, and pretty towns like Asselborn, which houses a 1,000-year-old watermill. Across the border in Wallonia, Belgium's French-speaking heartland, forest trails connect you to historic battlefields such as Houffalize, which was a focal point of the Battle of the Bulge during World War II. But it's the gentle tranquility of this delightfully unassuming trail that lingers longest in your memory once the hike is over.

The Belgian town of Houffalize, on the banks of the Ourthe River

ELEVATION PROFILE

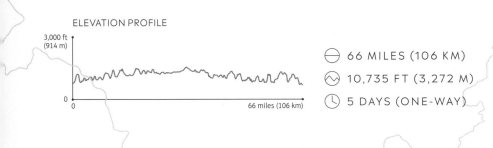

3,000 ft
(914 m)

0

0   66 miles (106 km)

⊖ 66 MILES (106 KM)

◯ 10,735 FT (3,272 M)

◷ 5 DAYS (ONE-WAY)

MAKE IT LONGER
The Full Route

The route described is a section of the full 227-mile (365 km) Moselsteig trail. Divided into 24 stages, it traces the Mosel from Perl, where Germany borders Belgium and Luxembourg, to the confluence with the Rhine at Koblenz.

60
Moselsteig

BERNKASTEL-KUES TO COCHEM, GERMANY

Savor a magical stretch of Germany's most winding river along a path through verdant vineyards.

74 MILES (119 KM)

14,688 FT (4,477 M)

5-7 DAYS (ONE-WAY)

Like wine and walking? You'll love the Mosel. This most serpentine of rivers is a bibulous delight: Germany's oldest and, arguably, finest wine-growing region surrounds the river and has produced tasty drops for some 2,000 years since the Romans introduced viticulture. There's no end of opportunities to sample a glass or two on this route, which follows the Mosel's sensuous bends between Bernkastel-Kues and Cochem.

Thanks to typically efficient German infrastructure—ample characterful accommodation lines the path, and bus, train and boat connections link key stops—it's a dream to organize a multiday trek here. In between the vineyards lie intriguing glimpses of the region's history, including Roman sites and 17th- and 18th-century castles built to guard the waterway. The trail itself frequently strays from the riverbank to conquer hilltops with far-reaching views. And once you've worked up a sweat, you'll find a Weinstube (wine bar) or Weingut (winery) around every bend, serving refreshing local Rieslings to slake your thirst.

Climb through dense woods to the viewpoint at **CALMONT**, which affords panoramic vistas across reputedly Europe's steepest vineyards and over a tight loop of the Mosel.

Mosel

Cochem

Bruttig-Fankel

Beilstein

Calmont

Neef

Senheim

GERMANY

Reil

Zell

0 ·········· km ·········· 5
0 ·········· miles ·········· 5

Enkirch

Zeltingen-Rachtig

Trabem-Trarbach

Mosel

Bernkastel-Kues

ELEVATION PROFILE

3,000 ft
(914 m)

0

0   74 miles (119 km)

BEILSTEIN's medieval core of venerable timbered houses is guarded by a hilltop Carmelite church and the ruined Metternich Castle.

Ascend from the river and explore the medieval market square of **BERNKASTEL**, with its decorated timbered houses.

61

The Malerweg

LIEBETHAL TO PIRNA, GERMANY

For hundreds of years, the region of Saxon Switzerland in Germany has inspired artists to capture its natural beauty on canvas. Walk the Malerweg (Painters' Way) and you might find yourself wanting to do the same.

72 MILES (116 KM)

13,390 FT (4,081 M)

8 DAYS (ONE-WAY)

126

Liebethal

Pirna   Elbe

The magnificent Elbe Sandstone Mountains extend from Saxon Switzerland in eastern Germany into neighboring Bohemian Switzerland in the Czech Republic. The area was popularized by 18th-century Romantic painters, among them German artists Caspar David Friedrich and Ludwig Richter, who were captivated by the beauty of the landscapes here. And for good reason, too. This region is unlike any other in Germany: ancient rock formations tower overhead, an imposing mountaintop fortress looms in the distance, and vast forested valleys and mountains are carved in two by the Elbe River. Today, the Malerweg takes you to the heart of Saxon Switzerland and pays homage to the artists and the landscapes that inspired them.

The trail has been carefully developed based on the historic route that these artists followed, and display boards along its eight stages detail the artworks that were conceived at those very locations. Look at the famous Bastei rock formations through the eyes of Caspar David Friedrich;

consider the Kuhstall, Saxon Switzerland's largest cave, from the perspective of Johann Carl August Richter; admire Ludwig Richter's wonderful copper etching of Schmilka mill (used to inform the mill's restoration almost 200 years later); and compare the Pirna of today to the Italian artist Bernardo Bellotto's oil painting of the marketplace.

The area's romantic allure continues to draw visitors to the Malerweg, and it is, rightly so, one of Germany's most popular hikes. While it's generally a pretty easygoing trail, some rocky ascents require a small dose of courage. But you'll be well rewarded with unforgettable views—and perhaps even a few reflective moments to get your sketchpad out.

ELEVATION PROFILE

3,000 ft
(914 m)

0

0   72 miles (116 km)

Looking out over the inspiring scenery of the Elbe Sandstone Mountains

The towering sandstone **BASTEI** rock formations are linked by a stone bridge, built in 1851.

ANOTHER WAY
Take the Tram
Spend the night in the riverside spa town of Bad Schandau, just a few miles from Altendorf at the end of stage 3, and then rejoin the trail via the historic Kirnitzschtal tramway, which travels 5 miles (8 km) through the romantic Kirnitzsch Valley to Lichtenhain Waterfall.

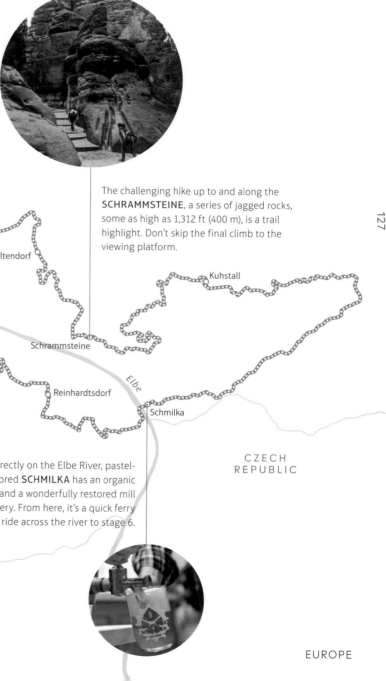

The challenging hike up to and along the **SCHRAMMSTEINE**, a series of jagged rocks, some as high as 1,312 ft (400 m), is a trail highlight. Don't skip the final climb to the viewing platform.

127

Hocksteinturm

Rathewalde

Stadt Wehlen

Bastei

Rauensteinweg

Waitzdorf

GERMANY

Altendorf

Kuhstall

Königstein Fortress

Königstein

Schrammsteine

Papstein

Elbe

Reinhardtsdorf

Schmilka

Factor in extra time to visit the mountaintop **KÖNIGSTEIN FORTRESS**, which has a history dating back to the 13th century. It was used as a state prison until the early 20th century.

CZECH REPUBLIC

0 ·············· km ·············· 3
0 ·············· miles ·············· 3

Sitting directly on the Elbe River, pastel-colored **SCHMILKA** has an organic brewery and a wonderfully restored mill and bakery. From here, it's a quick ferry ride across the river to stage 6.

62

Heidschnuckenweg

FISCHBEK TO CELLE, GERMANY

*The Heidschnuckenweg (Moorland Sheep Way) passes through gently
undulating landscapes of heath, forest, and open fields, with the local
sheep that lend this trail its name providing company along the way.*

Covering a large area of Lower Saxony in northern
Germany, the Lüneburg Heath (Lüneburger Heide) is
largely a car-free nature reserve. Through it winds the
well-signposted Heidschnuckenweg, a trail that runs from
Hamburg's southwestern neighborhood of Fischbek
to the quaint town of Celle in Lower Saxony, just 25 miles
(40 km) northeast of the state capital Hanover.

The unique landscape this route passes through
is maintained year-round by herds of Heidschnucke,
distinctive gray-horned moorland sheep from northern
Germany. The sheep graze on wild herbs, grass, and young
shoots of birch and pine trees, allowing the heather to
grow and thrive. Hiking here is possible year-round, but
it is in late summer—when the heather blooms all shades
of purple—that the Heidschnuckenweg is undoubtedly
at its most beautiful.

ELEVATION PROFILE

1,500 ft
(457 m)

0

0   140 miles (226 km)

⊖ 140 MILES (226 KM)

◔ 6,230 FT (1,899 M)

🕐 13 DAYS (ONE-WAY)

Fischbek

Buchholz in
der Nordheide

Wilsede

Totengrund

Bispingen

Soltau

Wietzendorf

Müden

Celle

GERMANY

WILSEDER BERG
(555 ft/169 m), near
the tiny village of
Wilsede, is the high-
est point on the
trail; it offers views
of the heathland
and, on clear days,
as far as Hamburg.

Pause to look
down at the wonderful
TOTENGRUND valley; it's
particularly scenic when
the heather is in bloom.

0 ········ km ········· 15
0 ········ miles ········ 15

The trail concludes in the
riverside town of **CELLE**. It
has hundreds of restored half-
timbered houses dating from
the 16th to 19th centuries.

63

Inn Valley High Trail

PATSCHERKOFEL TO SCHWAZ, AUSTRIA

On this hut-to-hut hike through the Tux Alps in Tyrol, exquisite Alpine panoramas are upstaged only by the hearty and satisfying regional cuisine.

Tip

Book in advance in peak months—there are no sleeping and eating alternatives in the mountains.

43 MILES (70 KM) | 12,792 FT (3,899 M) | 6 DAYS (ONE-WAY)

Running from Patscherkofel to Schwaz, Tyrol's multiday Inn Valley High Trail passes above the Inn Valley and through the Tux Alps, mostly at heights of between 5,906 ft (1,800 m) and 9,186 ft (2,800 m). Along the six-stage route, you'll take in ancient pine forests, blue lakes, dramatic peaks and ridges, and endless Alpine vistas—not to mention a chain of mountain huts famed for serving up delicious Tyrolean and Austrian specialties. Expect fortifying dishes such as *Speckknödel* (bread dumplings in broth),

Kasspatzl (egg noodles with cheese), and *Kaiserschmarren* (shredded pancakes)— after which a Schnapps is surely in order.

Clearly signed and best undertaken in the warmer months from June to September, this is an easy to intermediate hike—good news if you're here only for the food. More difficult sections can be bypassed if need be, and, at any stage, it's possible to descend to the valley and cut the trail short—though with views and food like this, it's unlikely you'll want to.

129

ELEVATION PROFILE

10,000 ft (3,048 m)

0

0   43 miles (70 km)

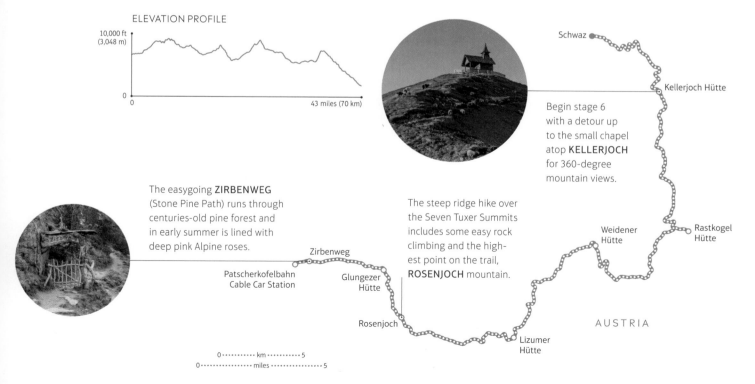

The easygoing **ZIRBENWEG** (Stone Pine Path) runs through centuries-old pine forest and in early summer is lined with deep pink Alpine roses.

The steep ridge hike over the Seven Tuxer Summits includes some easy rock climbing and the highest point on the trail, **ROSENJOCH** mountain.

Begin stage 6 with a detour up to the small chapel atop **KELLERJOCH** for 360-degree mountain views.

Schwaz

Kellerjoch Hütte

Rastkogel Hütte

Weidener Hütte

Zirbenweg

Patscherkofelbahn Cable Car Station

Glungezer Hütte

Rosenjoch

Lizumer Hütte

AUSTRIA

0 ········· km ········· 5
0 ········· miles ········· 5

EUROPE

ANOTHER WAY

Innsbruck to Ehrwald

If you'd prefer a slightly less challenging introduction to the Adlerweg, you can try the three stages from Innsbruck to Ehrwald instead. They follow either intermediate or easy grades of path, and you get a head start on the ascent by taking a cable car up to the track from Innsbruck.

0 ········ km ········ 5
·0 ·········· miles ·············· 5

AUSTRIA

Ehrwald

Lorea Hütte

Anhalter Hütte

Boden

Hanauer Hütte

Württemberger Haus

Memminger Hütte

Grossbergspitze

Parseierspitze

Kaiserjochhaus

Haas-Weg

Ansbacher Hütte

St Christoph am Arlberg

Built in 1888, the wonderfully positioned **KAISERJOCHHAUS**, on the main ridge of the Lechtal Valley, has a reputation for excellent regional cuisine.

A high ridge walk leads to the top of **GROSSBERGSPITZE**, where panoramic views of the surrounding peaks will stop you in your tracks. This is the view you came here for.

The rugged **HAAS-WEG** involves rocky scrambling, steep drop-offs, and a few stomach-lurching moments. Hang on to the fixed cables and try to enjoy the challenge.

There are more than 600 peaks in the Lechtal Alps, but only the imposing **PARSEIERSPITZE** (9,961 ft/3,036 m) reaches over 9,800 ft (3,000 m).

64

Adlerweg

EHRWALD TO ST CHRISTOPH
AM ARLBERG, AUSTRIA

Experience the Alpine beauty of the Lechtal Alps on a
challenging hike along a section of Austria's epic Eagle Walk.

65 MILES (104 KM)

26,401 FT (8,047 M)

8 DAYS (ONE-WAY)

Traversing the entire state of Tyrol from east to west, the long-distance Adlerweg (Eagle Walk) is the region's most famous trail. It's actually not one but two hikes, which aren't directly connected to each other but together span 33 stages, 257 miles (413 km), and 101,706 ft (31,000 m) of elevation gain. Each stage has been designed to end at a mountain hut or village, where you can pull off your boots for the night, fill up on hearty regional cuisine and swap stories with fellow hikers before doing it all over again the next day.

The full trail takes over a month to complete, but a testing yet rewarding taster is offered by the eight stages through the Lechtal Alps in North Tyrol. Stretching from Ehrwald to St. Christoph am Arlberg, with a total elevation gain of more than 26,400 ft (8,000 m), this is one of the more difficult sections of the Adlerweg and should not be attempted by hikers without technical or high-altitude experience. While many miles tread along flat tracks that are easy to follow, some sections involve picking your

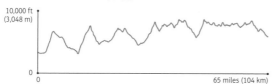

ELEVATION PROFILE

10,000 ft
(3,048 m)

0

0   65 miles (104 km)

Skirting around a lake in the beautiful
surrounds of the Lechtal Alps

131

way along narrow trails and ridgelines, scrambling up rocky stretches and scree slopes, and pulling yourself along or up the mountainside using iron cables—suffice to say, sure-footedness and a head for heights are mandatory.

The trail is as beautiful as it is difficult. At one point, you might be strolling through a deep-green forest, at another traversing the edge of a steep hillside that tumbles away into a lush valley below. The route passes through pretty Alpine meadows, which pop with color when wildflowers are in bloom and past crystalline lakes that reflect the surrounding landscape. Watching over all of these scenes are the Lechtal Alps themselves, an ever-constant presence, their rugged peaks stretching ever up toward the sky.

Tip
Book your beds early
as the season runs
short, from July to
mid-September.

Rifugio Locatelli/
Drei Zinnen Hutte

0 ···········km···········1
0 ···········miles···········1

At the rustic **RIFUGIO LOCATELLI/DREI ZINNEN HUTTE**, enjoy coffee, a giant slice of apple strudel, and epic views of the three peaks.

Langalm Hut

Forcella Lavaredo

ITALY

As you approach **FORCELLA LAVAREDO**, look closely at the mountain to your left to spy sections of a walkway carved into the rock by soldiers during World War I.

Rifugio Lavaredo

Col di Mezzo

Rifugio Auronzo

Snap a photograph of the three peaks reflected in the clear, turquoise waters of the pools near **LANGALM HUT**.

65

Tre Cime di Lavaredo

RIFUGIO AURONZO, ITALY

Spend a day amid the unfailingly spectacular scenery of the Dolomites, circling a trio of hulking peaks on one of the region's most iconic hiking routes.

⊖ 6 MILES (10 KM)

〰 1,420 FT (433 M)

🕐 1 DAY (LOOP)

ELEVATION PROFILE

10,000 ft
(3,048 m)

3,000 ft
(914 m)
0   6 miles (10 km)

Erupting from the rocky ground like the ragged teeth of some mythical beast, the soaring pinnacles of the Tre Cime di Lavaredo could have stepped straight out of a fairy tale. Dominating the surrounding landscape, these imposing rocky spires are an emblem of the region—think of the Dolomites and it's probably Tre Cime di Lavaredo that springs to mind.

While the lofty summits are most definitely out-of-reach to all but expert climbers, a loop of the mountain's base is surprisingly straight-forward. Tracing a clockwise path around these majestic stony monoliths, a well-maintained if undulating trail offers up beautiful views in abundance: rocky Alpine meadows dotted with wildflowers; mirrorlike crystalline pools in shades of turquoise and teal; the pointed peaks of the Cadini di Misurina and the Paternkofel; and, of course, the famed Tre Cime di Lavaredo itself. Even better, the path is liberally dotted with wooden-shuttered *rifugios*— perfect spots for soaking up the scenery with a reviving espresso.

66
Faulhornweg

SCHYNIGE PLATTE TO FIRST,
SWITZERLAND

Stride along the spine of the Swiss Alps on a ridge walk that rewards with unparalleled 360-degree views of soaring peaks.

10 MILES (16 KM)   2,910 FT (887 M)   1 DAY (ONE-WAY)

It's hard to think of many short hikes that are as accessible and achievable, and yet as dramatic as this classic route winding above Interlaken in the heart of the Bernese Oberland. Not only is the path of the Faulhornweg—named after the 8,796 ft (2,681 m) peak marking its apogee and rough midpoint—easy to follow, but it also eschews any particularly demanding ascents or descents. Besides, if you should happen to get tired en route, you can always call at one of Switzerland's two

The snaking First Cliff Walk at the end of the Faulhornweg

most alluring mountain huts, at either Männdlenen or Faulhorn, for a delicious chilled *radler* (shandy) as a pick-me-up. And that's not even to mention the jaw-dropping scenery, which includes the twin meres of Brienzersee and Thunsee, and a parade of peaks featuring that most characterful and infamous trio: the Eiger (Ogre), Mönch (Monk), and Jungfrau (Maiden).

You could be forgiven at this point for asking what the catch is—but the wonderful thing about this hike is that there truly isn't one.

ELEVATION PROFILE

10,000 ft
(3,048 m)

3,000 ft
(914 m)

0   10 miles (16 km)

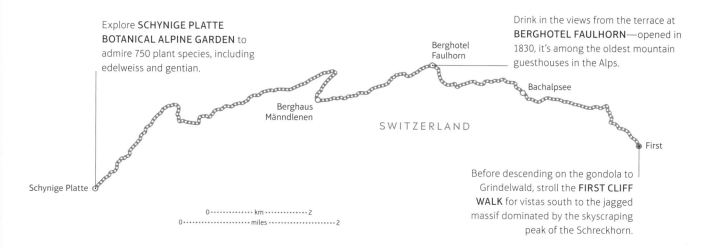

Explore **SCHYNIGE PLATTE BOTANICAL ALPINE GARDEN** to admire 750 plant species, including edelweiss and gentian.

Schynige Platte

Berghaus
Männdlenen

0 ········· km ········· 2
0 ········· miles ········· 2

Berghotel
Faulhorn

SWITZERLAND

Bachalpsee

First

Drink in the views from the terrace at **BERGHOTEL FAULHORN**—opened in 1830, it's among the oldest mountain guesthouses in the Alps.

Before descending on the gondola to Grindelwald, stroll the **FIRST CLIFF WALK** for vistas south to the jagged massif dominated by the skyscraping peak of the Schreckhorn.

0 ·········· km ········· 5
0 ·········· miles ········· 5

At **CHAMPEX**, there's an option to take an alternative route via the vertiginous col known as the Fenêtre d'Arpette, for jaw-dropping views over the Glacier du Trient.

Watch (and listen) for marmots, chamois, and even big-horned ibex among the rocks and conifers of the **AIGUILLES ROUGE NATURE RESERVE**.

Col de Portalo

Champex

Aiguillette des Posettes

Fenêtre d'Arpette

Admire the clearest face-on views (clouds permitting) of Mont Blanc from the panoramic terrace at **LE BRÉVENT**.

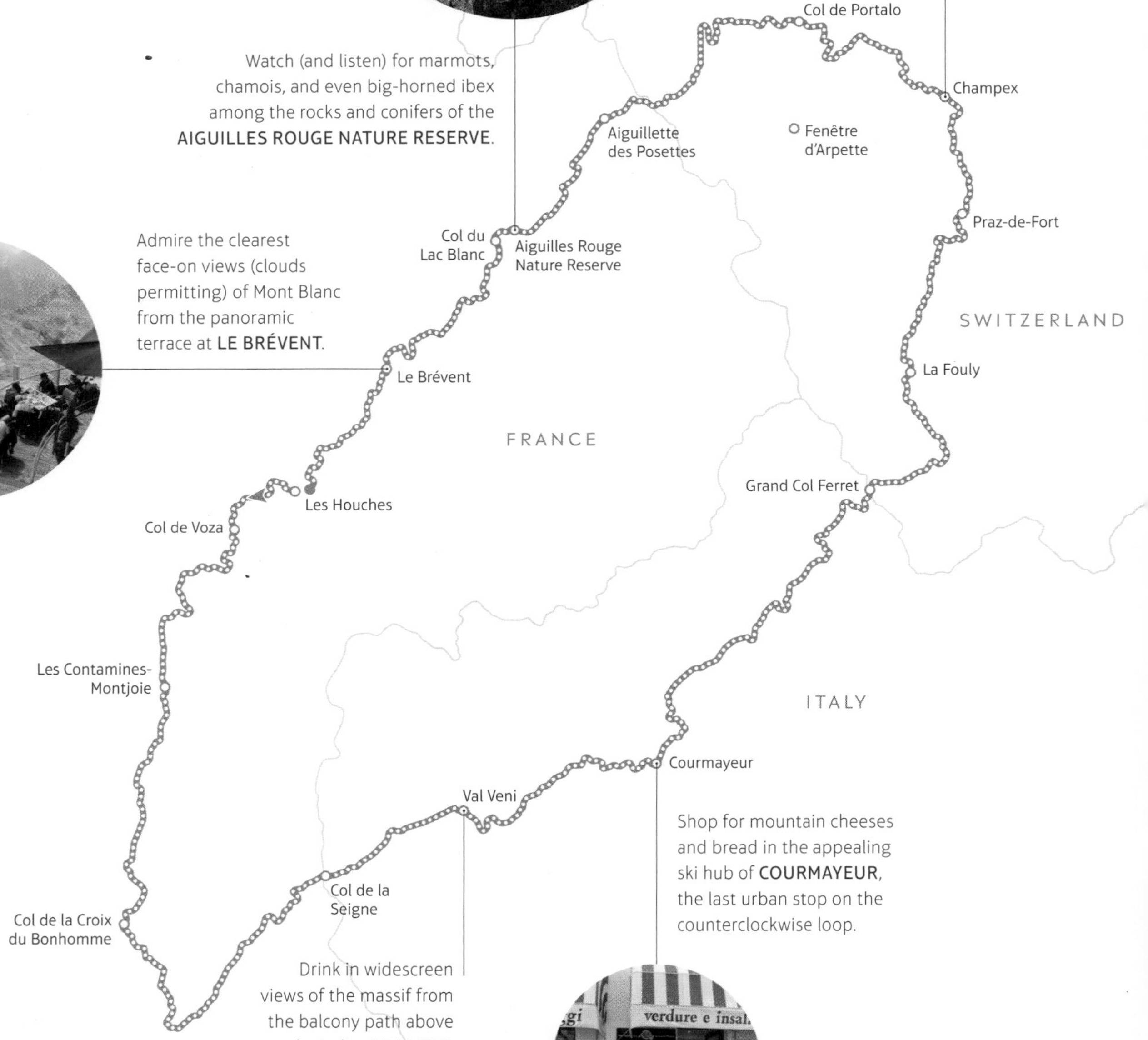

Col du Lac Blanc

Aiguilles Rouge Nature Reserve

Praz-de-Fort

SWITZERLAND

Le Brévent

La Fouly

FRANCE

Les Houches

Grand Col Ferret

Col de Voza

Les Contamines-Montjoie

ITALY

Courmayeur

Val Veni

Shop for mountain cheeses and bread in the appealing ski hub of **COURMAYEUR**, the last urban stop on the counterclockwise loop.

Col de la Seigne

Col de la Croix du Bonhomme

Drink in widescreen views of the massif from the balcony path above the Italian **VAL VENI**, between the French border at Col de la Seigne and Col Chécroui.

67

Tour du Mont Blanc

LES HOUCHES, FRANCE

Passing through three countries, this classic Alpine route takes you on a loop around the tallest peak in Western Europe, offering the chance to admire the myriad faces of the White Mountain as you go.

102 MILES (164 KM)

34,104 FT (10,395 M)

9–14 DAYS (LOOP)

Over two and a half centuries ago, Horace-Bénédict du Saussure, a wealthy Swiss geologist studying the Alps, discovered that walking around the Mont Blanc massif—topped by its 15,774 ft (4,808 m) peak, Western Europe's tallest—is, well, actually quite enjoyable. In many ways, little has changed in the birthplace of Alpine tourism since he completed that first lap. True, visitors have proliferated while glaciers have sadly receded, but the experience of gazing at the White Mountain from every angle, and the exhilaration of traversing trails with vistas to rival any on the planet, remain as elemental as ever. Today, the Tour du Mont Blanc, now a waymarked 102-mile (164 km) route typically broken down into 10 or 11 stages, is deservedly one of the world's most popular long-distance treks.

Unsurprisingly, given its long heritage, the practicalities are straightforward. Mostly well-made paths, repurposed from ancient

Stopping to enjoy the view while undertaking the Tour du Mont Blanc

shepherds' tracks, link a generous network of mountain huts, *gîtes d'etape* (lodges) and rustic guesthouses and hotels offering more or less comfortable accommodations and hearty food along the trail. Bag transfers are also available if you'd prefer not to lug all your gear between overnights. But despite these comforts, there's no getting away from the fact that the Tour du Mont Blanc is as challenging as it is spectacular—to complete the whole circuit, you'll have to tackle some 34,000 ft (10,000 m) of ascents and descents. ▶

ELEVATION PROFILE

10,000 ft
(3,048 m)

0

0   102 miles (164 km)

IN FOCUS
Pioneer of the Peaks

Horace-Bénédict de Saussure became obsessed with Mont Blanc after visiting the surrounding area to collect plant specimens. In 1767—supported by an entourage of mules, porters, and guides—he pioneered a circuit around the peak, following much the same route as the modern tour. Today, his statue gazes across Chamonix from the bridge by Place Balmat.

With the highest point on the official route topping out at over 8,200 ft (2,500 m), the trail is reliably open only between mid-June and September. Although the weather is best in July and August, with passes almost always snow-free, these are also the busiest months, and the latter is prone to afternoon thunderstorms—as a result, it's often the shoulder months that offer the most enjoyable hiking.

The traditional starting point of the tour is Les Houches, near Chamonix in the Savoy Alps—in part because of its historic importance but also because it's easily accessible. Most hike counterclockwise from Les Houches, though of course it's possible to walk in the other direction and begin at different points; Champex is recommended as a starting place for clockwise hikers, to avoid a first day of constant steep ascent. On many stages, variant routes offer a choice of terrain; often one path is gentler, perhaps along the flanks of a verdant valley or through pinewoods, while the other may involve steep scrambling to a loftier col (pass), rewarded with greater satisfaction and even farther-reaching vistas of those granite crags and ridges.

Whichever direction, starting point, and variants you choose, days typically follow a similar pattern. After breakfasting in your overnight refuge, you'll follow a path through wildflower meadows and pastures speckled with butterflies, zigzagging up to a col that reveals the glories to come that day. You'll detect subtle differences along the way, of course. Not just between the three countries you traverse—France, Italy, and Switzerland—but also from one valley to the next, in the landscapes and flora, architecture and cuisine, even costs.

One thing that remains unchanging, though, is the mountain itself—or, rather, mountains; the massif stretches some 29 miles (46 km) from the southwest to the northeast. It's ever-present on the hike, revealing disparate features as you progress around: the stark grandeur of the south face, glaring across at the Italian Val Veni; waterfalls striping forested slopes in the Swiss section above La Fouly; the vast Mer de Glace dripping between northern crags like icing from a gargantuan birthday cake. It's truly a feast for the eyes, soul, and soles alike.

Gazing up at the jagged ridges of the Mont Blanc massif from a footpath in Val Ferret on the Swiss section of the trail

EUROPE

68
Loire Valley

BLOIS TO CHINON, FRANCE

Stroll through old-world France on this section of the much longer Grande Randonnée 3, discovering a world of lush vineyards, towering châteaux, and historic cities—all linked by the sinuous Loire River.

90 MILES (145 KM)

5,554 FT (1,693 M)

8 DAYS (ONE-WAY)

Covering just 90 miles (145 km) of France's long-distance Grande Randonnée 3 (GR3), this hike is but a mere snippet of the whole— yet what a snippet. Grand châteaux gleam in the sunshine, their manicured gardens a rolling tapestry in which not a stitch is out of place, and vineyards stretch over undulating slopes, punctuated by historic cities too charming to feel real.

It's little surprise that the central Loire's nickname "The Valley of the Kings" has stuck with it throughout the centuries. Few places feel more royally decadent than this ribbon of France. There are no vertiginous climbs or days to push you to your limits—this is a trail of sensory delights, its gentle contours leading you through the passages of time. No sense is left out of the experience: dip into a vineyard and taste the crisp richness of a Vouvray, or bathe in the chorus of the surrounding forest. This is a world where both nature and people have everything just-so and the resulting perfection is ample recompense for each day's walk. ▶

ELEVATION PROFILE

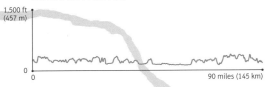

1,500 ft (457 m)

0

0   90 miles (145 km)

Visit the impressive castle and historical center of **CHINON**, before heading to one of the surrounding vineyards to sip on a glass of dry Vouvray wine.

Chinon

The city of Tours, stretching along the banks of the Loire

138

The Valley of the Kings

The striking châteaux that line the Loire Valley play no small part in earning the region its nickname, "The Valley of the Kings." Indeed, this stretch of France was a royal favorite for centuries, with seven kings and 10 queens of France alone naming the Royal Château in Blois an official residence.

Stop in the charming historic city of **BLOIS** to admire its Renaissance château; it incorporates four architectural styles and now houses two museums.

The grand estate of the **CHÂTEAU DE VILLANDRY** is a horticulturalist's dream, thanks to the immaculately restored chessboard of 16th-century gardens that blend French and Italianate styles.

Nicknamed the Gateway City of the Loire, **TOURS** has a beguiling charm with its half-timbered houses, cobbled streets, and striking architecture.

A visit to the stately château of **DOMAINE DE CHAUMONT-SUR-LOIRE** is as much about the 79-acre (32 ha) gardens and views of the Loire as it is about the fairy-tale castle itself.

Blois

Loire

Chouzy-sur-Cisse

Onzain

Domaine de Chaumont-sur-Loire

Limeray

Amboise

Loire

Tours

Montlouis-sur-Loire

FRANCE

Château de Villandry

Château d'Azay-le-Rideau

One of the best examples of French Renaissance architecture, the **CHÂTEAU D'AZAY-LE-RIDEAU**'s evolution between the 16th and 19th centuries resulted in a grand fortress, an undisputed highlight of the Loire.

139

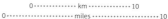

0 ·············· km ·············· 10
0 ·············· miles ·············· 10

Ripening grapes
in a vineyard near
Château de Chinon

This hike begins at Blois, which alone has enough attractions to cause you to dally. Sitting on a rocky outcrop overlooking the wide river valley, it's one of the biggest cities in the Loire and the capital of the Loir-et-Cher region. The starting point is the Jacques Gabriel Bridge, its graceful arches rising over the serene waters that will guide your steps for the next eight days. Following their lead, the path brings you through the medieval center to several of Blois's other attractions—the Royal Château de Blois and The Church of Saint Nicholas—so expect to get off to a slow start as you pause to admire their charms.

As Blois's stony streets recede into the distance, they're replaced with gravel tracks then dirt paths that lead you to the village of Chouzy-sur-Cisse, with its 8th-century abbey, and from here on toward Onzain. After the relaxed opening chapter of the first stage of the hike, the more pronounced contours of the next leg toward Limeray may come as something of

a shock to the system. It's all relative, though; a short pull uphill, a little downward spell, you'll encounter nothing too drastic in the Loire.

Like many river walks, the GR3 follows its waterway loosely, dancing closer to and away from the Loire, affording ample views of the water as it courses—almost imperceptibly—through the valley, light sparkling on its surface. When the trail does more closely hug the river, the sight of the traditional flat-bottomed boats is a reminder of a time when this was the region's main trading route.

Vineyards abound, of course, the rustling vine leaves laden with plump grapes readying for the harvest.

Grande Randonnée 3

If you have significantly more time, tackle the whole length of the GR3, whose 776-mile (1,248-km) route runs from Mont Gerbier-de-Jonc to La Baule. It takes around two months to complete and features several variations to allow you to explore different aspects of the valley, such as troglodyte caves and wildlife, depending on your interests.

Vineyards abound, of course, the rustling vine leaves laden with plump grapes readying for the harvest. The day's walk between Limeray and Amboise more than lives up to the area's wine-loving reputation—no sooner do you leave the boundaries of one vineyard than you cross into another. Resist the urge to stop at them all unless you plan on taking things at a very slow pace.

From here, it only gets better. Tours—a maze of half-timbered houses and narrow cobbled streets, themselves a journey through the history of France— brings the architectural delight of a well-preserved medieval city. As abundant as its history is, this is not a place stuck in the past; its cultural heritage rubs easily with the cosmopolitan panache of modern France.

It's a stride along the river from Tours to Villandry, with its magnificent château and gardens. Not content to be outdone by its neighbor, the château at Azay-le-Rideau is similarly impressive—nestled on an island and rising from the water, phoenix-like from centuries past.

By the time you finish at Chinon, home of the great French writer Rabelais, the character of the Loire, and the people and places that have flourished around it for centuries past and present, will feel like old friends.

Looking towards historic Blois, one of the Loire's largest cities

69

GR20

CALENZANA TO CONCA, CORSICA, FRANCE

Head to the Mediterranean's most mountainous island for a hike across craggy summits, past snow-covered cirques, and through ancient river valleys on one of Europe's most challenging treks.

109 MILES (176 KM)

37,064 FT (11,297 M)

15 DAYS (ONE-WAY)

The Mediterranean island of Corsica feels like a world removed from other parts of France. Rugged mountains cover two-thirds of its territory, and in many of the old stone villages, you can still hear the mellifluous tones of Corsican, a language that sounds more Italian than French.

This unique island is home to one of Europe's most demanding multiday hikes, the Grande Randonnée (GR) 20, which courses over the chiseled spine of the interior on grinding ups and downs. It's tough—less than half of those who set out on the trail manage to complete it. Solid preparation, both physical and mental, is the key to success on this alpine roller coaster, which involves some 62,336 ft (19,000 m) of elevation changes.

Despite the arduous terrain, the rewards of hiking the GR20 are immense. You'll experience an astonishing variety of landscapes as you hike up boulder-strewn ridges and descend into deep valleys, traveling past pine forests,

boggy marshland, and misty lakes. The weather can be just as mixed, with searing heat, thick fog, rain, and even hail all possible on a single summer day, thanks to Corsica's unusual microclimates.

Most hikers start the journey in Calenzana and make their way south. That way you cover the hardest parts of the trail in the beginning and can enjoy a (comparatively) more gentle finish on the lower peaks outside of Conca. Your first days take you across rushing rivers, over suspension bridges above churning waterfalls, and up to dizzying heights where saw-toothed peaks and precipitous

ELEVATION PROFILE

10,000 ft
(3,048 m)

0

0   109 miles (176 km)

Trekking past the granite formations of Aiguilles de Bavella on the GR20

MAKE IT SHORTER

Vizzavona Finish

If you have just a week to spare, end your hike at the small town of Vizzavona, which marks the halfway point of the GR20. From here, you can catch an onward train or bus to the cities of Ajaccio or Bastia.

The trail bounces across the iconic **SPASIMATA SUSPENSION BRIDGE**, which stretches over the eponymous river.

Calenzana

Spasimata suspension bridge

Haut-Asco

Monte Cinto

The main trail passes along the flanks of **MONTE CINTO**, but if you have the stamina, make the side trip up Corsica's highest peak for mesmerizing views.

Lac de Nino

Set in the Camputile Plateau, the crystal-clear **LAC DE NINO** is fringed by green pastures where you can sometimes see wild horses grazing.

Vizzavona

CORSICA

143

Capanelle

```
0 ········· km ········· 15
0 ········· miles ········· 15
```

valleys stretch in every direction. The later-stage descents are no less dramatic, taking you through thick maquis (Mediterranean scrub) and past mirrorlike glacial lakes, where you might spy wild horses on nearby meadows. Sheep and goats—and shepherds' huts—are also part of the landscape, along with golden eagles and other birds of prey that soar above.

As you make your final descent into Conca, you'll have no doubts left about how the GR20 got its Corsican name of Fra li Monti (Across the Mountains). From this point, it's a short hop to the glorious beaches of the southeast—a well-earned treat for successfully completing one of Europe's most notorious hikes.

Aiguilles de Bavella

Bavella

Conca

En route to the mountain hamlet of Bavella, you'll wind past the towering red-rock spires of **AIGUILLES DE BAVELLA**.

0 ·······km······· 2
0 ······miles······ 2

Poncebos

To really take in the drama of the Cares Gorge, pause on the **PUENTE DE LOS REBECOS** bridge and gaze up and downstream.

Puente de los Rebecos

SPAIN

Caín de Valdeón

Visit **ERMITA DE CORONA**, the hermitage where Don Pelayo was reputedly crowned first king of Asturias in AD 718.

Ermita de Corona

Mirador del Tombo

Drink in the dramatic vistas up to the high peaks and north along the Valdeón Valley from the **MIRADOR DEL TOMBO**.

Posada de Valdeón

70

Cares Gorge

POSADA DE VALDEÓN TO PONCEBOS, SPAIN

Delve between vertiginous rock walls to trace the Cares River on an exhilarating and hugely popular walk through the spectacular ravine known as the "Divine Gorge."

12 MILES (20 KM)
3,658 FT (1,115 M)
1 DAY (ONE-WAY)

Vertigo sufferers be warned: though the path through the Cares Gorge isn't particularly challenging, the drop-off at its edge, which plunges down to the river dashing over rocks far below, is heart-in-mouth sheer. The corollary, though, is that the surrounding Picos de Europa mountains, rising to some 8,530 ft (2,600 m), are jaw-to-floor spectacular.

The Ruta del Cares, or PR-PNPE 3 as it's more prosaically known, is a beautiful bite-size taster of this gleaming limestone massif. Heading north from the attractive village of Posada de Valdeón, its streets punctuated with traditional *horreos* (wooden granaries on stone legs), the route initially traverses a peaceful, verdant valley guarded by sharp peaks. The drama intensifies at Caín, where the path is injected into the narrow Cares Gorge. From here, the route follows a trail hewn into the rock face, introducing a stretch that's by turns claustrophobic and—of course—vertiginous.

ELEVATION PROFILE

3,000 ft
(914 m)

0

0   12 miles (20 km)

71

Sámara Circuit

TEIDE NATIONAL PARK, TENERIFE, SPAIN

Bonsai forests of pine erupt from the black volcanic earth on this circular route, with spectacular views of Tenerife's Mount Teide.

3 MILES (5 KM) 790 FT (241 M) 0.5 DAYS (LOOP)

Tenerife is synonymous with sunshine, a vernal land where electric blue lizards zip across the volcanic soil and the scent of Canary juniper hangs in the balmy air. But an unearthly atmosphere shrouds the cloud-wreathed peak of Teide, Spain's highest mountain, which rises from the heart of the island. "Lunar" is a word that's often used to describe the peak and its surrounding landscape, and it

Exploring the otherworldly landscape of Teide National Park in Tenerife

certainly fits the crater-pitted lava fields and hoodoo-like rock formations here.

Beginning and ending at the Mirador de Sámara viewpoint, this easygoing loop trail takes you on a tour of another world. Miniature forests of pine sprout gamely from the barren black earth, their bright green fronds providing a striking contrast to the rust-red summit of Teide in the distance. It's a surreal and beautiful sight that's not so much from another planet as another galaxy entirely.

ELEVATION PROFILE

8,200 ft (2,499 m)

3,000 ft (914 m)

0   3 miles (5 km)

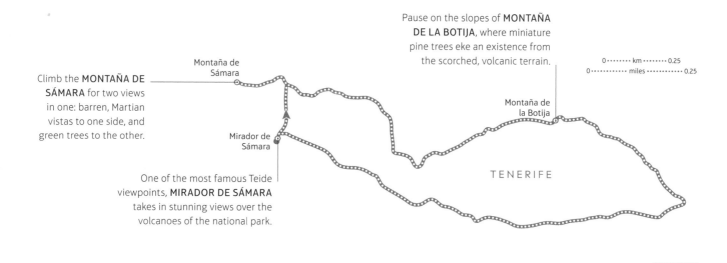

Pause on the slopes of **MONTAÑA DE LA BOTIJA**, where miniature pine trees eke an existence from the scorched, volcanic terrain.

Climb the **MONTAÑA DE SÁMARA** for two views in one: barren, Martian vistas to one side, and green trees to the other.

Montaña de Sámara

0 ········· km ········· 0.25
0 ········· miles ········· 0.25

Montaña de la Botija

Mirador de Sámara

TENERIFE

One of the most famous Teide viewpoints, **MIRADOR DE SÁMARA** takes in stunning views over the volcanoes of the national park.

All roads lead to the cathedral at **SANTIAGO DE COMPOSTELA**, a magnificent sight that is just reward for all those weeks on the road.

Santiago de Compostela · Melide · Sarria · O Cebreiro · Ponferrada

72
Camino de Santiago

SAINT JEAN PIED DE PORT, FRANCE,
TO SANTIAGO DE COMPOSTELA, SPAIN

Embark on one of the most iconic long-distance walks in the world, an epic pilgrimage to the capital of Galicia that has been a tradition for centuries.

480 MILES (772 KM) 〇
41,935 FT (12,782 M) 〰
4–5 WEEKS (ONE-WAY) 🕐

Pilgrims have been walking the Camino de Santiago, the Way of St. James, for nearly 900 years, tramping across Spain to pay their respects at the Cathedral of Santiago de Compostela, the reputed final resting place of St. James. They come from all directions—the Camino is really several routes that have emerged over the centuries, leading north from Andalusia, west from the French Basque Country, or up the coast of Portugal.

Whatever route you decide to take, you'll have the same goal in sight: the magnificent 13th-century Cathedral of

ELEVATION PROFILE

6,500 ft
(1,981 m)

0
0   480 miles (772 km)

Passing a trail marker on the Camino de Santiago

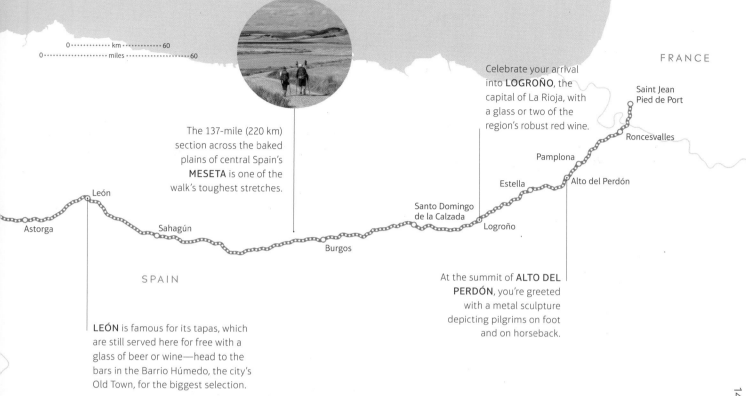

The 137-mile (220 km) section across the baked plains of central Spain's **MESETA** is one of the walk's toughest stretches.

Celebrate your arrival into **LOGROÑO**, the capital of La Rioja, with a glass or two of the region's robust red wine.

FRANCE

Saint Jean Pied de Port

Roncesvalles

Pamplona

Alto del Perdón

Estella

Logroño

Santo Domingo de la Calzada

León

Astorga

Sahagún

Burgos

SPAIN

LEÓN is famous for its tapas, which are still served here for free with a glass of beer or wine—head to the bars in the Barrio Húmedo, the city's Old Town, for the biggest selection.

At the summit of **ALTO DEL PERDÓN**, you're greeted with a metal sculpture depicting pilgrims on foot and on horseback.

Santiago de Compostela, the Way's official finish (although some hardy souls—with even hardier soles—strike on to Finisterre and the coast, where Spain runs out and they can walk no further). The longest, and arguably the most scenic, of the pathways is the Camino del Norte, or Northern Way, which weaves for 514 miles (827 km) along the Bay of Biscay from San Sebastián to Oviedo and then on to Santiago. The shortest is the Camino Inglés, the English Way, which starts in A Coruña, 68 miles (110 km) from the end. Looking for a challenge? Then the Camino Primitivo, the Original Way, is the one for you. Deemed to be the toughest of all the trails, it threads up through the mountains of Asturias.

The most popular route, however, and the most historic, is the Camino Frances, or the French Way. It was first documented in the Codex Calixtinus (the first-ever guidebook to the pilgrimage) in 1135 and became the most important Christian pilgrimage route in medieval Europe. ▶

IN FOCUS
St. James

St. James is the patron saint of Spain and was one of the Twelve Apostles chosen by Jesus to spread the word of God. The first of the disciples to be martyred, James was beheaded in 44 CE on the orders of Herod Agrippa I, King of Judea, and his body was said to have been transported from Jerusalem to Santiago de Compostela.

Tip

Pick up a pilgrim passport and collect stamps en route to get an official certificate of completion.

Top A poppy-lined stretch of the Camino Frances through Castile and León

Bottom left Stopping for a drink from the wine fountain at Bodegas Irache

Bottom right One of the scallop shell markers that guide the way along the trail

Today, around 250,000 walkers tackle this trail each year—as many as once walked the route in its 12th- and 13th-century heyday. There are 33 stages in all, covering 480 miles (772 km) across the northern Iberian Peninsula, from the pretty town of Saint Jean Pied de Port in France to the far corner of northwest Spain. Your constant companion throughout the journey will be a scallop shell, an unusual but ubiquitous sight on all of the routes and the historic symbol of the Camino. Several myths associate St. James with the scallop—mainly around the miraculous survival of drowning brides or knights, who were rescued from the sea, covered in shells—and scallop shells were once presented to pilgrims on their arrival in Santiago as proof of their achievement. Today, they act as directional markers, set into the pavement, carved into walls and onto the sides of churches, and splashed across the routes' official signposts.

Most pilgrims also carry a scallop shell or two with them as they walk, tied to their backpack or strung together in a necklace, as a sign to other hikers that they are undertaking the whole Way. The shells also come in handy as a kind of drinking vessel, used—as recent tradition dictates—for quaffing from the wine fountain at Irache, near the town of Estella, which has been offering pilgrims a free sample of the bodega's red wine since 1991.

You'll certainly be needing a drink by that point. The Camino Frances isn't a route you ease into slowly—the first stage is probably the hardest of the entire walk—a calf-straining climb out of Saint Jean, across the border and up over 4,100 ft (1,250 m) into the Pyrenees to the Spanish village of Roncesvalles.

The good news is that it's then mostly downhill all the way to the bull-running city of Pamplona, from where the route opens up across Spain. You'll be averaging just over 15 miles (24 km) a day, taking in medieval walled towns and mountain villages, wheat fields, and olive groves—as well as cultural highlights like the straw-roofed roundhouses of O Cebreiro and the show-stopping cathedrals of Burgos and León. Over time, the peaks of the Pyrenees give way to the vast, scorched plains of the *meseta* (plateau) and then the rain-soaked hinterlands of Galicia—the signal that you're on the home stretch to Santiago. Whether your motivation for doing the walk is spiritual or otherwise, the sight of its cathedral will make your soul sing.

ANOTHER WAY
Camino dos Faros

An interesting alternative to the pilgrim trails, the Camino dos Faros (Lighthouse Way) is a striking coastal route that runs 124 miles (200 km) along the windswept clifftops and Atlantic beaches of the Costa da Morte, from Malpica south to Finisterre.

73
Levada das 25 Fontes

RABAÇAL, MADEIRA, PORTUGAL

Follow centuries-old water channels through rare forests to an enchanting lagoon on the west side of Madeira. Valley views, wildflowers, and silvery waterfalls are all part of the allure.

3 MILES (5 KM)   968 FT (295 M)   0.5 DAYS (RETURN)

Often described as "the land of eternal spring," the volcanic island of Madeira has a near-perfect subtropical climate with year-round sunshine and verdant forests blanketing its mountainous interior. The Portuguese isle is also the land of the *levada*—a complex irrigation system that channels water from the upper mountain slopes to the parched lowlands.

Hiking along these *levadas*, particularly the stunning Levada das 25 Fontes, is one of the best ways to experience the island's beauty. This path follows a moss-covered stone channel from the 1800s, passing through tunnel-like clusters of high-altitude heathers and dense forest, before skirting along wildflower-fringed ledges and down fern-covered hillsides. It ends at a tiny emerald-hued lagoon, fed by trickling waterfalls—the picturesque "25 fountains" that give this walk its name.

MAKE IT LONGER
Scenic Side Trip

About 0.25 miles (400 m) along the trail lies a 1-mile (1.6 km) return detour to the towering Risco waterfall (labeled "PR6.1, Risco"). A lookout provides a picture-perfect view of the forest-fringed cascade, which has a 328 ft (100 m) drop down a steep cliff face.

ELEVATION PROFILE

5,000 ft (1,524 m)

1,500 ft (457 m)

0 — 3 miles (5 km)

The **LAGOA DAS 25 FONTES** (25 Fountains Lagoon) makes a great spot for a picnic. If you're feeling intrepid, you can even take a dip in the icy waters.

Around 1 mile (1.6 km) along the trail, you'll be treated to sweeping views over the **RIBEIRA DA JANELA VALLEY**, which is dominated by an ancient laurel forest.

Viewpoint

Lagoa das 25 Fontes

MADEIRA

Near trail's start, you can see the **TÚNEL DO RABAÇAL**, an 2,625 ft (800 m) passageway used to transport water through the mountain.

Rabaçal

0 ········· km ········· 0.25
0 ········· miles ········· 0.25

Praia de Vale Centianes

PORTUGAL

Backed by towering cliffs and reached by a tunnel, the **PRAIA DO CARVALHO** is a great spot for a picnic.

Praia da Marinha

Farol de Alfanzina

Praia do Carvalho

Praia de Benagil

The iconic red-domed **FAROL DE ALFANZINA** (Alfanzina Lighthouse), which was built in 1920, makes a fine focal point in photos of the rugged coastline.

0 ·········· km ·········· 0.5
0 ·········· miles ·········· 0.5

At the trail's end, enjoy a refreshing dip at **PRAIA DA MARINHA**, which is ranked among Portugal's loveliest beaches.

74

Seven Hanging Valleys Trail

PRAIA DE VALE CENTIANES TO PRAIA DA MARINHA, PORTUGAL

Hike the clifftops of Portugal's sun-kissed Algarve region on a trail that takes in rocky coves, sandy beaches, and jaw-dropping views over the Atlantic.

4 MILES (6 KM)   607 FT (185 M)   1 DAY (ONE-WAY)

Much of the beauty of the Seven Hanging Valleys Trail lies in this coastal path's blissful simplicity. The route is well marked and never really gets especially strenuous, so you can just unwind and savor the salt-tinged air and sunny skies. (With more than 300 days of sunshine a year in the Algarve, the weather rarely disappoints.)

But the true heart of this hike's appeal rests in its spectacular seaside views. Upon stepping out onto the boardwalk above the sands of Praia de Vale Centianes, the panoramas get progressively better as you go along: expect myriad photo opportunities of chiseled limestone formations arching into the ocean, wave-kissed shores directly beneath your feet, and a lone lighthouse glimmering in the distance. As you walk, keep an eye out for side paths leading down to enticing golden beaches—where you'll be kicking yourself if you forgot to bring along your swimsuit.

ELEVATION PROFILE

650 ft
(198 m)

0

0   4 miles (6 km)

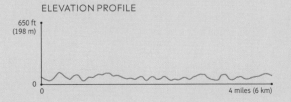

ANOTHER WAY
Bogshoeing

On a guided tour (available through the Estonian Tourist Board), you can leave the trail's boardwalk and hike through Viru on a bogshoeing expedition. Bogshoes act in the same way as snowshoes do, allowing you to navigate the soft, squelchy vegetation without sinking in up to your knees.

You can follow a branch off the path to an old **PEAT CUTTING FIELD**. Peat production was stopped in 1985, but the bog is still yet to recover here.

At the start of the trail, make sure you study the **INFORMATION BOARD** that details the bog's unusual flora.

Peat cutting field

ESTONIA

Car park

Observation tower

About a quarter of the way into the walk, climb up the **OBSERVATION TOWER** for a bird's-eye view of the bog pools.

0 ···········km··········· 0.5
0 ···········miles··········· 0.5

75

Viru Bog Trail

LAHEMAA NATIONAL PARK, ESTONIA

Delve into the swampy landscape of Estonia's largest national park from the comfort of a sturdy wooden boardwalk.

Bogs often get a bad rap. In movies, they're frequently portrayed as slimy, stinking swamps—remember *Labyrinth*'s Bog of Eternal Stench?—even though they don't actually smell. In fact, these beleaguered wetlands are some of the cleanest habitats around, which is something you'll discover on this fascinating walk through Viru Bog in Estonia's Lahemaa National Park. Raised up on a wooden boardwalk, the trail cuts through a sea of spongy vegetation, bog pools, and reedy fen. Occasional viewing

platforms give you close-up views of the mossy carpet that covers Viru—it's 20 ft (6 m) deep in parts and is constantly thickening, as the plant matter on top grows and the peaty bottom decomposes. Mist often hangs over the landscape, adding an eerie ambiance to your walk—and giving more than a touch of credence to the story of Soovana, Estonia's mythological Guardian Spirit of the Wetlands, whose shining eyes are said to lure wanderers deep into the bog.

ELEVATION PROFILE

650 ft
(198 m)

0

0   4 miles (6 km)

⊖ 4 MILES (6 KM)

◯ 123 FT (37 M)

🕑 0.5 DAYS (LOOP)

152

76

Wooden Architecture Route

LACHOWICE TO GRYWAŁD, POLAND

Ramble from wooden churches to grand old timber manors on this tranquil section of Poland's Wooden Architecture Route—an odyssey through the country's historical building traditions.

95 MILES (153 KM)

15,629 FT (4,764 M)

7 DAYS (ONE-WAY)

The Wooden Architecture Route winds its way through Małopolska (Lesser Poland), a jewelry box of quaint wooden churches, rural cottages, and manor houses. While the whole trail is a lengthy 932 miles (1,500 km), much of the route's charm can be experienced on this shorter stretch from Lachowice to Grywałd.

The trail's architectural gems sparkle from the start, with the Baroque splendor of Lachowice's UNESCO-listed, onion-domed church. Each trim farming village that follows is endowed with its own unique architectural intrigue.

At St. Anne's in Nowy Targ, rosettes bloom from the church vaults, while in Trybsz, further southeast, a squat 16th-century church is capped with a pointed roof that rather resembles a witch's hat.

In between the timber churches and creaky heritage houses, you'll skirt the banks of glassy Lake Czorsztyńskie and tramp right through the heart of Pieniny National Park. But while these natural settings have their own treasures, it's the promise of more unusual buildings around the corner that spur you to hike ever onward to Grywałd.

153

Lachowice

Zawoja

Arriving in the village of Orawka, step inside the **CHURCH OF ST. JOHN THE BAPTIST** to contemplate its paintings and late-Baroque altar.

Stroll through Łopuszna to the **MUSEUM OF NOBLEMAN CULTURE**, housed in an opulent 18th-century manor house.

Raba Wyżna

Orawka

POLAND

Nowy Targ

Łopuszna

Reaching Grywałd, you'll soon spot the **AUXILIARY CHURCH OF ST. MARTIN**, with its sharp spire and bellhouse.

Grywałd

0 ········· km ········· 10

0 ········· miles ········· 10

ELEVATION PROFILE

6,500 ft (1,981 m)

0

0

95 miles (153 km)

Trybsz

Niedzica-Zamek

Pieniny National Park

Take time to admire the enigmatic **WOODEN CHURCH** at Petriș. Built in 1748, it features a silver-capped tower and timbered walls.

Feast within the chandeliered dining hall of **CASTEL DRACULA**, a hotel-restaurant homage to Bram Stoker's fanged creation. It's in Piatra Fântânele, less than an hour's walk off the main trail.

Recharge with a day or two at fir-lined **LAKE COLIBIȚA**, where you can swim, fish, and boat by day and bed down in simple lakeside inns by night.

Linger in Brâncovenești to visit 800-year-old **CASTELUL KEMÉNY**, complete with Renaissance-style windows and distinctive turrets.

MAKE IT LONGER

Terra Siculorum

Delve into Romania's Hungarian history by continuing along the next section of the trail: Terra Siculorum (Latin for Székely Land, the home of Transylvanian Hungarians). It runs from Câmpu Cetății south to Archita and takes eight full days to complete.

Lunca Ilvei

Poiana Stampei

Poiana Negrii

Castel Dracula

Bistrița-Bârgăului

Lake Colibița

ROMANIA

Mărișelu

Jeica

Monor

Petriș

Săcalu de Pădure

Brâncovenești

Gurghiu

Câmpu Cetății

154

0 ·············· km ·············· 10
0 ·············· miles ·············· 10

Via Transilvanica

POIANA NEGRII TO CÂMPU CETĂȚII, ROMANIA

Tracing a section of the colossal Via Transilvanica, this highland hike reveals the multifaceted charms of Romania's natural beauty and cultural heritage.

136 MILES (219 KM)

18,428 FT (5,617 M)

10 DAYS (ONE-WAY)

An 497-mile (800 km)—and growing—trail network across Transylvania, the Via Transilvanica is a portal into a rural idyll. It passes through primeval forests, time-trapped farming villages, and open fields grazed by fluffy sheep. Cabbage rolls and homemade *pálinka* (plum brandy) provide the fuel, while farmstays and rustic guesthouses offer cozy lodgings along the way.

There are several distinctive sections to this mighty trail, of which the Highland Route, from Poiana Negrii to Câmpu Cetății, promises the most dramatic mountainscapes. Inevitably, this means a few calf-stiffening uphills, but the bucolic surroundings deserve a slow pace to take everything in, anyway. Orange-and-white markers lead through forests, marshes, and peat reserves, which gradually open out into wide meadows with views of the Călimani and Rodnei mountains.

By now you're deep into Romanian farming country, a timeless landscape of rustic wooden buildings standing watch over green fields. Alongside the path are excitable sheepdogs and signs indicating

Farm buildings and haystacks in the rural surroundings of Piatra Fântânele

local produce for sale—*caș* (crumbly cow's milk cheese) and *urdă* (soft whey cheese) are both delicious snacks.

As the hike continues, meadows merge into old-growth forests, home to brown bears and wild boar, giving the trail a fairy-tale feel. This is made only more vivid by the traditional Saxon-style houses at Jeica, inhabited by Transylvania's German-speaking community since medieval times (look for ornate inscriptions above the doors), and the Hungarian-style castles at Brâncovenești and Gurghiu. It's hard to return to the realities of everyday life upon reaching the trail's end at Câmpu Cetății, but there's always more of the Via Transilvanica to explore if you want to keep going.

ELEVATION PROFILE

6,500 ft (1,981 m)

0

0   136 miles (219 km)

155

If you can, time your ascent of **PLANINICA** so you arrive at the summit by late afternoon, when the views dazzle in the soft light.

0 ·········· km ·········· 1
0 ·············· miles ·············· 1

Jelovačka Pećina

Zminje Jezero

Car park

Gornja Ališnica

Donja Ališnica

MONTENEGRO

Crno Jezero

Planinica

The high alpine meadow of **GORNJA ALIŠNICA** is a great place to admire nearby Bubatov Kok, the highest peak in Durmitor.

Just 10 minutes' walk from the park entrance, the dark glacial lake of **CRNO JEZERO**, or Black Lake, marks the hike's trailhead.

Malo Jezero   *Veliko Jezero*

78

Planinica

DURMITOR NATIONAL PARK, MONTENEGRO

Follow a little-trodden trail up to a glacial cirque among the mountains of Montenegro's finest national park.

Mountains and meadows, pine forests, and glacial lakes—the hike up to the mountain amphitheater of Planinica, in Montenegro's Durmitor National Park, has a little bit of everything. Part of the Dinaric Alps, which rumble down through the Western Balkans from Slovenia, the limestone massif of Durmitor remains off the radar for most hikers, despite its surrounding national park being inscribed onto UNESCO's World Heritage list in 1980. The walk to Planinica starts just outside the village of Žbaljak

and leads through thick pine forest and past inky black glacial lakes, known locally as "mountain eyes." Soft grasses carpet the carved valleys of Donja Ališnica and Gornja Ališnica, which in summer are grazed by horses and cows. There are views throughout that will make your heart sing, but the best are saved for last: Planinica towers over the beautiful Veliko Jezero and Malo Jezero lakes, and from its summit you can gaze in awe at Sareni Pasovi (Colorful Layers), a Viennetta of rippled rock layers, compressed into snaking lines that run up to its peak.

ELEVATION PROFILE

10,000 ft
(3,048 m)

0

0   12 miles (19 km)

⊖ 12 MILES (19 KM)

⊗ 3,248 FT (990 M)

◔ 1 DAY (RETURN)

156

Samaria Gorge

XYLOSKALO TO AGÍA ROUMÉLI,
CRETE, GREECE

Walk the length of this towering gorge—the jewel in the crown of Crete's White Mountains National Park—for stunning scenery every step of the way.

As Crete is an island known for its clear blue skies, bright sunshine, and warmth, it comes as a relief to learn that most of this downhill walk is in the shade, with numerous natural springs along the way to refill your water bottle. The day begins with a long, steep descent into the gorge, but your aching knees are soon relieved by a gentle amble as the gradient improves. Now all you need to think about is the rugged beauty of the surroundings—soaring cliffs on either side, historic sites such as the abandoned village of Samaria, and, best of all, fabulous flora and fauna.

In spring, you'll see a colorful display of wildflowers, including dazzling peonies and endemics such as the Cretan bee orchid. Throughout the year, the curvy-horned Cretan goat, or kri-kri, may make an appearance, and the dandyish hoopoe, majestic golden eagle, and bone-crushing bearded vulture might be spotted in the skies. Whenever you visit, though, you're guaranteed a backdrop of awe-inspiring crags.

ELEVATION PROFILE

6,500 ft
(1,981 m)

0

0   9 miles (14 km)

⊖ 9 MILES (14 KM)

⊘ 397 FT (121 M)

◷ 1 DAY (ONE-WAY)

ANOTHER WAY
Vikos Gorge

In the Pindus Mountains of northern Greece lies a similarly imposing and alluring gorge: Vikos Gorge. It has all kinds of pathways with varying degrees of difficulty and holds the Guinness World Record for the deepest canyon in proportion to its width.

The rustic **AGIOS NIKOLAOS CHURCH**, built on the site of a temple to Apollo, makes an ideal spot for a rest. Shade is easy to find, thanks to the tall Cypress trees here.

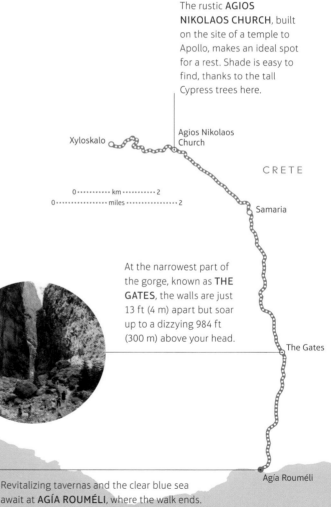

Xyloskalo

Agios Nikolaos Church

CRETE

0 ········· km ········· 2
0 ········· miles ········· 2

Samaria

At the narrowest part of the gorge, known as **THE GATES**, the walls are just 13 ft (4 m) apart but soar up to a dizzying 984 ft (300 m) above your head.

The Gates

Agía Rouméli

Revitalizing tavernas and the clear blue sea await at **AGÍA ROUMÉLI**, where the walk ends. You can catch a ferry from here to Hora Sfakion, then travel onward to your accommodations.

157

80
Carian Trail

İÇMELER TO HISARÖNÜ, TURKEY

Traverse pinewood paths and rocky promontories studded with historic ruins and almond groves overlooking the Aegean on a testing trail through the land of the ancient Carians.

◯ 94 MILES (152 KM) 〰 21,010 FT (6,404 M) ◷ 8 DAYS (ONE-WAY)

Anatolia's southwesternmost extremity is not, it's fair to say, widely known as a hiking region. While sun worshippers flock to beaches around Marmaris to the north, the lumpy, long-isolated Bozburun Peninsula mainly attracts Turkish tourists in the know. From 2012, though, a series of mostly forgotten footpaths—byways well trodden by villagers and shepherds for centuries, but latterly abandoned and overgrown—were rehabilitated. Bushwhacked and waymarked as part of the wider Carian Trail project across southwest Turkey, they now allow on-foot access to an area rich in natural beauty and intriguing archaeological sites: the region known in ancient days as Caria.

This patch of Anatolia between the Dalaman and Büyük Menderes rivers was mentioned in texts dating back to the second millennium BC as the home of seafaring warriors. According to the ancient Greek poet Homer, Carians fought alongside Priam at Troy, and they're also known to have served as mercenaries in Egypt. Various powers have taken control here over the centuries, including the Hittites, Alexander the Great, and nearby Rhodes, as well as the Persian, Roman, Byzantine, Selçuk, and Ottoman empires. Between them, they left a legacy of temples, citadels, and tombs, the remains of which today pepper the Bozburun Peninsula. ▶

ELEVATION PROFILE

6,500 ft
(1,981 m)

0

0   94 miles (152 km)

Rambling alongside the azure waters of the Aegean on the Carian Trail

REFUEL
Honey

Be sure to try the various flavors of local honey, redolent with the aromas of the carob, pine, rosemary, and thyme blooms on whose nectar the bees sup. You'll pass pale blue beehives at many points along the trail, placed under flowering trees or among herbs, and can pick up pots of honey from roadside stalls.

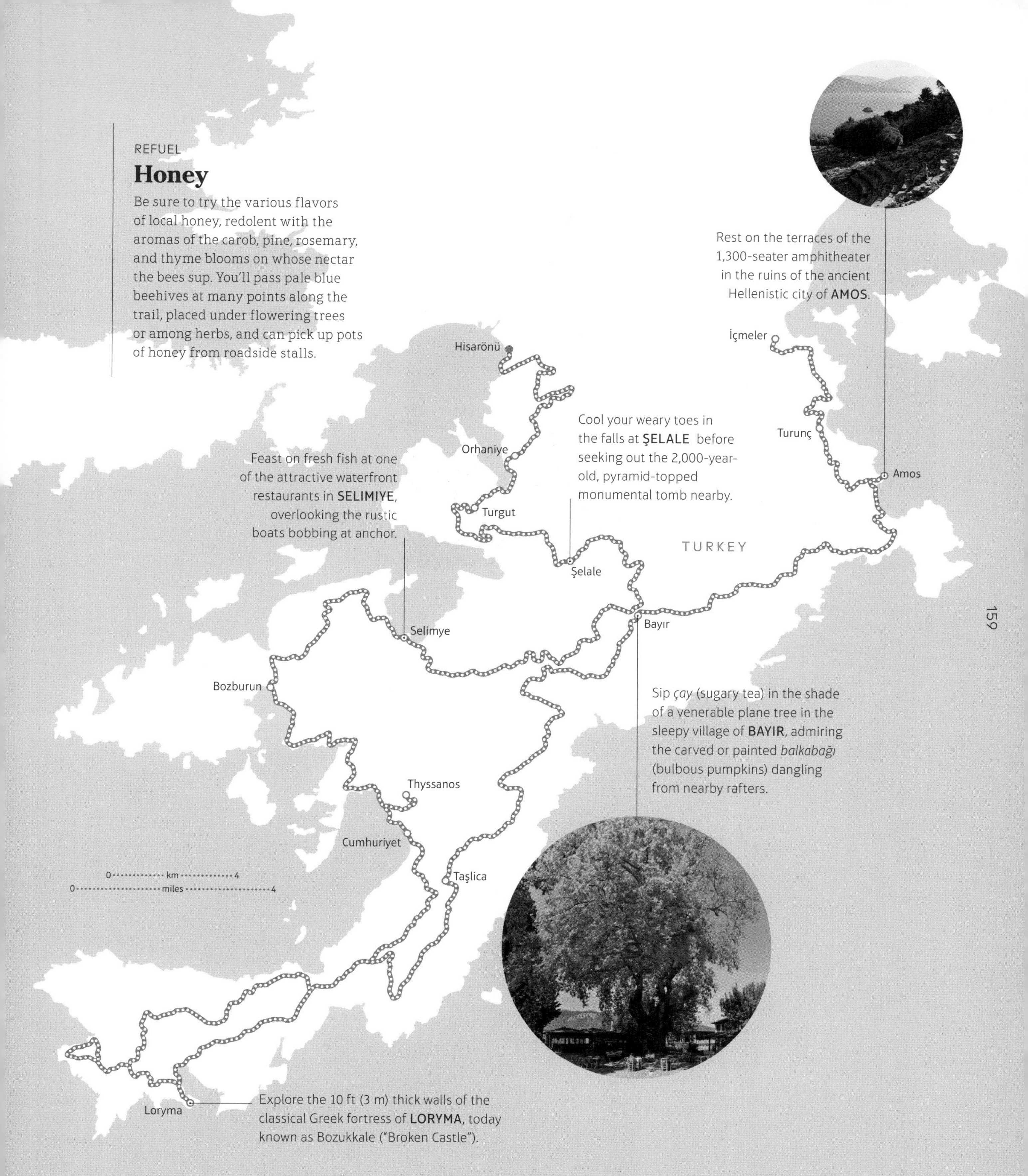

Rest on the terraces of the 1,300-seater amphitheater in the ruins of the ancient Hellenistic city of **AMOS**.

Feast on fresh fish at one of the attractive waterfront restaurants in **SELIMIYE**, overlooking the rustic boats bobbing at anchor.

Cool your weary toes in the falls at **ŞELALE** before seeking out the 2,000-year-old, pyramid-topped monumental tomb nearby.

İçmeler

Hisarönü

Orhaniye

Turunç

Turgut

Şelale

TURKEY

Amos

Selimye

Bayır

Bozburun

Sip çay (sugary tea) in the shade of a venerable plane tree in the sleepy village of **BAYIR**, admiring the carved or painted *balkabağı* (bulbous pumpkins) dangling from nearby rafters.

Thyssanos

Cumhuriyet

Taşlica

0 ········· km ········· 4
0 ········· miles ········· 4

Loryma

Explore the 10 ft (3 m) thick walls of the classical Greek fortress of **LORYMA**, today known as Bozukkale ("Broken Castle").

The resort of İçmeler, where the route around the Bozburun Peninsula begins

These are the historical highlights of the Bozburun section of the Carian Trail, a demanding but rewarding multiday route that snakes south from the resort of İçmeler to the tip of the promontory before pivoting nearly 180 degrees and finishing on the west coast at Hisarönü. The route is a ticket to time travel in more ways than one. Not only does the trail (waymarked with red-and-white stripes) visit the remains of settlements dating back well over two millennia, but it also provides insights into a way of life little changed in centuries. On the trail, you'll pass herds of goats foraging beneath olive trees and almond groves sprouting between the tumbledown stones of long-deserted settlements and citadels. And in timeless hamlets, you'll join old men conversing and playing dominoes while drinking endless tulip-shaped glasses of çay (sugary tea) on café terraces.

Indeed, another joy of hiking here is the range of traditional flavors you'll sample along the trail, from çağla (unripe almonds) plucked from trees as you pass, to the fresh fish served in harborside tavernas and the delights of meze: gül dolması (roses stuffed with rice and herbs), mücver (spicy zucchini fritters), cigar-shaped cheese filo böreği, and garlicky grilled peppers.

When it comes to the actual walk, this most craggy of capes, stretching into the Aegean, is in many ways a route of two halves. The northern section is greener, the path shaded in parts by pine, cypress, and wild carob trees rising from dense maquis scrub. Here, the air is herb-scented with wild rosemary, thyme, and pine oil, released as your boots tramp needles on the path; cicadas buzz, and crickets chirp, and purple patches near the shore betray blossoming rock roses and oleanders.

South of Bayır, the village in the center of the peninsula, the landscape is rockier, more exposed, and dramatic, its forums and fortifications affording far-reaching views across impossibly azure waters. Occasionally, the path drops to the shore, where you can dash into the sea to cool off; more often, it climbs to lofty ridges and plateaus.

> ## The route is a ticket to time travel in more ways than one.

Throughout this region, you'll need strong stamina and a good supply of water, with both shade and supplies scarce on long stretches. That's one reason why it's advisable to avoid hiking in summer, from mid-June to early September, when the heat can be brutal; short and wet winter days aren't ideal, either. Instead, time your walk for wildflower-strewn spring (March–May) or fall, when temperatures are more moderate and hotels and restaurants are open—the best seasons in which to sate your hunger for hiking, history, and timeless Turkish cuisine.

Left Walking along a gravel track on the Carian Trail

Right Boats moored at Bozburun Marina

MAKE IT LONGER
Branch Out

The Bozburun Peninsula is one of five main sections that make up the full Carian Trail, which totals around 510 miles (820 km) between Dalyan in the east and Bodrum on the Aegean. The other four are linked (though not in a linear way), offering plenty of opportunity to explore the region further.

Just beyond the village of **LATSUMBA**, a short detour off the trail leads to an old church with far-reaching views over the Enguri Valley.

Utviri Pass · Nakra · Latsumba · Chuberi

81

Upper Svaneti

CHUBERI TO USHGULI, GEORGIA

Cross the beautiful Upper Svaneti region, surrounded by the mighty Greater Caucasus mountains.

86 MILES (138 KM)

28,691 FT (8,745 M)

6–7 DAYS (ONE-WAY)

Nestled within the Greater Caucasus mountains, with the Svaneti range snaking along its border to the south, Upper Svaneti is surrounded by some of Georgia's highest peaks. These mighty mountains have acted as a historical barrier, preserving the region's stone villages (some of whose buildings date back to the 12th century) to such an extent that they were declared a UNESCO World Heritage Site in 1996.

· The poster child for Upper Svaneti is the community of Ushguli: a picture-perfect jumble of houses between two velvety green slopes, with the white-capped ridges of a formidable mountain range rising up behind. It's an appropriate end point for this 86-mile (138 km) up-and-down hike, which showcases the intriguing history and distinctive culture of this long-inaccessible area—not to mention its jaw-dropping beauty.

The trail to Ushguli starts in the village of Chuberi, in the Neskra Valley and crosses five major mountain passes—you'll reach 9,692 ft (2,954 m) cresting the Guli Pass on day four, on the climb between Mazeri and Mestia, where snow lingers on the path well into July. It's not all lofty peaks, though, with forested valleys and high alpine meadows providing dramatic changes to the landscape along the way. You'll follow old logging trails and Soviet

ELEVATION PROFILE

10,000 ft
(3,048 m)

0
0   86 miles (138 km)

Hiking toward the mountain village of Adishi in Upper Svaneti

The powerful **ADISHCHALA RIVER** can be tricky to navigate when it's in full flow; one of the locals will take you across on horseback for a few lari.

Guli Pass

Bak Pass   Mazeri

Pari

Mestia

GEORGIA

Zhabeshi

MESTIA is the largest settlement in the Upper Svaneti and a good place to stock up on provisions for the rest of your hike.

Adishi

Adishchala River

Davberi

Ushguli

Jeep tracks in and out of medieval-looking villages and abandoned hamlets, crossing streams on fallen logs and makeshift bridges or, where the Mulkhura River flows through Zhabeshi, whizzing across on a zip line set up by an entrepreneurial local mountain guide.

It's possible to camp en route, but the villages are set close enough together that you can spend each night in a local guesthouse, enjoying traditional Georgian hospitality and home-cooked cuisine by a warming log fire. The signature Svan dish is *kubdari*, a delicious flatbread filled with beef and onions, but look out, too, for *chvishtari* (fried cornbread stuffed with cheese) and *tashmijabi*, a kind of stretchy, cheesy mashed potato. It's hearty comfort food that will fuel you all the way to Ushguli (technically a group of villages), and its cluster of more than 200 tower houses, churches, and castles. Arriving in this medieval scene is one of those rare occasions when real life lives up to—if not exceeds—the promise of the postcards.

The trail ends in **USHGULI**, its picturesque towers backdropped by the majestic Greater Caucasus mountains.

MAKE IT LONGER
Transcaucasian Trail

This hike forms part of the 1,860-mile (3,000-km) Transcaucasian Trail, which will eventually run through Armenia, Georgia, and Azerbaijan. With Georgia under your belt, why not continue on into Armenia on the 517-mile (832 km) route from Lake Arpi to Meghri?

MOROCCO

◎85

WESTERN SAHARA

MAURITANIA

SENEGAL

GAMBIA

GUINEA-BISSAU

GUINEA

SIERRA LEONE ◎86 CÔTE D'IVOIRE

LIBERIA

AFRICA AND THE MIDDLE EAST

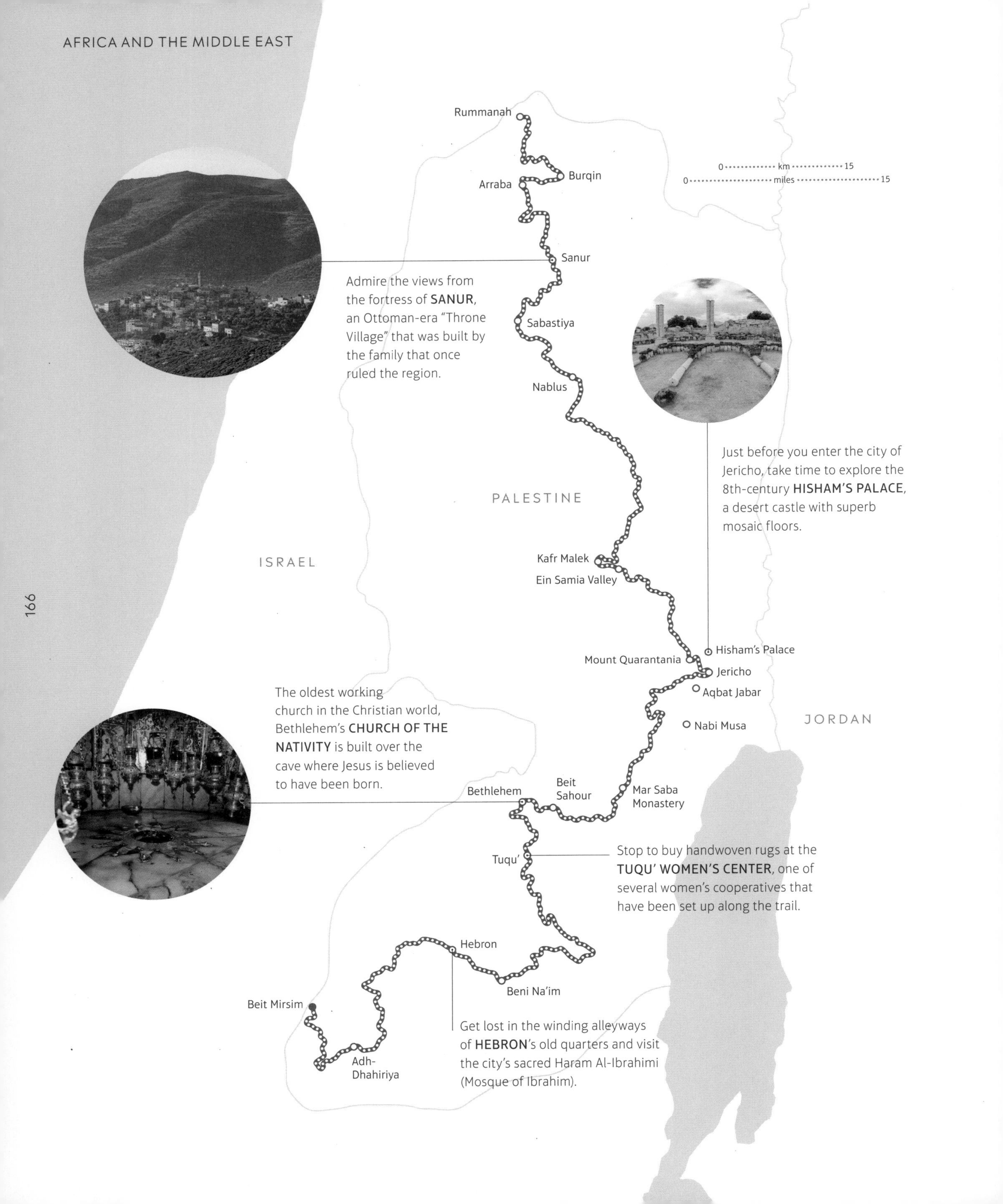

Rummanah

Burqin

Arraba

Sanur

Admire the views from
the fortress of **SANUR**,
an Ottoman-era "Throne
Village" that was built by
the family that once
ruled the region.

Sabastiya

Nablus

PALESTINE

ISRAEL

Just before you enter the city of
Jericho, take time to explore the
8th-century **HISHAM'S PALACE**,
a desert castle with superb
mosaic floors.

Kafr Malek

Ein Samia Valley

Mount Quarantania

Hisham's Palace

Jericho

Aqbat Jabar

The oldest working
church in the Christian world,
Bethlehem's **CHURCH OF THE
NATIVITY** is built over the
cave where Jesus is believed
to have been born.

Nabi Musa

JORDAN

Beit
Sahour

Mar Saba
Monastery

Bethlehem

Stop to buy handwoven rugs at the
TUQU' WOMEN'S CENTER, one of
several women's cooperatives that
have been set up along the trail.

Tuqu'

Hebron

Beni Na'im

Beit Mirsim

Get lost in the winding alleyways
of **HEBRON**'s old quarters and visit
the city's sacred Haram Al-Ibrahimi
(Mosque of Ibrahim).

Adh-
Dhahiriya

0 ·········· km ·········· 15
0 ·········· miles ·········· 15

82

Palestinian Heritage Trail

RUMMANAH TO BEIT MIRSIM, PALESTINE

Traverse the Holy Land on a walk that blends scenes from the Bible with traditional Palestinian hospitality.

Tip

If you'd like to walk with a group, you can join one of the guided thru-hikes that take place every March and November.

202 MILES (325 KM)

31,214 FT (9,514 M)

21 DAYS (ONE-WAY)

Starting in the village of Rummanah, northwest of Jenin, and ending in Beit Mirsim, southwest of Hebron, the Palestinian Heritage Trail, or Masar Ibrahim al-Khalil, is a long-distance discovery of Palestine's rich cultural heritage—and a walk through thousands of years of regional history.

Following dirt tracks, shepherds' trails, and footpaths still used by local Bedouins, you'll walk through almond groves, vineyards, and clusters of trees weighed down with shiny olives. Fertile valleys give way to open plains and rolling fields, deep canyons become desert landscapes, and the sight of farmers in fields is superseded by that of stallholders in old city souks.

Dotted throughout are architectural landmarks that signpost almost every major era since civilization began. In the north alone, you can explore ancient Canaanite sites in the Ein Samia valley, Ottoman

Mar Saba Monastery, built into the cliffs of the Kidron Valley in the Judean Desert

palaces at Arraba, and the sprawling Roman ruins of Herod's Temple in Sabastiya. Byzantine churches are a regular sight, and there are centuries-old mountain monasteries throughout—none more impressive than Mar Saba, a Greek Orthodox monastery that staggers down a rocky cliff in barren wilderness halfway between Jerusalem and the Dead Sea. Many of these sites are steeped in religious significance—this is the Holy Land, after all—and as you work your way south, you'll hike from one biblical reference to the next. ▶

ELEVATION PROFILE

6,500 ft
(1,981 m)

0

0   202 miles (325 km)

Left The Greek Orthodox church at the Shepherds' Fields in Beit Sahour

Below The Church of St. George, at the site where Jesus healed a group of men suffering from leprosy

Bottom The shrine of Nabi Musa, believed to be the tomb of Moses

As you work your way south, you'll hike from one biblical reference to the next.

The town of Burqin, reached at the end of your first day's walk, is home to the 4th-century Church of St. George, built on the spot where Jesus reportedly healed 10 men suffering from leprosy. North of Jericho, you can climb up Mount Quarantania, the Mount of Temptation, where Jesus was tested by the devil while he fasted for 40 days and nights in the desert; south of the city, the complex of Nabi Musa is believed to house the tomb of Moses (Musa in Arabic). On your approach into Bethlehem, you'll follow the trail through the Shepherds' Fields in the town of Beit Sahour, where two chapels (one Greek, the other Catholic) mark the spots where the shepherds first saw the Star of Bethlehem. Many hikers break their journey in Bethlehem itself, using their rest days to visit Manger Square, the Church of the Nativity, and the Milk Grotto, where Mary, Joseph, and Jesus are said to have hidden before their flight to Egypt.

But this hike isn't all about historical buildings and Bible stories. In fact, the trail was inaugurated in part to help the everyday people who live alongside the route, and there are plenty of opportunities to stay with local families and engage in pioneering community-based tourism projects. You'll soon discover that food is at the heart of Palestinian hospitality, whether that's dining under the stars to the haunting sounds of the stringed *rababa* at a Bedouin camp in Al-Auja, stopping for a home-cooked meal and stay in a guesthouse courtesy of the Aqbat Jaber Refugee Camp Women's Center, or enjoying a lunch of grape leaves stuffed with meat and spiced rice, fresh from the vineyards of a family in Beni Na'im. In the final stages of the trail, make sure to call at Adh-Dhahiriya, just 12 miles (20 km) from the route's end. Here, you can pick up some *maftoul* (Palestinian couscous) or herby *za'atar* mix from the local women's cooperatives—tasty reminders of your time on the trail that will last long after the walk has come to an end.

MAKE IT LONGER

Dead Sea Viewpoint

A beautiful detour off the main trail takes you 5 miles (8.5 km) from 'Arab al-Rashayida down to a viewpoint over the Dead Sea. The turquoise waters are a spectacular sight against the backdrop of hazy purple peaks in distant Jordan.

83
Wadi Ghuweir Trail

MANSOURA TO WADI USHAYQIR, JORDAN

In the parched desert of northern Jordan, discover a verdant oasis of palms and grasses hidden within the depths of an ancient river valley.

9 MILES (14 KM) · **705 FT (215 M)** · **1 DAY (ONE-WAY)**

Cinematic in its beauty, stark, and strange, the scorched earth of Jordan's rocky desert makes a spectacular setting for this magical one-day trek. Following a winding path, it begins amid a landscape of black-streaked red rocks and sheer canyon walls—but it's not long before this Martian panorama morphs into something more unexpected.

As you descend into Wadi Ghuweir, the trail plunges into a lush green garden that has seemingly been conjured out of thin air. It's an effect made believable by the fact that the river that created the gorge remains largely unseen, making only occasional cameo appearances as it snakes beneath boulders and tumbles over tiny waterfalls. The life-bestowing properties of water have never been more apparent: the red and ocher valley walls burst with palm trees and wild grasses, and the rocks are dyed green by algae and moss. It's a surreal and exhilarating sight, which feels ever more fantastical as you leave the gorge and emerge back into the desert.

ELEVATION PROFILE

6,500 ft
(1,981 m)

0

0 — 9 miles (14 km)

Keep an eye out at **WADI USHAYQIR** for goats plucking at the few hardy shrubs that survive among the sun-baked rocks streaked with black lines.

0 ········ km ········ 1
0 ········ miles ········ 1

As you enter **WADI GHUWEIR** ("Descending Valley"), the rock walls of the gorge take on a strange rippling look, like the grain of olive wood.

Wadi Ushayqir

JORDAN

Wadi Al-Nakheel

WADI AL-NAKHEEL, or the "Valley of the Palms," is a true desert oasis, where palm trees, spiky grasses, and pink wildflowers sprout from the parched valley walls.

Wadi Ghuweir

Trailhead

Walking through a section of Wadi Ghuweir, toward a lush oasis

Climb up the terraced slopes above the village to explore **BI'R DAKHILYA**, an inviting lake beneath a rocky overhang.

Bi'r Dakhilya

As-Sab

At the end of your outbound hike, take time to explore the crumbling stone buildings scattered throughout the deserted village of **AS-SAB**.

OMAN

0 ······· km ······· 0.5
0 ······ miles ······ 0.5

Al Khitaym

84

The Balcony Walk

AL QANNAH PLATEAU, OMAN

Hike through the Western Hajar mountains, along the rim of Oman's "Grand Canyon."

4 MILES (7 KM)

1,050 FT (320 M)

0.5 DAYS (RETURN)

One of the finest hikes in Oman, Route W6 follows an old donkey track along the edge of Wadi An Nakhur, Oman's "Grand Canyon," to the abandoned village of As-Sab. The trail is much better known as The Balcony Walk, an apt description for a route that totters along the canyon's craggy western flank, allowing stupendous views throughout: down into the abyss of An Nakhur and as far away as Al Hamra, a village 23 miles (37 km) to the south.

The path is narrow and etched into the cliff face, with sheer drop-offs for company, so you'll need a good head for heights. But it's much less treacherous than it may appear from a distance—the goats that follow you along the way take it all very much in their stride. Lying in wait at the end is the village of As-Sab, once home to a dozen or so families who somehow farmed these precipitous slopes but now abandoned to the ravages of the wind. It's a remarkable place but one that you'll have to leave all too soon, as the return journey back along the canyon awaits.

The walk starts in the village of **AL KHITAYM**, where a few tiny houses cling to the edge high above the canyon floor.

ANOTHER WAY

Route W4

For a longer walk nearby, hike Route W4 to the southern summit of Jebel Shams (9,833 ft/2,997 m), the country's highest peak, following the rim of the Saydran Gorge. It's a steep 6-mile (9 km) trek, taking around 10 hours.

ELEVATION PROFILE

6,500 ft (1,981 m)

3,000 ft (914 m)

0   4 miles (7 km)

85

The Toubkal Circuit

IMLIL, MOROCCO

This challenging tour through the far-flung Berber villages of the starkly beautiful Toubkal Massif ends with an ascent of North Africa's highest peak.

47 MILES (75 KM)

19,495 FT (5,942 M)

6 DAYS (LOOP)

Cutting a crown through Morocco's High Atlas mountains, the demanding Toubkal Circuit is one of the most interesting multi-day treks in Africa. Jebel Toubkal (the range's highest peak) is the ultimate goal—regular views of its summit remind you of such—and some hikers cut to the chase and head straight for the summit from the starting village of Imlil. But this six-day circuit is about so much more than scaling one particular mountain. The slow-going ups and downs give you time to enjoy fascinating glimpses of rural Berber life. Mud-brick villages cling to the sides of bare mountains, the houses stacked on top of each other like oversized earthy Jenga blocks. Local children roam far from home as they shepherd their goats through isolated valleys, while Berber women, dressed in flowing headscarves, tend their crops of barley and corn on gravity-defying terraces.

Taking your time also gives you a chance to acclimatize to the heady altitude and linger over the magnificent mountain scenery. For the most part, the High Atlas are bone-jarringly barren, a Mars-like landscape of loose scree and boulders, where sunbaked trails snake through deep gorges and up over windswept passes. But there are welcome splashes of vibrancy among the rocky terrain—a lush valley here, a gurgling stream there, as well as almond trees, olive groves, and turquoise mountain lakes. And the panoramic views are sublime: across summer pastures, over jagged ridges, down into vast bowling valleys, and, from the top of Jebel Toubkal itself, a sweeping vista of the entire

ELEVATION PROFILE

16,000 ft (4,876 m)

0

0   47 miles (75 km)

A simple stone *gîte*, located on the snowy, rocky slopes of Jebel Toubkal

Tip
It's strongly advisable to hire a licensed guide to safely navigate the circuit.

172

Climb Ouanoukrim

If you have an extra day, you could add on a side trip to climb Ouanoukrim, the Toubkal Massif's second-highest peak. Situated at the very end of the High Atlas, it affords great views over the oasis valleys and desert plains of southern Morocco.

Tacheddirt

Imlil

Aroumd

Sidi Chamarouch

Summiting mighty **JEBEL TOUBKAL**, at 13,671 ft (4,167 m), will literally be the highlight of your trek.

With terraced slopes and a beautifully clear mountain stream, the pastureland of **AZIB LIKEMT** is a lovely place to set up camp.

Azib Likemt

MOROCCO

173

Jebel Toubkal

Toubkal Massif and the Haouz plains that roll back to Marrakesh beyond.

Make no mistake: this is a demanding trek, with long, grueling climbs and equally long—and equally grueling—descents. But the chance to engage with Berber culture is unbeatable. You'll bunk down in stone shelters set up for shepherds, camp on riverbanks, or spend the night in simple village *gîtes*. You'll have pancakes for breakfast, couscous for lunch, and filling tagines for dinner. Indeed, the hospitality here is so warm and welcoming that you'll barely notice the ache in your legs.

Lac d'Ifni

Take a dip in the green waters of **LAC D'IFNI**, a striking sight against a backdrop of parched mountainsides.

Stock up on provisions at the village of **AMSOUZERT**, where there are several shops, plus cafés serving mint tea.

Ait Igrane

Amsouzert

0 ·········· km ·········· 3
0 ·········· miles ·········· 3

AFRICA AND THE MIDDLE EAST

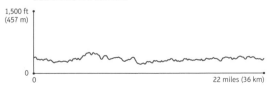

The trail passes the banks of the Moa River, before arriving at **TIWAI ISLAND WILDLIFE SANCTUARY**, a place known for the pygmy hippopotamus.

Tiwai Island
Wildlife Sanctuary

SIERRA
LEONE

Moa River

In Gola South, one of seven chiefdoms surrounding the park, stay overnight with the Mende people in **NEMAHUNGOIMA VILLAGE**.

Nemahungoima
Village

0 ·········· km ·········· 5
0 ·········· miles ·········· 5

Sileti

174

The **RAINFOREST** here holds 49 mammals; some of these are critically endangered, including the western chimpanzee as well as species of shrew, rodents, and bats.

86
Gola Rainforest to Tiwai Island

SILETI TO TIWAI ISLAND, SIERRA LEONE

Embark on a walk through caverns of evergreen forest to explore a world of primates, hippos, and birds.

Once the scene of conflict during the civil war that ravaged Sierra Leone in the 1990s, Gola Rainforest National Park is today a beacon of hope for conservation and sustainable resource management. This biodiverse spot—the country's largest remaining area of intact lowland rainforest—is home to almost 1,000 plant species and numerous endemic animals, and there are aims that one day this "green diamond of the nation" will hold UNESCO World Heritage Site status.

The trek to Tiwai Island Wildlife Sanctuary begins in the southern region of the rainforest, at the Sileti substation close to the Liberian border. As you hike in the tropical heat, accompanied by curious insects drawn to your sweat, you'll come across Diana monkeys and other primates clambering through the trees. From the lush thicket comes the call of birds—white-necked rockfowl, rufous fishing owl, and Gola malimbe—who represent a mere fraction of the vast aviary that exists here. The final stretch to Tiwai Island brings the chance to see one of the rarest creatures of all: the endangered pygmy hippopotamus, which grazes on the swampy vegetation of the river here.

⊖ 22 MILES (36 KM)

⊗ 2,165 FT (660 M)

🕒 3 DAYS (ONE-WAY)

ELEVATION PROFILE

1,500 ft
(457 m)

0

0   22 miles (36 km)

The vertiginous vista across the 1,640 ft (500 m) deep chasm to **JINBAR WATERFALL** is almost overwhelming in spectacle.

Imet Gogo

Chennek Camp

Gich

Jinbar Waterfall

Sankaber Camp

ETHIOPIA

Buyit Ras

Ras Bwahit

Arguably the keynote of the entire trek is the hike along the escarpment from Gich to **IMET GOGO**. At the summit is a 360-degree viewpoint.

The final day of the trek is a challenging early morning ascent of the 14,534 ft (4,430 m) **RAS BWAHIT**. The surrounding highlands offer the best chance to spot the Ethiopian wolf.

87

Simien Mountains National Park

BUYIT RAS TO RAS BWAHIT, ETHIOPIA

Take a tough hike across the magnificent Simien Mountains massif, one of Africa's most extraordinary landscapes.

26 MILES (42 KM)

9,275 FT (2,827 M)

4 DAYS (ONE-WAY)

A mere five minutes along this circuit through the UNESCO-listed Simien Mountains National Park, the wonders of the park's namesake massif are clear to see. The ragged tablelands before you host a dozen peaks topping 13,000 ft (4,000 m), the most notable of which is Ras Dashen—at 14,928 ft (4,550 m), it's Ethiopia's highest. Beyond their contours, lush Afroalpine grasslands cover the hills, with erica bushes and giant lobelia trees dotting exposed bluffs inhabited by gelada baboons.

The trail spends four challenging days coursing along the massif's craggy escarpments, occasionally dipping into a cool valley for respite en route to the next idyllically positioned campsite. The Simiens are known as the "roof of Africa," and as you progress to Ras Bwahit, scaling summits like Imet Gogo, you're certain to feel on top of the world.

MAKE IT LONGER
Ras Dashen

Enthusiastic peak baggers will want to extend their hike by at least a day to include an ascent of Ras Dashen, Ethiopia's highest—and Africa's 14th-highest—mountain. Interestingly, due to a strange trick of perspective, the surrounding peaks actually look higher when standing on its lofty, rocky summit.

ELEVATION PROFILE

16,000 ft (4,876 m)

6,500 ft (1,981 m)

0

26 miles (42 km)

PFUNDA TEA ESTATE produces some of the world's best teas. Book a tour of the plantation to learn how the leaves are picked and processed.

Pfunda Tea Estate

Rubavu

RUBONA BAY, just outside Rubavu, is a popular beach resort with a bustling small harbor.

Cyimbiri

A boat ride to **NYAMIRUNDI ISLAND** is a must for coffee lovers. Visit a plantation and enjoy sipping a cup while soaking up the stunning views.

Nyamirundi Island

Kinunu

DEMOCRATIC REPUBLIC OF THE CONGO

Bumba

Lake Kivu

Karongi Town

RWANDA

If you want to regroup and take a breather, tranquil **KUMBYA**, located on a small peninsula, makes the perfect retreat.

Mugonero

Don't miss the night fishing experience on Lake Kivu from **KARONGI TOWN**. The local fishermen whistle and sing to call each other to the lake, where they then hunt for isambaza fish.

Karengera

Kumbya

Rugabano

Shangi

Kamembe

0 ·········· km ·········· 15
0 ·········· miles ·········· 15

Tip

Visit the Kivu Belt website *(kivubelt.travel)* for a detailed guide to the trail and the tours available en route.

88

Congo-Nile Trail

RUBAVU TO KAMEMBE, RWANDA

Follow the footpaths of local communities to experience Rwandan culture on this undulating hike along the emerald banks of Lake Kivu.

110 MILES (178 KM)

22,614 FT (6,893 M)

10 DAYS (ONE-WAY)

The first thing that hits you on the Congo–Nile Trail is just how green Rwanda is. The countryside here is a rumpled patchwork quilt of every shade imaginable: vivid lime-colored tea bushes, orderly rows of emerald banana fronds, and bamboo forests of leafy jade, to name just a few. Stitching them all together is a network of red-earth footpaths and roads, carved steadily over the years by locals going about their daily lives—and which today form the basis of this beautiful and inspiring trail.

The creation of the route is part of Rwanda's long road to recovery from the events of 1994. Between April and June of that year, more than 800,000 Tutsi and

moderate Hutus were murdered by bands of Hutu militia in one of the most brutal genocides of the 20th century. These days, the country is safe and the leadership keen to encourage visitors, hence the launch of this 110-mile (178 km) hiking trail as one of its flagship tourism projects. (The route also has alternative options for traveling by mountain bike or kayak.) Opened in 2011, it has swiftly gained a reputation as one of Africa's most accessible long-distance hikes. ▶

REFUEL

Sorghum Beer

Sorghum is commonly used to make *kigage*, a thick and nutritious beer that Rwandans enjoy during traditional ceremonies. Outside Karongi is a village that offers a sorghum beer experience, where you learn how to make beer from scratch—from harvesting the crop to fermenting it—and then sit and enjoy a glass with your new friends in the village.

ELEVATION PROFILE

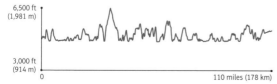

6,500 ft (1,981 m)

3,000 ft (914 m)

0   110 miles (178 km)

The villages you pass through and the people you meet are at the very heart of what makes this trail special.

Despite the name, the trail doesn't follow either the Congo or the Nile. In fact, it traces the watershed divide between the two rivers, running along the edge of Lake Kivu, one of the African Great Lakes. This vast body of water straddles the border between Rwanda and the Democratic Republic of the Congo, and its emerald expanse is your constant companion from Rubavu (previously known as Gisenyi) to Kamembe. Boats carrying tourists to its many islands are a common sight during the day, while at night the lake comes alive with the songs of fishermen, as they row out into the center on traditional three-hulled boats.

The villages you pass through and the people you meet are at the very heart of what makes this trail special. The route has been specifically designed to encourage engagement with local communities, and there are plenty of opportunities to dive more deeply into Rwandan culture. Organize a traditional healing tour to learn about the medicinal powers of local plants in Cyimbiri, have a lesson in handcrafts with a women's cooperative near Gishwati Forest, and sip Rwanda's famed coffee on a visit to the washing station at Kinunu. Everywhere you go, people will be eager to show you the fruit of their hands, from traditional pottery to freshly harvested honey. The language barrier can be tricky at times, but it's easy to make friends by learning a few words of Kinyarwanda—*muraho* (hello) and *urabeho* (goodbye) will give you a good start.

In between the villages, you'll pass sprawling fields of tea, coffee, and rice and hike through montane rainforest filled with the chatter of monkeys and chirp of rainbow-colored birds. The terrain throughout is decidedly undulating—Rwanda isn't nicknamed "the Land of a Thousand Hills" for nothing—so be prepared for a workout. Happily, there's no need to carry a tent as each stage of the trail is bookended by welcoming guesthouses (although it's possible to camp if you want to), and there are plenty of small shops where you can pick up supplies.

This is a trail that suits a slow pace, anyway, so take your time to enjoy the vistas of the rolling green hills and glittering Lake Kivu. And take every opportunity you can to experience all that the local communities have to offer—drink banana beer, eat *mbuzi choma* (roasted goat meat), and listen to the stories of Rwanda from the people who carved the path on which you're walking.

178

Right Crops growing on the rolling hills around Lake Kivu

Below The tranquil waters and green shoreline of Lake Kivu

AFRICA AND THE MIDDLE EAST

89

Ngare Ndare Forest

NGARE NDARE FOREST, KENYA

Uncover one of Kenya's hidden treasures on an enchanting forest walk to a pair of heavenly waterfalls.

4 MILES (7 KM)

650 FT (198 M)

0.5 DAYS (RETURN)

180

People come from all corners of the globe to visit Kenya's expansive savanna and abundant wildlife, landing in Nairobi before swooping off to the country's famed national parks. But few have ever heard of—let alone visited—Ngare Ndare Forest.

Ngare Ndare is one of only a few indigenous forests in Kenya whose canopy cover is expanding (thanks to local conservation and tree-planting projects). Long an important elephant corridor, it's a majestic setting of butterflies, birds, and ancient African olive and red cedar trees, which cast playful shadows as the sun's beams frolic among their branches. Black rhino and leopard tracks are writ in dry mud along the narrow dirt path, and clumps of misshapen tall grass are perhaps a sign that prowling lions have been by.

As you stroll between the tall trees on this steep yet manageable hike, the forest is charmingly quiet, with just the gentle rustle of leaves in the breeze. But the sound of thunder calls from a distance, eventually materializing in the form of two beautiful waterfalls. These are what the forest is known for—Ngare Ndare means "water for the goats" in the Maa language of the Maasai—and a dip into their bracingly cold azure pools is as unforgettable as the natural beauty that surrounds them.

ELEVATION PROFILE

8,200 ft (2,499 m)

3,000 ft (914 m)

0   4 miles (7 km)

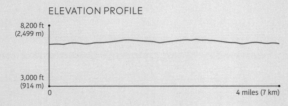

Trailhead

0 ·········· km ·········· 0.5
0 ·················· miles ·················· 0.5

Near the start of the trail is a basic **CAMPSITE**. It's near here that you'll meet your mandatory guide before setting out.

KENYA

The **WATERFALLS** are a popular local swimming spot, but be warned: the water remains icy cold all year round.

The **FOREST** is home to over 200 bird species, including the Hartlaub's turaco and the Narina trogon—see how many you can spot along the trail.

Waterfall

Waterfall

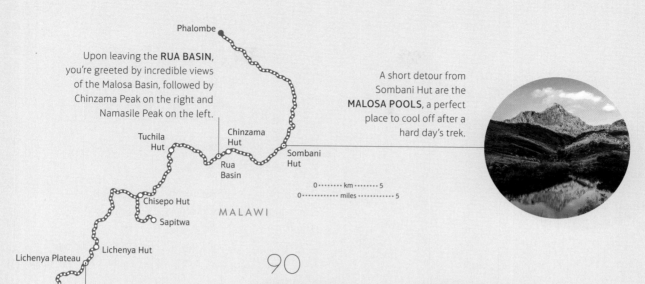

Phalombe

Upon leaving the **RUA BASIN**, you're greeted by incredible views of the Malosa Basin, followed by Chinzama Peak on the right and Namasile Peak on the left.

A short detour from Sombani Hut are the **MALOSA POOLS**, a perfect place to cool off after a hard day's trek.

Tuchila Hut

Chinzama Hut

Sombani Hut

Rua Basin

0 ·········· km ·········· 5
0 ·········· miles ·········· 5

MALAWI

Chisepo Hut

Sapitwa

Lichenya Plateau

Lichenya Hut

Mulanje

The **LICHENYA PLATEAU** is a tranquil area of expansive grassland that overlooks bright green tea estates.

90

Mulanje Grand Traverse

MULANJE TO PHALOMBE, MALAWI

Mount Mulanje is known locally as the "island in the sky," and a trek across this massif will certainly take you to the heavens.

Looking up at Mount Mulanje, a massive granite monolith that towers over southern Malawi, you can't help but be impressed by its sheer size and power. The massif's highest peak, Sapitwa, stands 9,849 ft (3,002 m) tall and is often draped in voluminous clouds. Local legend has it that the gods or ancestral spirits live here, and making the grueling trek along Mount Mulanje's length will lead you within reach of their realm.

The Grand Traverse trail begins among the vivid green tea estates of Mulanje town. Following the narrow path, you'll cross streams, gaze over sloping gorges laced with waterfalls, and even spy neighboring Mozambique on the horizon. The vegetation changes as you progress ever further across the massif, transforming from grasslands to forests of pine trees and endemic Mulanje cedar on the upper slopes.

It's sometimes a tight scramble over the foreboding rocks and rivers, reaching an apex on day three with the hike to the top of Sapitwa. The peak's name is the Chichewa word for "no-go zone," and it's said that you must appease the gods if you're to have a successful ascent—local lore advises eating any edible food you come across, as it's believed to be a good omen from the deities. Be sure to thank them as you soak up the stunning views from the top, before beginning the descent back down to the mortal world.

⊖ 35 MILES (57 KM)

⌃ 13,294 FT (4,052 M)

🕐 5 DAYS (ONE-WAY)

ELEVATION PROFILE

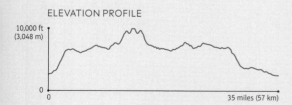

10,000 ft
(3,048 m)

0

0   35 miles (57 km)

The **LOOKOUT PLATFORM** found at the end of the Andamozavaky Circuit offers 360-degree views across a forest of rocky needles.

Loookout platform

0 ·········· km ·········· 0.5
0 ················ miles ················ 0.5

Canyons

Tight passages weave through the bottom of the **CANYONS** on the Broadway Circuit, requiring you to crawl in places.

Trailhead

MADAGASCAR

Hanging bridge

The **HANGING BRIDGE** on the Ranotsara Circuit dangles 230 ft (70 m) above the ground.

Trail end

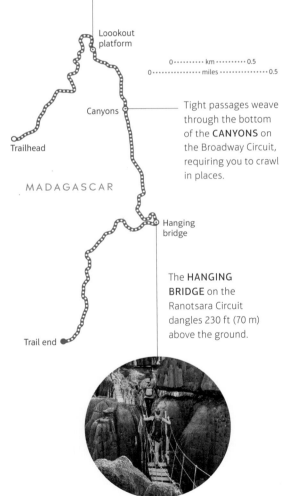

91
Grands Circuits

TSINGY DE BEMARAHA NATIONAL PARK, MADAGASCAR

Enjoy fabulous wildlife and a far-out landscape in Madagascar's most memorable national park.

Has there ever been a place more aptly named than Madagascar's Tsingy de Bemaraha National Park? Tsingy means "walking on tiptoe" in the Malagasy language, which is exactly how you should navigate the razor-sharp pinnacles that dominate the bizarre landscape here. Carved out by groundwater and sculpted by monsoon rains, they rise like karst spires above the surrounding trees; it's easy to see why local guides call them "limestone cathedrals."

You can enjoy a full day of strenuous hiking by connecting the three circuits that thread through the Grands Tsingy, the most impressive section of the park. You'll need a head for heights—in parts, you'll have to climb steep metal ladders that are bolted to the rocks—but the pay-off is staggering views and a bewildering variety of flora and fauna, nearly half of which are found only in this region. The highlight, of course, is the lemurs—including Decken's sifaka and the fat-tailed dwarf lemur—which you'll see gingerly leaping from one jagged rock to the next, more jumping on tiptoes than walking on them.

⊖ 3 MILES (4.5 KM)

⊘ 272 FT (83 M)

🕐 1 DAY (ONE-WAY)

ELEVATION PROFILE

1,500 ft (457 m)

0

0   3 miles (4.5 km)

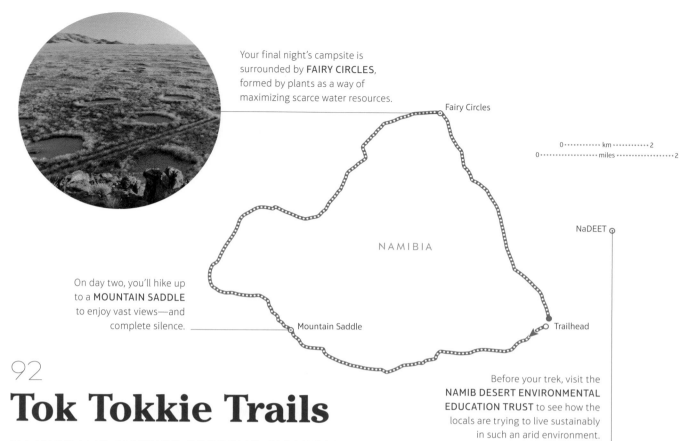

Your final night's campsite is surrounded by **FAIRY CIRCLES**, formed by plants as a way of maximizing scarce water resources.

Fairy Circles

NaDEET

NAMIBIA

On day two, you'll hike up to a **MOUNTAIN SADDLE** to enjoy vast views—and complete silence.

Mountain Saddle

Trailhead

0 ········· km ········· 2
0 ········· miles ········ 2

Before your trek, visit the **NAMIB DESERT ENVIRONMENTAL EDUCATION TRUST** to see how the locals are trying to live sustainably in such an arid environment.

92

Tok Tokkie Trails

NAMIBRAND NATURE RESERVE, NAMIBIA

Take a guided walking trail through this starkly beautiful private desert reserve, full of unusual wildlife.

Created in 1994, the NamibRand Nature Reserve now forms a pristine part of the Namib Desert, the oldest living desert in the world. But this is not the desert as you may know it. Sure, there are rolling dunes and scrubby flats, but also grassy plains, camel-thorn trees, and fleets of rocky mountains gathered on the horizon. While the wildlife might not be the big game you'd normally associate with Africa, it's varied and unusual—you might spot golden moles, bat-eared foxes, barking geckos, or a wheel spider, cartwheeling down the dunes.

You'll be walking in the early morning and late afternoon to avoid the heat of the day, hiking over dunes, across plains, and through dried-up riverbeds, charting the desert's shifting hues as the day progresses. At night, you'll sleep out on stretcher beds, or at least you'll try to—it's difficult to keep your eyes closed when the sky is alight with a billion of the brightest stars you've probably ever seen.

ELEVATION PROFILE

6,500 ft
(1,981 m)

0

0   15 miles (24 km)

⊖ 15 MILES (24 KM)

⊘ 1,588 FT (484 M)

◷ 3 DAYS (LOOP)

93

Otter Trail

STORMS RIVER TO NATURE'S VALLEY, SOUTH AFRICA

Experience a more adventurous side of South Africa's famed Garden Route on this iconic multiday coastal tramp.

The only residential community within South Africa's national park system, **NATURE'S VALLEY** eases you back into civilization gently with its low-key vibe.

Nature's Valley

Andre Hut

184

23 MILES (37 KM)

5,532 FT (1,686 M)

5 DAYS (ONE-WAY)

Hugging a wonderfully wild stretch of South African coast known as the Garden Route, the Otter Trail is the nation's oldest multiday hiking trail and also one of its most popular. With only 12 walkers allowed on the 23-mile (37 km) route each day, expect to connect to nature on an all-new level.

Weaving up, down, and along the wave-pummeled cliffs and beaches of Tsitsikamma National Park—a biodiversity-rich protected area known for its lush temperate forests, mighty rivers, flourishing fynbos (indigenous evergreen heathland), and idyllic rocky coves—this challenging hike links the recreation area of Storms River with the village of Nature's Valley. The adventure begins before you even set off: with only two hours of walking on the first day, there's time to warm up your legs with a stroll across the 253 ft (77 m) long

Crossing the lengthy suspension bridge that stretches across Storms River

suspension bridge that spans the mighty mouth of the ultra-scenic Storms River.

Steep inclines, rocky scrambles, several river crossings, and possible rain year-round mean that the Otter Trail is far from a casual undertaking. But it's not all hard work; there are plenty of opportunities along the way for ocean and waterfall swims, photographing rare blooms and dramatic seascapes, and spotting myriad marine life. While the

ELEVATION PROFILE

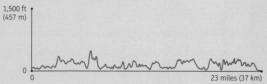

1,500 ft
(457 m)

0

0   23 miles (37 km)

Strip down to your swimwear and get ready to potentially float your pack across the **BLOUKRANS RIVER** on day four.

0 ·············· km ·············· 3
0 ·············· miles ·············· 3

Bloukrans River

SOUTH AFRICA

Take the short detour at the 1.2-mile (1.9 km) mark on day two to enjoy sweeping views along the coastline at the **SKILDERKLIP VIEWPOINT**.

Oakhurst Hut

Many Otter Trail alumni claim the scenery peaks on day three. Take time to soak up your surrounds, and stop to swim in the rivers and rockpools en route to **OAKHURST HUT**.

Scott Hut

Jerling River Waterfall

Skilderklip Viewpoint   Ngubu Hut

Storms River

185

Cascading into a large pool halfway along the first leg of the trail, the **JERLING RIVER WATERFALL** is the perfect spot for a break and a rather bracing swim.

trail's namesake—the Cape clawless otter—is famously elusive, you can pretty much bank on seeing seals and dolphins. Migrating whales join the party between June and October, and on land, you might even glimpse a rare blue duiker, South Africa's smallest antelope species.

Another perk comes in the form of the log cabins that bookend each leg of the trail, so you don't need to carry a tent—camping isn't even allowed. Make new friends over a *braai* (barbecue) dinner as the sun sinks behind the horizon, casting a serene orange glow over the Southern Ocean. It's all part of the pleasure of this delightfully scenic hike.

IN FOCUS
Khoisan Heritage

Named for a Khoisan word meaning "place of much water," Tsitsikamma National Park was an important place for South Africa's first peoples. The national park protects various cultural heritage sites, including caves, middens, rock art, remnants of fishing settlements and forestry industries, and grave sites.

RUSSIA

KAZAKHSTAN

MONGOLIA

109 ⊚

UZBEKISTAN

⊚ 94

KYRGYZSTAN

107 ⊚

NORTH
KOREA

TURKMENISTAN

TAJIKISTAN

110 ⊚

95 ⊚

SOUTH
KOREA

AFGHANISTAN

CHINA

97 ⊚

111 ⊚

PAKISTAN

99 ⊚

⊚ 100

106

NEPAL

⊚ BHUTAN

⊚ 108

⊚ 106

96 ⊚

BANGLADESH

105

TAIWAN

INDIA

MYANMAR

⊚ 103

LAOS

⊚ 104

THAILAND

102 ⊚

VIETNAM

CAMBODIA

PHILIPPINES

SRI
LANKA

101 ⊚

98 ⊚

BRUNEI

MALAYSIA

SINGAPORE

INDONESIA

TIMOR-
LESTE

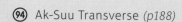

187

ASIA

94

Ak-Suu Transverse

JYRGALAN VILLAGE TO JETI-OGUZ HOT SPRINGS,
KYRGYZSTAN

*Climbing up eight mountain passes, the Ak-Suu Transverse is a challenging trek
into some of the most remote—and spectacularly beautiful—parts of Kyrgyzstan.*

It's not every day that you get to experience hiking in a wild pocket of Central Asia. But the Ak-Suu Transverse lets you do just that, taking you on a journey through the remote valleys and rugged peaks of the Ak-Suu region of Issyk-Kol, an area home to nomadic Kyrgyz communities.

The route is physically strenuous, taking in multiple mountain passes that total around 23,000 ft (7,000 m) of ascent, plus the inevitable knee-pounding descents that follow. You'll have to be relatively self-sufficient, too, carrying plenty of supplies with you in a heavy pack and spending your nights in a tent or yurt.

It's tough, but the staggering alpine scenery more than makes up for any hardship. As you push ahead into this remote region, you'll hike through verdant, tree-dotted valleys cut through by gushing streams; make camp alongside quiet lakes surrounded by blooming wildflowers; and take in views of sharp and soaring massifs draped with icy glaciers. At points the route winds through green-and-gold grasslands, which in summer are often dotted with

herds belonging to the area's seminomadic Kyrgyz people; if you meet with a shepherd, don't be surprised if you're invited for tea, bread, or *kumis* (fermented horse milk).

One of the most scenic sections of the route is arguably also one of the toughest. Leaving Arashan Valley, the trail climbs up toward the 12,818 ft (3,907 m) Ala-Kol Pass. The last couple of miles to the top, on a steep, scree-laden slope, are literally breathtaking. But at the summit, you'll quickly forget your heaving lungs and burning legs—from here, stunning views of the bright turquoise Ala-Kol Lake unfold before you, surrounded by the ridged peaks of the Turgen Ak-Suu range that stretch into the distance.

⊖ 65 MILES (105 KM)

⊘ 23,173 FT (7,063 M)

🕓 7 DAYS (ONE-WAY)

Hiking along the end of
the Ak-Suu Transverse
toward Ala-Kol Lake

188

REFUEL
Altyn Arashan

Around halfway along the route is the small settlement of Altyn Arashan. Here, you can get a delicious hot meal, dorm-style accommodations, and a refreshing cool beer. Even better, there's a small hot spring where you can rest your weary pins in the steaming water.

Before you set off from **JYRGALAN** village, catch a game of *kok-boru*—a sport on horseback that's similar to polo.

Stay at Kara-Kyz yurt camp, found in the open and flat **JERGEZ VALLEY**, to experience the nomadic lifestyle of the Kyrgyz people.

At the end of your journey, soak in the warmth of the **JETI-OGUZ HOT SPRINGS**.

KYRGYZSTAN

Admire a cluster of alpine pools at **BOZ UCHUK LAKES**; they once formed part of a massive glacier.

Jyrgalan

Terim Tor
Bulak Pass

Boz Uchuk
Lakes

Jergez Valley

Allanysh
Pass

Altyn Arashan

Anyrtor
North Pass

Ala-Kol Pass

*Ala-Kol
Lake*

Jeti-Oguz
Hot Springs

Telety Pass

0 ········· km ········· 10
0 ········· miles ········· 10

ELEVATION PROFILE

16,000 ft
(4,876 m)

3,000 ft
(914 m)

0   65 miles (105 km)

ASIA

95

K2 Base Camp Trek

ASKOLE, PAKISTAN

The journey to K2 Base Camp is one of the most spectacular on earth. Nowhere else can hikers see such a concentration of sky-scraping mountains—seven of the planet's 19 highest peaks line the route.

111 MILES (178 KM) ⊖

12,310 FT (3,752 M) ⊗

12–14 DAYS (RETURN) ⏱

Bid adieu to the cozy teahouses, colorful prayer flags, and welcoming villages of Nepal's Everest base camp trek. The trail to the foot of K2, earth's second-highest peak, is more challenging, more remote, and, ultimately, more sensational.

Located in Pakistan's Karakoram Mountains, the most heavily glaciated region outside of the poles, the trek to K2's base traverses genuine wilderness. Compared to Nepal's Everest region, Pakistan's Central Karakoram National Park receives just a trickle of visitors, which means its trails are gloriously traffic-free. However, as a consequence, the region does also lack the facilities and infrastructure seen in other trekking destinations around the world.

Foreign visitors cannot enter the Central Karakoram National Park without a guide and must hire a team of porters and cooks from a list of government-approved tour operators. This will all need to be organized in Skardu, the gateway city to the Karakoram, which is a six-hour drive away from Askole, where your trek begins.

Life on the trail is basic, to say the least. Comforts are few and far between, with camping the only accommodation available throughout—including several nights of pitching directly on the freezing glacier. Toilets and hot water are rare and showers nonexistent. ▶

The campsite at Concordia, with K2 standing majestically in the distance

Askole

Jhola Campsite

JHOLA CAMPSITE is nestled in the lee of the distinctive 19,061 ft (5,810 m) peak of Bakhor Das, known locally as Mango Peak due to its curiously shaped summit cone.

ELEVATION PROFILE

16,000 ft
(4,876 m)

6,500 ft
(1,981 m)

0   111 miles (178 km)

The soaring granite spires of **TRANGO TOWERS** have some of earth's most formidable cliffs. At 4,396 ft (1,340 m), the east face of Great Trango Tower is the world's greatest "nearly vertical" drop.

○ Trango Towers

Your prize for days of intense trekking is to stand at the foot of **K2** and gaze up at 3 km (2 miles) of rock and ice rising vertically above.

○ K2 Base Camp

Broad Peak
Base Camp

PAKISTAN

Concordia

Goro 2

Urdukas

Khoburtse

Baltoro Glacier

Paiju

The **BALTORO GLACIER** is the mighty highway of ice that guides you along a spectacular natural corridor to within striking distance of K2.

CONCORDIA, positioned at the confluence of the Baltoro and Godwin-Austen glaciers, is one of just a handful of places in the world where you can see four 26,000 ft (8,000 m) peaks.

0 ·········· km ·········· 5
0 ·········· miles ·········· 5

The terrain can also be deeply challenging, with routes constantly changing as the ice shifts and crevasses open up, so a degree of off-trail hiking is required in places. It's also not uncommon for rivers to swell and wash away footbridges – be prepared to get your feet wet.

So why do it? For an unrivalled look at one of nature's most incredible spectacles. Following the Braldu Valley onto the shifting Baltoro Glacier, you're immediately surrounded by enormous snow-cloaked granite peaks. The extraordinary summits get progressively higher and more imposing as you move up the valley, making you feel progressively smaller and insubstantial in return. Finally, when the Baltoro and Godwin-Austen glaciers converge at the

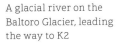

A glacial river on the Baltoro Glacier, leading the way to K2

Trekkers are eventually greeted by one of the most stupendous scenes on the planet: the colossal pyramidal peak of K2.

immense mountain amphitheatre that is Concordia, K2 and its satellite peaks begin to appear.

The K2 massif is home to the world's densest gathering of high mountains – even more than the Everest massif in Nepal – and if you felt ant-like before then you'll feel positively microscopic now. Among these goliaths are the Gasherbrum Range, a collection of five peaks over 7,000 m (23,000 ft), including two over 8,000 m

(26,000 ft) – Gasherbrum I and II – which are, respectively, the world's 11th and 13th highest mountains. Broad Peak, which at 8,051 m (26,414 ft) is the world's 12th highest peak, also abuts the chain with its enormous 1.5-km (1-mile) summit ridge from which it takes its name.

After labouring along the moraine-strewn Godwin-Austen Glacier, trekkers are eventually greeted by one of the most stupendous scenes on the planet: the colossal pyramidal peak of K2. The sheer size of the mountain is utterly overwhelming. K2 may be second in status to Everest, but it displays a grace and symmetry that arguably makes it even more impressive.

Once you've reached the modest rockpile that marks Base Camp, the 8,611 m (28,251 ft) mass of rock and ice before you makes the ranges of Western Europe look like mere hills in comparison. Stood here, you're already higher than anything in the Alps, yet are still, inexplicably, nearly 3,500 m (11,483 ft) below K2's summit.

The K2 Base Camp trek may well be the most gratifying journey you ever take. It is a huge undertaking through one of the most remote regions on the planet. But the burdens of the trek wash away like meltwater when you first glimpse the crown of the Karakoram. It is the most humbling of scenes, and one which will still your step on the ice – that is the power, the magnificence, of K2.

MAKE IT LONGER

Gondogoro La Pass

Instead of returning down the Braldu Valley, more experienced mountaineers can tackle the challenging 5,560-m- (18,241-ft-) high Gondogoro La Pass. Found to the south of the K2 Base Camp, it requires the use of an ice axe and crampons. Although a shorter return journey in terms of distance, this route extends the trek by around two days due to the challenging terrain.

IN FOCUS
Saving the Tiger

There are few animals more iconic than the Bengal tiger. These beautiful predators are among the most beloved—and endangered—creatures in the world. Conservation efforts have seen India's tiger population double since 2010, but in Chhattisgarh the numbers continue to decline—proof that the fight is far from over.

Pink lotus flowers bloom on the surface of **TEDIYABAANDH**, a gorgeous serene lake found very close to where you begin, in the village of Ramgarh.

Tediyabaandh

Ramgarh

INDIA

0 ·········· km ·········· 2
0 ········· miles ········· 2

Turrapaani

Viewpoint

After a day following the Parai River, you'll pitch up for the night at **GIDHAR**, where a wide, sandy beach makes a scenic campsite.

Gidhar

The last full day sees you trekking along a dry riverbed littered with large red rocks to the village of **TURRAPAANI**.

Khalas Pahad

Around the midpoint of the trek, the small hill of **KHALAS PAHAD** rises above you, its rippling rocks resembling pink marble. The 10-minute climb affords views over Guru Ghasidas National Park.

Chhattisgarh Jungle Trek

GURU GHASIDAS NATIONAL PARK, INDIA

Known as the "Jungle Book Trek," this four-day trail winds through the dense forests of India's Guru Ghasidas National Park, taking in the primeval landscapes that inspired Rudyard Kipling to write his masterpiece.

29 MILES (46 KM)

2,831 FT (863 M)

4 DAYS (LOOP)

Chhattisgarh is a land that time forgot. Nearly half of this central Indian state is covered in thick jungle, and what you'll discover within is potent kindling for the imagination: turquoise waterfalls tumbling through vast rock corridors, river beaches of honey sand and old growth, creeper-strewn sal trees stretching 98 ft (30 m) into the skies to form a cooling canopy. No wonder, then, that it lit a creative spark for writer Rudyard Kipling (who lived in India as a child), providing the setting for his literary classic *The Jungle Book*.

This trek into Chhattisgarh offers the rare opportunity to walk on foot through an Indian national park (in this case, Guru Ghasidas). It can only be done as part of a guided tour, which usually entails hiking 6–9 miles (10–14 km) per day and sleeping in tents deep within the forest—surrounded,

as Kipling put it, by "night noises that, taken together, make one big silence." The trails are varied and occasionally involve fording rivers, so while this isn't a technically difficult trek, basic fitness is a must. The most important requirement, though, is a sense of openness and curiosity: something reciprocated by the villagers you meet along the way, who have forged a living in communion with the dangers, beauties, and bounties of this forest land.

Throughout the trek, as in Kipling's famous tales, the animals of Chhattisgarh are your characterful companions: spotted sambar deer watch warily through stands of trees, monitor lizards slither beneath river rocks, and Indian pitta birds flash a rainbow of feathers as they forage for bugs on the forest floor. Even more tantalizing are the clues you will find of the forest's more elusive inhabitants: the paw prints, scat, and claw marks left behind by Indian leopards and the kings and queens of the jungle, the Bengal tigers. Get very lucky and you may even catch a glimpse of the latter—an experience that will stay with you vividly for life.

ELEVATION PROFILE

6,500 ft
(1,981 m)

0

0   29 miles (46 km)

195

ASIA

The flora-lined path through India's spectacular Valley of Flowers

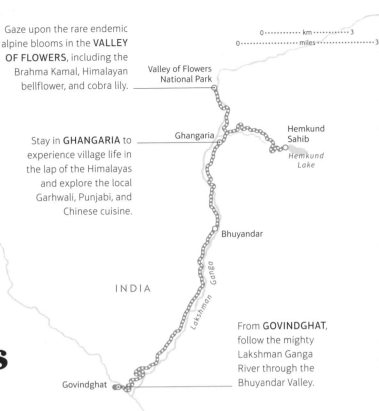

Gaze upon the rare endemic alpine blooms in the **VALLEY OF FLOWERS**, including the Brahma Kamal, Himalayan bellflower, and cobra lily.

Stay in **GHANGARIA** to experience village life in the lap of the Himalayas and explore the local Garhwali, Punjabi, and Chinese cuisine.

From **GOVINDGHAT**, follow the mighty Lakshman Ganga River through the Bhuyandar Valley.

Valley of Flowers National Park

Ghangaria

Hemkund Sahib

Hemkund Lake

Bhuyandar

Lakshman Ganga

INDIA

Govindghat

97
Valley of Flowers

GOVINDGHAT, INDIA

Trek through India's prettiest national park, known for its meadows bursting with colorful alpine flowers.

25 MILES (41 KM)
9,623 FT (2,933 M)
4 DAYS (RETURN)

In 1931, a party of British mountaineers and botanists, who found themselves lost following a successful expedition to Mount Kamet, stumbled across a valley blanketed with wildflowers. After they shared their story, the Valley of Flowers shot to international fame, and today it's the backdrop to one of the best-loved hikes in India. Happily, you don't need to be an expert explorer to enjoy the route—it's easy enough for amateur trekkers thanks to its mellow terrain and well-maintained path.

Following a verdant valley, the trail heads through deep-green forest, across gurgling rivers, and past tumbling waterfalls. The scenery is stunning, but it's the wildflowers that really steal the show. During the summer, particularly in July and August, nature's colorful palette extends across the valley floor, daubed with the blossoms of delicate purple orchids, bright blue poppies, and vibrant orange marigolds. There are an astounding 498 species of flowering plants found here, many of which are endemic to the area. Breathe in the sweet-smelling perfume as you admire the blooms—among the prettiest are the delicate florets of Himalayan thyme, the tiny bell-like flowers of whorled Solomon's seal, and the golden discs of showy Inula, whose petals look like sunbeams.

ELEVATION PROFILE

13,000 ft (3,962 m)

0

0   25 miles (41 km)

World's End and Baker's Falls

HORTON PLAINS NATIONAL PARK, SRI LANKA

Drink in world-beating views on this undemanding trail, which winds through mist-wreathed cloud forest and past cascading waterfalls, stopping for vistas over the fertile tea fields of Sri Lanka's Central Highlands.

5 MILES (8 KM)
719 FT (219 M)
0.5 DAYS (LOOP)

It may be called World's End, but there's nothing apocalyptic about the view from this cliff-top precipice in Sri Lanka's Horton Plains National Park. In fact, the sight of the lush green valley below, where cloud forest gives way to gentle tea plantations and highland villages, will have you reflecting on the wonders of the world and all the life that's in it—doubly so on a clear morning, when the view stretches all the way to the Indian Ocean.

The same could be said of the hike to the viewpoint, which follows a path through moss-smothered forest where golden senna flowers peek out from the floor and rare purple-faced langurs gaze curiously at you from the branches. A short climb further on from the viewpoint leads you to Baker's Falls, where the Belihul Oya River splits into spidery webs of water and plunges prettily over a wide rock face—you can't swim here, but the spray from the falls is beautifully refreshing after an invigorating morning's hike.

ELEVATION PROFILE

8,200 ft
(2,499 m)

3,000 ft
(914 m)

0   5 miles (8 km)

Make a final stop at **BAKER'S FALLS**, where the waters of the Belihul Oya cascade down a knobbly 66 ft (20 m) cliff face.

Baker's Falls

Belihul Oya

Chimney Pool

Horton Plains National Park office

0 ·········· km ··········· 1
0 ·········· miles ··············· 1

SRI LANKA

Mini World's End

The highlight of the trail is the incomparable **WORLD'S END VIEWPOINT** at the trek's halfway point.

World's End Viewpoint

The perfect place for a first resting point is **MINI WORLD'S END**, where the forest parts to reveal the peaks of surrounding mountains.

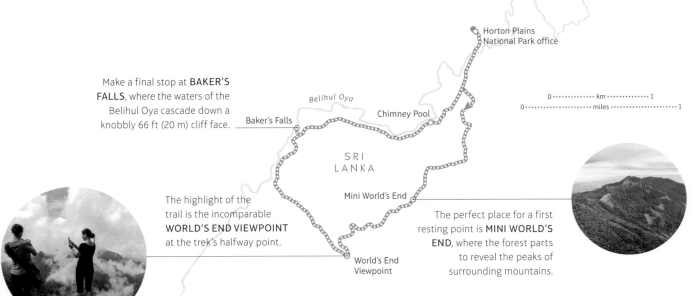

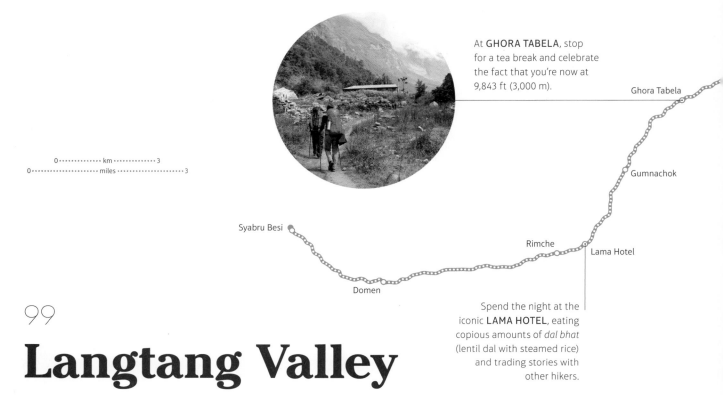

At **GHORA TABELA**, stop for a tea break and celebrate the fact that you're now at 9,843 ft (3,000 m).

Ghora Tabela

Gumnachok

Syabru Besi

Rimche

Lama Hotel

Domen

Spend the night at the iconic **LAMA HOTEL**, eating copious amounts of *dal bhat* (lentil dal with steamed rice) and trading stories with other hikers.

0 ·········· km ·········· 3
0 ·········· miles ·········· 3

99

Langtang Valley

SYABRU BESI, NEPAL

Hike in the shadow of some of the world's tallest mountains on this out-and-back route into the heart of Nepal's Langtang Valley.

35 MILES (56 KM) 9,672 FT (2,948 M) 5–7 DAYS (RETURN)

Found around 93 miles (150 km) north of Kathmandu, the remote Langtang Valley is a place of dramatic beauty. This multiday hike winds along its length, taking you from subtropical forest to glacier-clad mountains in a matter of days.

Despite following the valley floor, this route is still a big challenge. On the way, you'll ascend nearly 9,700 ft (3,000 m) and climb to a literally breathtaking altitude of almost 13,123 ft (4,000 m). Thankfully, an abundance of cozy teahouses dot the route, largely run by the area's Tamang people, offering up warm beds and reviving grub like moreish *momos* (Tibetan dumplings).

Setting off from Syabru Besi, a genuine end-of-the-road town, the trail follows a narrow path through a forest of oak, fir, and rhododendron, the lush foliage home to hooting langur monkeys and cut through by a tumbling glacial river. As the path weaves ever higher, the scenery transforms: the forest thins, giving way to rough alpine grasslands and mountains that seem to creep ever-more skyward.

ELEVATION PROFILE

13,000 ft (3,962 m)

0

0   35 miles (56 km)

198

Langtang
Lirung Glacier ⊙────────────────

○ Kyanjin Ri

Gumba ───────── Sindum

Langtang

⊙ Kyanjin Gompa

Thangsyap

Take in the majesty of the **LANGTANG LIRUNG GLACIER**; this hulking frozen river flows down the edge of Langtang Lirung.

NEPAL

KYANJIN GOMPA marks the hike's halfway point. Make for the Dorje Bakery Cafe here to grab a slice of its famed chocolate cake.

IN FOCUS
The 2015 Earthquake

The Langtang Valley was badly affected by the devastating earthquake (7.8 magnitude) that struck Nepal on April 25, 2015. A large landslide, made up of millions of tons of rock and ice, killed around 250 people and almost completely destroyed Langtang Village. The village has since been rebuilt 328 ft (100 m) above the old one, and a Buddhist memorial mani wall, inscribed with the names of those who lost their lives here, has been erected.

It's not just the scenery that catches your attention, though. Along the route, you'll meet with yak herders driving their shaggy animals to fresh pastures, the heads of both marked with yak butter for good luck, and spy donkey trains wending their way along the valley, laden with supplies. There's evidence of the region's Buddhist faith everywhere you look, too: colorful prayer flags flutter in the wind, solitary stupas point their gilded heads toward the sky, and intricately carved prayer walls line the trail.

As you get closer to the small settlement of Kyanjin Gompa, the hike's turning point, the landscape becomes much more rocky and regal, and an amphitheater of snow-capped mountains rises up on all sides. The smallest peaks here are around the same height as Mont Blanc, while the valley's highest mountain—the 25,351 ft (7,227 m) glacier-cloaked Langtang Lirung—rises almost 9,843 ft (3,000 m) higher than that famed European peak.

It's unsurprising, then, that most of the mountains here are out of reach to humble hikers—apart from Kyanjin Ri (15,655 ft/ 4,773 m). This majestic peak is well worth a detour from Kyanjin Gompa (you'll have to add on an extra day to your trip): from its summit, you'll enjoy incredible 360-degree views of the surrounding sharp-edged peaks and gray-blue glaciers. What more fitting climax to a trek through the Himalayas than by standing atop this majestic mountain?

Crossing a suspension bridge in the snow-dusted Langtang Valley

100
The Druk Path

PARO TO THIMPHU, BHUTAN

Discover the Buddhist culture of Bhutan along an ancient trading route in the mountainous Land of the Thunder Dragon.

28 MILES (45 KM)

9,905 FT (3,019 M)

6 DAYS (ONE-WAY)

It's no wonder that Bhutan is considered one of the happiest countries in the world. This tiny Buddhist kingdom of pristine forests and Himalayan peaks makes for some delightful trekking, and you'll have plenty of joyful moments as you navigate the Druk Path, an old mule trail that links the historical centers of Paro and Thimphu, the Bhutanese capital.

The whole hike is at high altitude, so the scenery of snow-topped mountains, alpine lakes, and forests of blue pine and rhododendrons is suitably spectacular. But this is also a walk where you can easily engage with religious life in Bhutan, pausing to visit *dzongs* (fortified monasteries), *lhakhangs* (temples), and *chortens* (stupas). The *dzongs* are eye-catching—immense whitewashed complexes perched at the heads of valleys and on mountain spurs. But the *lhakhangs* can leave an even stronger impression, especially if you're on the end of a blessing from one of the incumbent monks (it involves being boinked on the head with a large wooden phallus, seen as a talisman against evil spirits).

Traditional Buddhist prayer flags outside Phajoding Monastery

Compared to the better-known treks in nearby Nepal, visitor numbers to Bhutan are fairly low, which means you'll be sharing the pathway with just a few others at most, plus the occasional yak herder leading their animals to open pasture. The trail only starts to get (comparatively) busier as you approach Thimphu, where day-trippers make the climb out of the capital up to the 13th-century Phajoding Monastery, a ramble of *lhakhangs* and meditation retreats. The temple floats above a quilt of clouds in early morning; on a clear day, a panoramic vista of the eastern Himalayas awaits. Either way, the sight of it will leave you walking into Thimphu grinning from ear to ear.

ELEVATION PROFILE

16,000 ft
(4,876 m)

3,000 ft
(914 m)

0   28 miles (45 km)

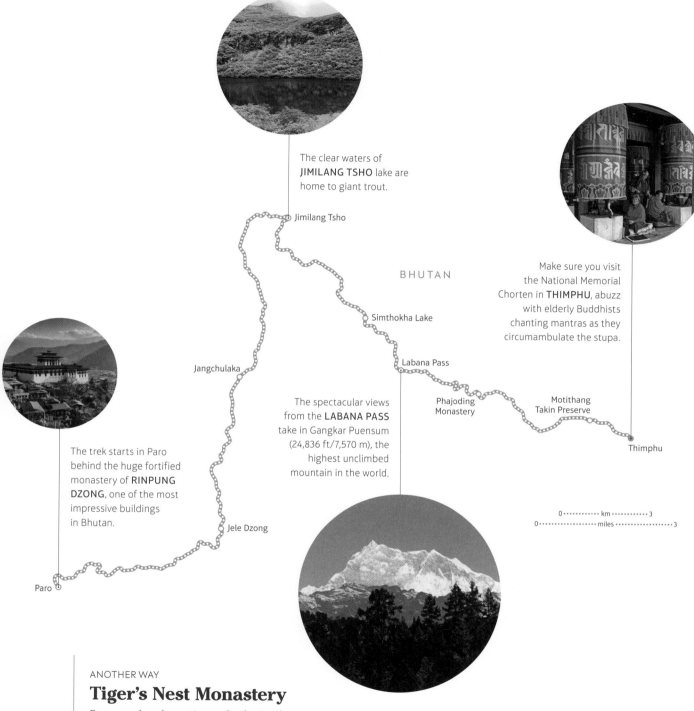

The clear waters of **JIMILANG TSHO** lake are home to giant trout.

Jimilang Tsho

BHUTAN

Simthokha Lake

Make sure you visit the National Memorial Chorten in **THIMPHU**, abuzz with elderly Buddhists chanting mantras as they circumambulate the stupa.

Jangchulaka

Labana Pass

Phajoding Monastery

Motithang Takin Preserve

The trek starts in Paro behind the huge fortified monastery of **RINPUNG DZONG**, one of the most impressive buildings in Bhutan.

The spectacular views from the **LABANA PASS** take in Gangkar Puensum (24,836 ft/7,570 m), the highest unclimbed mountain in the world.

Jele Dzong

Thimphu

Paro

0 ········· km ········· 3
0 ········· miles ········· 3

ANOTHER WAY

Tiger's Nest Monastery

For a one-day alternative, make the 4-mile (6-km) hike to Taktsang Monastery, reached via a 30-minute drive from Paro. Better known as the Tiger's Nest Monastery, it sits halfway up a cliff face, high above the Paro Valley, and seems to defy the laws of physics.

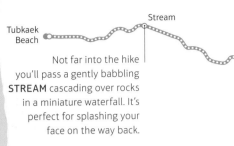

Stream

Not far into the hike you'll pass a gently babbling **STREAM** cascading over rocks in a miniature waterfall. It's perfect for splashing your face on the way back.

The jungle clears halfway along the path to reveal the **FIRST VIEWPOINT**, where you can pose for photos on a boulder and admire the green plains and karst formations of Krabi and Phang Nga Bay.

Tubkaek Beach

First viewpoint

THAILAND

0 ⋯⋯⋯ km ⋯⋯⋯ 0.5
0 ⋯⋯⋯ miles ⋯⋯⋯ 0.5

Ngon Nak

Dragon Crest Mountain

A sign for **NGON NAK** signals the second viewpoint, where a ladder helps you up onto a large rock from which you can reflect on a rewarding hike.

202

101
Tab Kak Hang Nak Nature Trail

TUBKAEK BEACH, THAILAND

Escape the tourist throngs on this wild nature trail up a jungle-covered hill, finishing atop a mountain summit that gazes out over Krabi's lush plains.

4 MILES (7 KM)   1,604 FT (489 M)   0.5 DAYS (RETURN)

In a country whose natural and cultural treasures are so widely celebrated, the beauty of this nature trail in Thailand's Krabi region is that it remains off the tourist radar—so you'll have more of its wildflowers, jungle, and sweeping views all to yourself.

Embrace your inner adventurer as you scramble across smooth rocks and over tree roots—sometimes these conspire to form a handy natural staircase; at other times, they're less obliging. In general, though, nature feels welcoming here: vast, protruding boulders seem to defy gravity in order to provide a shaded place

to rest, while burbling waterfalls collect in rocky pools waiting to soothe your tired feet. And at the summit of Dragon Crest Mountain, a rock overhang makes a natural seat on which to sit in solitude and savor the views of the emerald wilderness.

Looking out over lush green jungle on the Tab Kak Hang Nak Nature Trail

ELEVATION PROFILE

3,000 ft (914 m)

0

0   4 miles (7 km)

102

Kulen Mountain

PREAH ANG CHOUB PAGODA, CAMBODIA

Cinematic waterfalls and jungle-shrouded sacred sites are all in a day's walk on Kulen Mountain, a little-known treasure trove of ancient Khmer history.

The Linga

The linga symbol appears across the Hindu world as a representation of Shiva, the god of destruction and rebirth. It varies in appearance but often has a disc-shaped, rounded property; Shiva is associated with fertility, and some, though not all lingas, are phallic in their design.

5 MILES (8 KM) 846 FT (258 M) 1 DAY (RETURN)

Cambodia's ancient history does not end, or begin, with Angkor Wat. Found just 28 miles (45 km) from this world-famous site, Kulen Mountain is where the Khmer Empire was founded in the 9th century AD, and its slopes are littered with cultural and religious relics. You'll encounter a number of these on this relatively easy forest trail, which winds through forests of cashew trees, past the idyllic Phnom Kulen Waterfall. Highlights include Kbal Spean, or the Valley of 1,000 Lingas—a stretch of riverbed and rocks elaborately carved with linga symbols and scenes from Hindu mythology—and Prasat Krau Romeas, a ruined 9th-century Khmer temple being slowly reclaimed by the jungle's strangler figs and vines. Best of all, they're free to enjoy without huge crowds.

The reclining Buddha is the classic symbol of Southeast Asian temples, and there's a fine one—the largest in Cambodia, in fact—at **PREAH ANG THOM PAGODA.**

ELEVATION PROFILE

3,000 ft (914 m)

0

0 — 5 miles (8 km)

CAMBODIA

Phnom Kulen Waterfall

Valley of 1,000 Lingas

Phnom Kulen

Preah Ang Thom Pagoda

Preah Ang Choub Pagoda

Though a river has been flowing over the **VALLEY OF 1,000 LINGAS** for 1,000 years, the iconography carved into the riverbed is remarkably distinct.

0 ········· km ········· 0.5
0 ········· miles ········· 0.5

Just off the start of the path, **PREAH ANG CHOUB PAGODA** is a peaceful Buddhist temple at the foot of Kulen Mountain, home to a very welcome swimming pool where you can cool off.

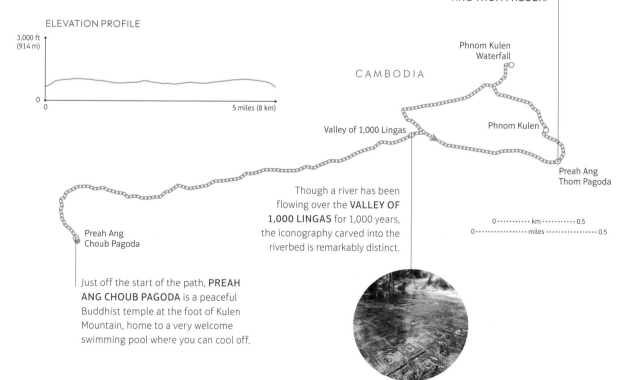

103
Viet Hai Trail

CAT BA NATIONAL PARK
HEADQUARTERS TO VIET HAI,
CAT BA ISLAND, VIETNAM

*Spy macaques, civets, and, if luck is on your side,
golden-headed langurs on a challenging jungle hike.*

⊖ 6 MILES (9 KM) ⊘ 1,296 FT (395 M) ⊕ 1 DAY (ONE-WAY)

204

Following rough paths, this trail laces its
way through the heart of Cat Ba National
Park, a UNESCO biosphere reserve. This
is true jungle and the route is hard going:
the atmosphere is hot and humid, leaving
you gasping for water, while the ground
underfoot is uneven, slippery, and often
crisscrossed with thick tree roots.
The path rises and dips, too, and at
points, you'll have to scramble up

The Cat Ba Archipelago, home to
Cat Ba Island and its national park

some steep sections, using your hands
to guide you skyward.

The challenge is more than worth it,
though. Here, lithe civets, agile macaques,
and giant black squirrels scurry through
the trees above you, camouflaged stick
insects hide in plain sight, and an array of
colorful butterflies flit easily through the
heavy air. And if you're especially lucky,
you might even spot a golden-headed
langur, the world's most endangered
primate—only 60 or so of these unique
creatures call this ancient jungle home.

ELEVATION PROFILE

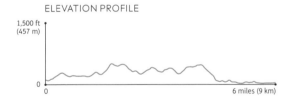

1,500 ft
(457 m)

0

0   6 miles (9 km)

Grab a snack from one of the
restaurants near the **CAT BA NATIONAL
PARK HEADQUARTERS**—you'll need
the energy for the hike ahead.

Stop off at **AO ECH**, a tranquil
lake dotted with trees; the
reflections here make it hard
to tell where the trees end
and the water begins.

Spend the night in a
homestay in the tiny
village of **VIET HAI**
before making your
way back to Cat Ba
Town by boat.

CAT BA
ISLAND

Ao Ech Lake

Viet Hai

Cat Ba National
Park Headquarters

0 ········· km ········· 1
0 ········· miles ········· 1

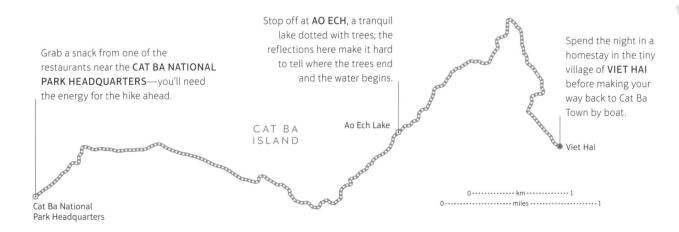

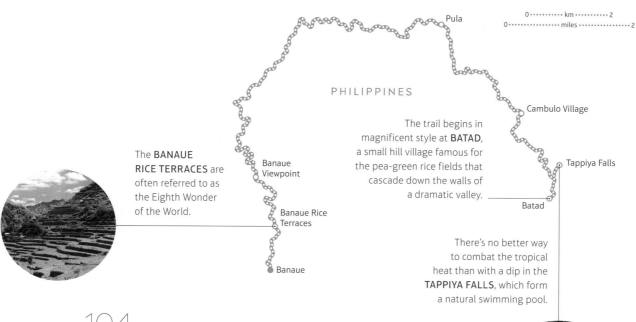

PHILIPPINES

Pula

Cambulo Village

The trail begins in magnificent style at **BATAD**, a small hill village famous for the pea-green rice fields that cascade down the walls of a dramatic valley.

Tappiya Falls

Batad

Banaue Viewpoint

The **BANAUE RICE TERRACES** are often referred to as the Eighth Wonder of the World.

Banaue Rice Terraces

Banaue

There's no better way to combat the tropical heat than with a dip in the **TAPPIYA FALLS**, which form a natural swimming pool.

104
Batad Rice Terrace Trail

BATAD TO BANAUE, PHILIPPINES

Glittering green shelves of rice paddies form the backdrop for this gentle two-day hike through the centuries-old culture of the Philippine countryside.

19 MILES (30 KM)

7,428 FT (2,264 M)

2 DAYS (ONE-WAY)

It's not often farmers' fields are inscribed as a UNESCO World Heritage Site, but the Batad Rice Terraces are no ordinary fields. Carved into the verdant hillside by hand around two millennia ago, they were—and are—a remarkable engineering feat by the Ifugao people, who remain the terraces' guardians today.

Over two days, this trail snakes through emerald amphitheaters stacked with layer upon layer of life-giving rice, past plunging waterfalls ripe for swimming, and traditional villages where a cup of tea or glass of rice wine are never far away. It's not just rice that's farmed here—take a closer look at the terraces, and you'll spot carp and snails thriving in the shallow water.

Though this is an easy trail, the steps can be steep in places. For safe passage, be sure as you pass them to bow to the *bulul*: ancestor statues who gaze across the fields as they stand silent guard over the precious crop.

ELEVATION PROFILE

6,500 ft
(1,981 m)

0

0   19 miles (30 km)

Pause at the largely deserted Punti village of **CHEK KENG** to seek out the Catholic Holy Family Chapel, founded by missionaries in the 19th century and now disused.

MAKE IT LONGER

The Full Trail

The whole MacLehose Trail snakes some 62 miles (100 km) across the New Territories from Sai Kung East to Tuen Mun in the west. It was named after Hong Kong's longest-serving British governor, Murray MacLehose, an expert hiker who established the then-colony's Country Parks.

Pak Tam Au

Chek Keng

Tai Long Au

HONG KONG

Ham Tin Wan

Sai Wan

0 ·········· km ·········· 1
0 ·········· miles ·········· 1

Kick off your boots for a paddle in the turquoise waves at **HAM TIN WAN**, one of Hong Kong's most beautiful white-sand beaches.

Sai Wan Shan

As you climb up **SAI WAN SHAN**—at 1,030 ft (314 m) the highest point on this route—look back for great views across Long Ke Beach to the islands in the bay beyond.

Long Ke Wan

At the start of the route, take a short detour along the **HIGH ISLAND GEO TRAIL** to marvel at the huge hexagonal basalt columns in the UNESCO Geopark area.

High Island Reservoir East Dam

105

MacLehose Trail

HIGH ISLAND RESERVOIR EAST DAM TO PAK
TAM AU, HONG KONG

*Explore the wilder side of Hong Kong's New Territories on a one-day hike
past glorious beaches and tumbledown hamlets.*

9 MILES (15 KM) · 2,556 FT (779 M) · 1 DAY (ONE-WAY)

There's more than one Hong Kong. Sure, there's the high-rise forest of concrete, steel, and glass sprouting from Kowloon and Hong Kong Island, all neon and traffic, bustling harbors, and clamoring voices. But then there's the New Territories to the north, a lush, undulating expanse stretching across the peninsula.

It's here that you'll find many Country Parks, created in the 1970s in an attempt to boost conservation and recreation. Today, the reforested hillsides are home to wildlife, including porcupines, pangolins, and Burmese pythons, as well as 230 types of butterflies and hundreds of bird species. Deserted villages—abandoned after their inhabitants migrated to urban areas—punctuate the landscape, along with traditional cemeteries and trenches and pillboxes from World War II.

One of these Country Parks, Sai Kung East, is the setting for stages 1 and 2 of the MacLehose Trail. The full 62-mile (100 km) trail is Hong Kong's longest hiking route, but a more laid-back taster can be created

by combining its opening segments into a wonderfully varied one-day hike. (Helpfully, it's also easy to access, thanks to an efficient public transportation system.)

Start as you don't mean to go on: skip the first few miles of Section 1. The stretch from Pak Tam Chung runs along an unshaded road and gets busy with day-trippers, particularly on weekends, so it's best to begin your trek at the High Island Reservoir East Dam instead.

The first half of the route tests calves and knees as it rises and falls steeply, albeit on mostly well-made (often concrete) paths. You'll ascend to viewpoints—many thankfully provided with shady pavilions under which to rest and catch your breath—before dipping down to a succession of lovely white-sand beaches lapped by the balmy waters of the South China Sea.

As the day progresses and the trail veers west, the landscape becomes progressively more wooded, with butterflies flitting around like confetti. Here, you'll encounter hamlets embedded in the foliage, some deserted and overgrown, others continuing a sleepy existence selling snacks and drinks to passing hikers. Keep strolling on and by the time you reach the end of Section 2, you may well want to continue further into the scenic splendor of Hong Kong's wild east.

ELEVATION PROFILE

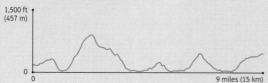

1,500 ft (457 m)

0

0   9 miles (15 km)

After your hike, pop into the **GOLD MUSEUM** to learn all about Taiwan's geology and its history of gold mining.

Gold Museum

Jinguashi

Chuen Ji Temple

TAIWAN

A photo op is in order at the **JINGUASHI GUANHAI PAVILION**, where there are stunning views of the bay.

Jinguashi Guanhai Pavilion

Teapot Mountain

Climb to the very top of **TEAPOT MOUNTAIN** through a small cave at its base; at the rocky summit, you'll feel on top of the world.

106
Teapot Trail

JINGUASHI, TAIWAN

Soak in postcard-worthy panoramas of glittering blue sea and lush green peaks on this hike to the top of the charmingly named Teapot Mountain.

3 MILES (5 KM) ⬭ 1,076 FT (328 M) ⬯ 0.5 DAYS (RETURN) ⬰

Ask any Taiwanese local where to find the best views of the country, and most will point you to the Teapot Mountain. This 1,969 ft (600 m) peak overlooks the country's lush northern coast, which shares a similar wild beauty to the more famous shores of Hawaii and California.

The trek begins at the Gold Museum in the town of Jinguashi, heading up a largely well-maintained path that winds its way to the top of the mountain. There are some steep, thigh-burning sections, especially when climbing the stony staircases that make up part of the route. Thankfully, two pavilions dot the path, offering a chance to rest your legs in the shade.

Looking out toward the sea from the top of Teapot Mountain

ELEVATION PROFILE

3,000 ft (914 m)

0

0   3 miles (5 km)

As you climb higher, Teapot Mountain rises before you, its rocky summit shaped like a teapot without the handle. Pause to admire the peak's curious shape before turning to take in the view: ridged emerald mountains flowing down to meet the striking Yin Yang Sea—a mineral-rich, blue-and-yellow colored bay—and beyond it, the shimmering ocean.

107
The Great Wall

JINSHANLING, CHINA

Walk atop a section of the world's most iconic wall as it snakes its way through northeast China.

3 MILES (5 KM)

1,007 FT (307 M)

0.5 DAYS (ONE-WAY)

You'll be glad to hear that you don't have to walk the entire length of the Great Wall to appreciate this jaw-dropping feat of engineering, which runs for over 13,000 miles (21,000 km) across China. You don't have to head too far from Beijing to avoid the swarms of tourists that can sometimes choke the sections closest to the capital, where souvenir shops and overzealous restorations can give the wall a bit of a theme-park feel. Simply make your way to the wild Jinshanling section, on the border of Beijing and Hebei provinces, where the wall is amazingly well preserved: a blue-gray ribbon of ramparts and battlements that winds its way over the mountains.

Starting at Jinshanling's West Gate, you'll rise and fall from one watchtower to the next, eventually climbing back off the wall at the East-Five Window Tower, a short hike from Jinshanling's East Gate. Although this may be only a relatively short stretch of the Great Wall, traversing these mammoth ramparts in quiet solitude is an experience you won't easily forget.

ELEVATION PROFILE

3,000 ft
(914 m)

0

0   3 miles (5 km)

209

0 ·············· km ·············· 0.5
0 ·············· miles ·············· 0.5

At the **ZHUANDUOKOU TOWER**, look for bricks engraved with Hanzi—the characters represent when that part of the wall was made and by which troops.

The **BLACK TOWER** is recognizable by its three floors (most towers have only two) and famous for its secret underground passage.

West Gate

East Gate

CHINA

Zhuanduokou Tower

General Tower

Black Tower

Houchuankou Pass

Big Jinshan Tower

East-Five Window Tower

The steep stretch from the **BIG JINSHAN TOWER** is the most rugged and requires some scrambling in parts.

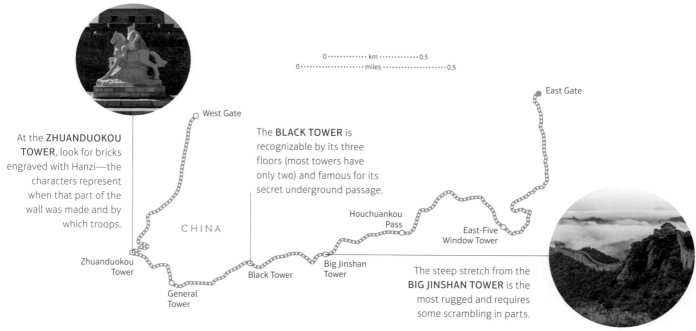

ASIA

108

Tiger Leaping Gorge Trail

QIAOTOU TO TIGER LEAPING GORGE VIEWPOINT, CHINA

Journey through one of the most spectacular landscapes in China, a deep gorge cut through by a roaring river and overlooked by jagged peaks.

17 MILES (28 KM)

5,381 FT (1,640 M)

2 DAYS (ONE-WAY)

Situated in China's Yunnan province, Tiger Leaping Gorge is one of the deepest canyons in the world—spanning 12,434 ft (3,790 m) from river to mountain peak. Gouged out by the powerful Jinsha River, a tributary of the Yangtze, it takes its name from a tale in local folklore, which states that a tiger once leapt across the narrowest part of the gorge—bounding off a rock in the middle of the river—during a fight with a hunter.

Starting from Qiaotou, this trail through the monumental gorge hugs its northern side. For the most part, the path is pretty straightforward, without too much climbing; there are some tricky sections, though, including the infamous "28 Bends," a series of leg-aching switchbacks that loop up the side of the gorge in the first section of the hike. The path is narrow at points,

too, and in places drops sharply away into the canyon—vertigo sufferers will need to brace themselves.

Any challenge on the route is quickly forgotten, however, in the midst of the scenic splendor. The mighty flow of the Jinsha River rushes through the canyon far below, while jagged mountains, including two over 16,400 ft (5,000 m)—the Jade Dragon Snow Mountain and Haba Snow Mountain—soar high above. As you go on, pockets of forest and terraced farmland emerge, and the path meanders past pretty waterfalls, as well as small villages and hamlets. The latter are home to the Nakhi, a matriarchal society descended from Tibetan nomads who made these valleys their home centuries ago and today farm the land here.

Eventually, your feet will lead you to Tiger Leaping Gorge Viewpoint, found just past the end of the trail. It was from this hulking rock, watched over by the imposing high walls of the canyon and surrounded by the rushing river, that the gorge's fabled big cat once leapt to freedom.

Walking through
the dramatic Tiger
Leaping Gorge

Take a photo beside the statue of the gorge's legendary tiger, and then enjoy the views of the **TIGER LEAPING GORGE VIEWPOINT** in the middle of the river.

Tiger Leaping Gorge Viewpoint

Jinsha River

Tibet Guesthouse

Guanyin Waterfall

Tumbling down the canyon wall is the **GUANYIN WATERFALL**. Pause to take in its majestic beauty and then visit the nearby temple, also of the same name, which is dedicated to the Buddhist Goddess of Mercy.

Halfway Guesthouse

Spend the night at the **HALFWAY GUESTHOUSE**, a perfect oasis nestled between the towering mountains; its picturesque courtyard is a perfect spot in which to wind down.

CHINA

Teahorse Guesthouse

```
0 ·········· km ·········· 3
0 ·········· miles ·········· 3
```

Naxi Family Guesthouse

Qiaotou

28 Bends

Jinsha River

Ascend the thigh-burning switchbacks of the **28 BENDS**, the steepest section of the hike, taking in the views of the sprawling mountains as you climb.

REFUEL

Naxi Family Guesthouse

About 3 miles (5 km) into your hike, stop at the Naxi Family Guesthouse to savor a taste of traditional Nakhi (Naxi) food. Relish a bowl of warm soup and glutinous rice as you explore the quiet courtyards overlooking the mountains.

·ELEVATION PROFILE

```
10,000 ft
(3,048 m)



3,000 ft
(914 m)
    0                              17 miles (28 km)
```

109

Great Baikal Trail

LISTVYANKA TO CAPE SKRIPER, RUSSIA

Trek through birch forests and along crystalline shores on this hiking route in Siberia, which wraps around Russia's most iconic lake.

16 MILES (25 KM)
3,468 FT (1,057 M)
1–2 DAYS (ONE-WAY)

212

A 311-mile (500 km) network of paths around the world's deepest and largest freshwater lake, the Great Baikal Trail was designed by eco-pioneers to connect walkers with Siberia's natural splendor. If you don't have time to walk the whole thing, then the first section from Listvyanka to Cape Skriper offers a sublime taste of pristine nature and Siberian village life.

Beginning in touristy Listvyanka, the first part of the walk demands energy: you'll hike uphill for 2.5 miles (4 km), climbing 1,312 ft (400 m) along a narrow, undulating path through forests of silver birch. These woodlands thrum with life: listen for trilling nightingales, and, if you're hiking in spring, admire the proliferation of Siberian flora, like dwarf lilies and vivid orange globeflowers.

Eventually the trees reveal a lookout point where you can survey shimmering Lake Baikal. Fed by more than 300 rivers,

the lake has dozens of endemic fish species and is aflutter with hundreds of types of bird, including cranes and rare swan geese. But the creature to watch for is the playful Baikal seal, a small pinniped often seen somersaulting in the lake's indigo depths.

The height you gained earlier comes with drawbacks on the next stretch for any hikers afflicted with vertigo: after the lookout point, the narrow pathway snakes along cliffs with a sheer drop down to the lake. You'll need to watch your feet, too,

ELEVATION PROFILE

3,000 ft
(914 m)

0
0   16 miles (25 km)

Hiking through birch trees along the shore of Lake Baikal

Before setting off, check out Listvyanka's **BAIKAL MUSEUM** to learn about the lake's unique ecosystem.

"Big Cats" isn't the only possible interpretation of **BOLSHIYE KOTY**'s name. It may also mean "Big Boots," a nod to the oversized footwear of gold washers during the village's prospecting days.

0 ·········· km ·········· 5
0 ·········· miles ·········· 5

RUSSIA

Bolshiye Koty

Cape Skriper

Baikal Museum ⊙

Listvyanka ⊙

Pebble beach

For the most memorable views of Lake Baikal, drink in the big blue panorama from **CAPE SKRIPER**.

The reward for trekking the uneven serpentine path through Listvyanka's birch forests is this restful **PEBBLE BEACH**, with seats overlooking Lake Baikal's sparkling waters.

on the pebbly pathway down to Bolshiye Koty (Big Cats). This erstwhile mining village still bears the imprint of its gold-prospecting past, but today it's utterly serene. An isolated place, shrouded by forest, it can be reached only on foot or across the water. It's free from roads and whisper-quiet, other than a few small businesses and a scattering of *dachas* (summer residences).

The final stretch to Cape Skriper, a craggy headland offering glorious lake views, is demanding, so consider bedding down in Bolshiye Koty and starting fresh in the morning. You may even find yourself energized enough to venture beyond Cape Skriper; after all, you've barely covered 6 percent of the trail's full length.

MAKE IT LONGER

On to Bolshiye Goloustnoye

Eager for more adventures along the Great Baikal Trail? The next section, from Bolshiye Koty/Cape Skriper to Bolshiye Goloustnoye, stretches for 19 miles (30 km) through aspen forests and along lake beaches. Unless you're very fit, it's a long day's walk; bring a tent and break it up across two days.

The beautiful 14th-century Gyeongbokgung Palace, which stands next to Seoul's city wall

A viewpoint at the summit of mighty **BUKAKSAN** affords panoramic views of Seoul, including the beautiful Gyeongbokgung Palace.

Once a poverty-stricken "moon village," **IHWA MAEUL** is now famous for its vibrant murals.

Korea's ancient culture echoes through **INWANGSAN GUKSADANG**, a shamanist shrine where priestesses perform rites to attract good fortune.

110
Seoul City Wall Trail

SEOUL, SOUTH KOREA

Follow the ridges of the four mountains that guard the Korean capital of Seoul, tracing chapters from the city's royal, religious, and workaday past.

Nowadays, Seoul is a peaceful place, where the high-tech steel-and-glass monoliths of a modern megalopolis abide in harmony with ancient temples and pavilion-roofed palaces. All that now remains of the warring dynasties of centuries past are ruins—including those of the Seoul City Wall, which make an evocative setting for a rewarding day's trek. From the crenelated walls and lookouts you'll take in the abodes of kings, such as the mighty Gyeongbokgung Palace, and pass through hilltop "moon villages" once inhabited by peasants and named for their beautiful vistas of the dark night sky.

With around 70 percent of the wall either still standing or rebuilt, the trail gives you a feel for how life in Seoul would have been in the 14th century. On the way, historic shamanist shrines and the surrounding boulder-strewn mountain landscapes echo with even more ancient history—all in striking contrast to the gleaming modern metropolis that always remains in view.

⊖ 13 MILES (21 KM)

⌢ 2,894 FT (882 M)

🕐 1 DAY (LOOP)

ELEVATION PROFILE

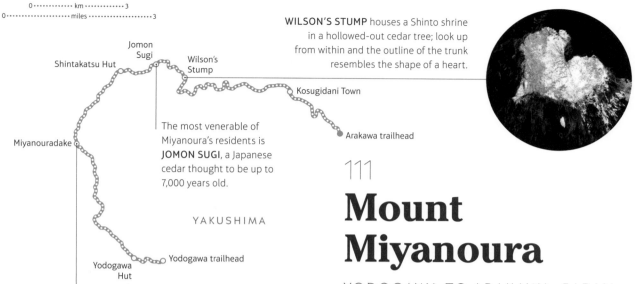

WILSON'S STUMP houses a Shinto shrine in a hollowed-out cedar tree; look up from within and the outline of the trunk resembles the shape of a heart.

The most venerable of Miyanoura's residents is **JOMON SUGI**, a Japanese cedar thought to be up to 7,000 years old.

YAKUSHIMA

The relatively gentle ascent doesn't make reaching **MIYANOURADAKE**—the mountain's summit—any less satisfying.

111
Mount Miyanoura

YODOGAWA TO ARAKAWA, JAPAN

Move through a sacred landscape of secret shrines and ethereal rock formations on this tranquil mountain trail.

13 MILES (21 KM)

2,828 FT (862 M)

2 DAYS (ONE-WAY)

In Japan's Shinto religion, mountains are considered sacred, and it's no different on the island of Yakushima. Here, the mountains are as gods, and Miyanoura, the island's highest peak, sits at the top of the pantheon.

Walk a pilgrim's path on this two-day hike, which leads to the top of the revered peak before plunging on through the lush landscape. On the way, you'll pass through primeval forests where spotted sika deer graze beside ancient cedar trees, thick with moss and gnarled with age, and where bizarre figures, naturally formed from granite, are said to resemble people and animals, frozen in time.

Nature and culture have grown together here over millennia. Red-faced Yakushima macaques peer out at you from shrines in the hollowed-out stumps of old trees, while nature has gained the upper hand over Kosugidani Town, a former logging village now being reclaimed by the forest. Sights like these do not draw you closer to nature so much as make you realize you were a part of it all along.

MAKE IT LONGER
Kuromidake

If summiting one mountain isn't enough for you, take a one-day (6-mile/10-km) detour to Kuromidake before Miyanouradake. You'll traverse crystal rivers and haul yourself up ropes toward the summit, where slabs of granite are neatly arranged, in true Japanese style, like a *mochi* cake sliced by the gods.

ELEVATION PROFILE

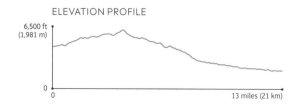

6,500 ft (1,981 m)

0

0   13 miles (21 km)

The jagged peaks of Jodogohama, along the Michinoku Coastal Trail

112

Michinoku Coastal Trail

HACHINOHE TO SOMA, JAPAN

All of life lies along the Michinoku Coastal Trail: bountiful nature, delicious food, and, in towns decimated by the 2011 tsunami, the echoes of tragedy and the embers of rebirth.

216

618 MILES (995 KM)

67,585 FT (20,600 M)

45 DAYS (ONE-WAY)

In centuries past, the Tohoku region was given the nickname "Michinoku," meaning "end of the road," due to its remoteness. Today, the area has passed on its moniker to this epic 618-mile (995 km) trail, which traces the edge of its untamed coastline.

Although the Michinoku Coastal Trail was opened only in 2019, long-distance walking in Japan is a venerable tradition going back thousands of years, often with a religious motivation. The Tohoku region in particular has drawn poetic wanderers and pious pilgrims since ancient times, and as soon as you set foot amid its wild, scenic beauty, you'll immediately see why. ▶

ELEVATION PROFILE

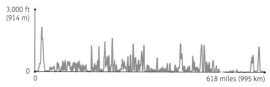

3,000 ft
(914 m)

0

0   618 miles (995 km)

Tip

The trail goes through black bear territory; though these creatures are shy, it's advisable to carry a bear bell.

Local Delicacies

One of the great joys of the trail is tasting the changing cuisine as you move down the coast. Near the start, you'll find exquisite tuna sashimi, followed by hearty seafood soup in Fukushima, and never-ending bowls of soba noodles in Iwate. Most days, you'll pass a restaurant, but always plan ahead and buy food in advance if necessary.

This is truly a land apart. Even in the modern age of mass tourism, just 2 percent of visitors make it to this northeastern corner of Honshu, Japan's main island. For long stretches of the trail, your only companions will be thick forest on one side and the Pacific Ocean, a near-endless stretch of blue, on the other.

The ocean in particular is a dominant presence, the relentless rhythms of its waves shaping not just the coastline itself but also the communities that make their homes along it. People have lived in tune with the sea here for untold centuries, from the *ama* of the Kosode Coast—female divers who have been collecting pearls by hand, with no oxygen or scuba gear, for some 2,000 years—to countless generations of fishermen hauling in seafood delicacies like abalone, sea squirts, and sea urchin.

But the ocean brings dangers as well as sustenance, as the region's recent history all too tragically attests. On March 11, 2011, the strongest earthquake ever recorded in Japan caused a catastrophic tsunami that decimated Tohoku's eastern coast, killing nearly 20,000 people, injuring thousands more, and forcing many others to abandon their homes. The cost—human, financial, and emotional—was devastating to the region and to Japan as a whole.

The Michinoku Coastal Trail offers many poignant opportunities to reflect on the effects of the disaster. Particularly moving are the remains of schools in Okawa and Arahama, now preserved as monuments, and the engraved "tsunami stones" that dot the route—such as the 10 ft (3 m) tall one in the village of Aneyoshi, which exhorts the locals never to build houses below that point.

Yet perhaps just as strongly, the trail also conveys the inspirational rebirth that followed these events; the resilience and spirit of the people forced to rebuild their shattered lives. ▶

A quiet stretch of coast near the city of Hachinohe

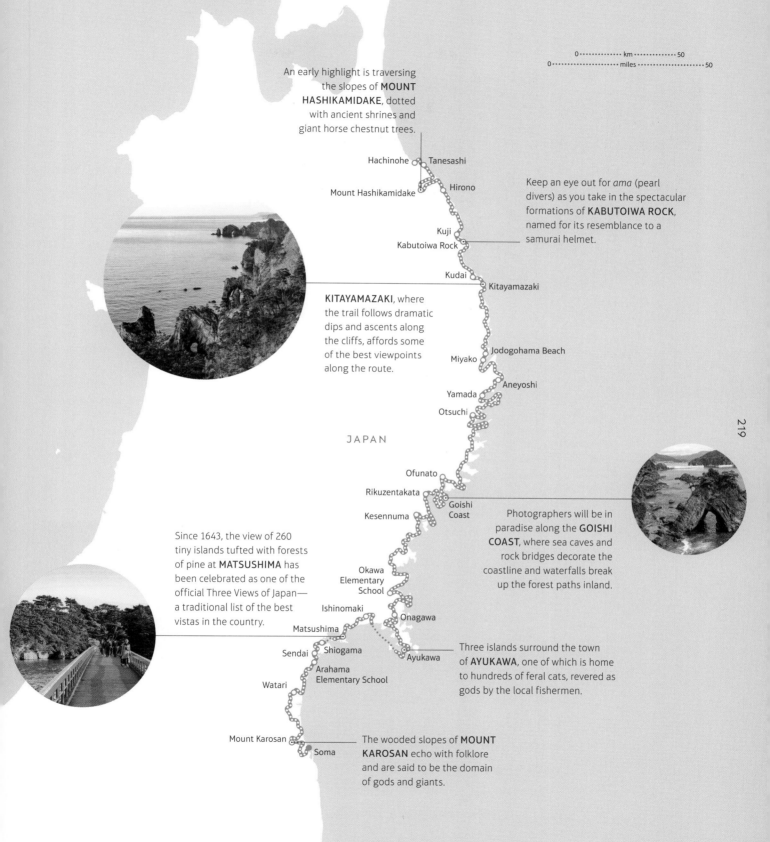

An early highlight is traversing the slopes of **MOUNT HASHIKAMIDAKE**, dotted with ancient shrines and giant horse chestnut trees.

Keep an eye out for *ama* (pearl divers) as you take in the spectacular formations of **KABUTOIWA ROCK**, named for its resemblance to a samurai helmet.

KITAYAMAZAKI, where the trail follows dramatic dips and ascents along the cliffs, affords some of the best viewpoints along the route.

Since 1643, the view of 260 tiny islands tufted with forests of pine at **MATSUSHIMA** has been celebrated as one of the official Three Views of Japan—a traditional list of the best vistas in the country.

Photographers will be in paradise along the **GOISHI COAST**, where sea caves and rock bridges decorate the coastline and waterfalls break up the forest paths inland.

Three islands surround the town of **AYUKAWA**, one of which is home to hundreds of feral cats, revered as gods by the local fishermen.

The wooded slopes of **MOUNT KAROSAN** echo with folklore and are said to be the domain of gods and giants.

Hachinohe
Tanesashi
Hirono
Mount Hashikamidake
Kuji
Kabutoiwa Rock
Kudai
Kitayamazaki
Jodogohama Beach
Miyako
Aneyoshi
Yamada
Otsuchi

JAPAN

Ofunato
Rikuzentakata
Goishi Coast
Kesennuma
Okawa Elementary School
Ishinomaki
Onagawa
Matsushima
Sendai Shiogama
Ayukawa
Arahama Elementary School
Watari
Mount Karosan
Soma

0 ········· km ········· 50
0 ········· miles ········· 50

Windswept trees standing over the golden sands of Shirahama Beach

Nature is integral to Japanese culture, both spiritually and physically, and there is a deep respect for its restorative powers. It's apt, then, that the Michinoku Coastal Trail spends much of its length immersed in Tohoku's wildly beautiful scenery. As soon as you leave the city of Hachinohe, you're plunged into the coastal meadows of Nakasuka, a riot of yellow and purple wildflowers, and the "singing sands" of Osuka Beach, which squeak tunefully with your every step. Natural beauty of a quieter kind awaits along the woodland trails of Tanesashi, lined with Mongolian oak and giant Japanese red pines, while further down the coast, at Shiofukiana, a spectacular blowhole spurts seawater 98 ft (30 m) into the air from an opening in a cave. Even more eye-catchingly at nearby Jodogohama, a row of towering shark's-tooth mountains shatters the surface of the sea, as if transplanted from the Japanese Alps or ripped from the mouth of some leviathan beneath the waves.

The towns you pass through blend past and present, with daily life carrying quietly on. Farmers' markets overflow with the seasonal bounty of the water and the land—strawberries, salmon, cherries—and atmospheric *ryokan* (inns) welcome weary hikers with traditional hospitality and warming food. Many *ryokan* are attached to *onsen* (bathhouses), a beloved pillar of Japanese life—and a much-needed balm for your tired feet. The town of Onagawa, around three-quarters of the way along the trail, offers the unusual opportunity to visit an *onsen* within

> As soon as you leave the city of Hachinohe, you're plunged into the coastal meadows of Nakasuka, a riot of yellow and purple wildflowers, and the "singing sands" of Osuka Beach.

One of the shrines found along the Michinoku Coastal Trail

a railroad station, where you can soak away any lingering aches and pains in the natural thermal waters.

After passing through Sendai, Tohoku's largest city, the trail eventually leads to Soma. This coastal city was badly affected by the 2011 tsunami and is home to a memorial hall that exhibits photographs of the region before and after the disaster. Miraculously, the nearby Tsu-jinja Shrine emerged unscathed from the earthquake that caused the tsunami—as well as two previous catastrophic earthquakes in 869 and 1611. It's a testament to Tohoku's resilience in the face of tragedy and a symbol that life here will continue to go on.

MAKE IT SHORTER
Pick a Section
Not everyone has the time or inclination to spend over a month walking the whole trail, but happily it's easy to do it in shorter sections. For the best coastal scenery, choose the North to Central Miyako Section (8 miles/13 km), and for wildlife go for the Ishinomaki South Oshika Peninsula Section (7 miles/12 km).

Looking over the islands of Matsushima from Mount Otakamori

114 ⊙

AUSTRALIA

113 ⊙

AUSTRALASIA

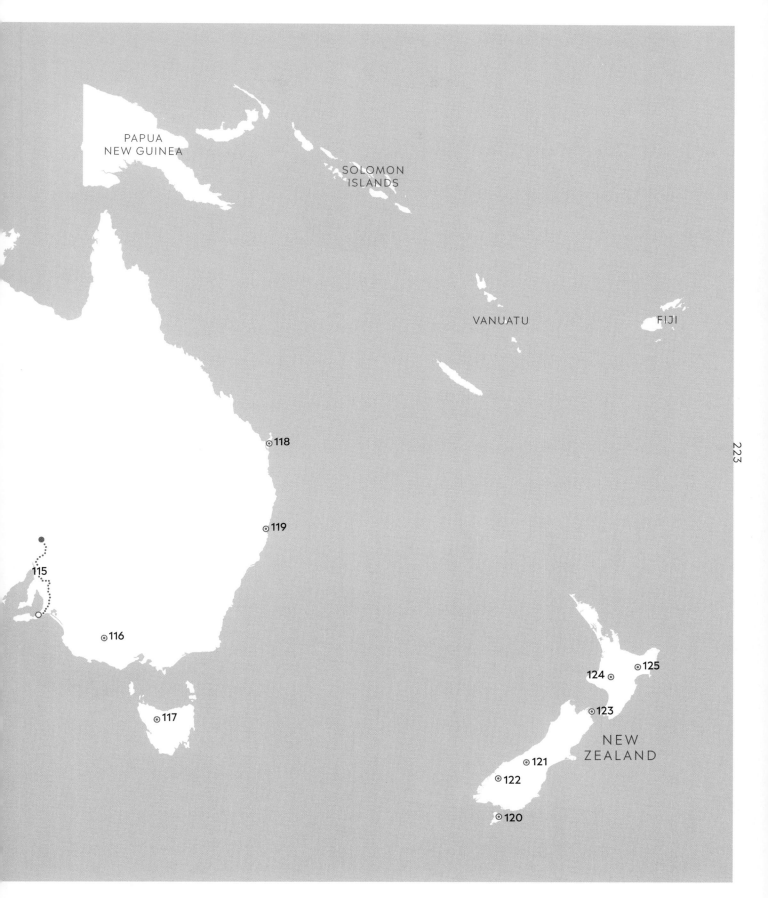

PAPUA
NEW GUINEA

SOLOMON
ISLANDS

VANUATU

FIJI

⊙ 118

⊙ 119

115

⊙ 116

⊙ 117

124 ⊙   ⊙ 125

⊙ 123

NEW
ZEALAND

⊙ 121

⊙ 122

⊙ 120

113

Cape to Cape

CAPE NATURALISTE TO CAPE LEEUWIN, AUSTRALIA

Traverse the scenic Margaret River Region on a coastal bushwalk that hugs the glittering waters of the Indian Ocean.

There's a satisfying symmetry to starting your hike at one lighthouse perched on the edge of a promontory and ending it, nearly a week later, at another. But the rest of this ramble along the coastline of Western Australia's beautiful Margaret River Region is wild and wonderfully varied.

The trail weaves along old 4WD tracks and around lengthy curves of white-sand beach, the shoreline punctuated by limestone cliffs and granite headlands shaped by surging ocean swells and the prevailing southwesterly winds. Coastal heath, springy with pink pimelea and blue fan-flowers, changes to woodland as you move over the Leeuwin-Naturaliste Ridge, with needlelike sheoak trees giving way to lofty karri forests as the trail continues south. Purple-crowned lorikeets and red-tailed black cockatoos are your regular (and noisy) companions, and you may even spot one of the region's magnificently named mammals, such as the ratlike quenda or the catlike chuditch. Throughout it all, the shimmering, cobalt-colored Indian Ocean is an eye-catching, ever-faithful presence on your right.

- ⊖ 79 MILES (127 KM)
- ⊘ 7,277 FT (2,218 M)
- ◷ 6 DAYS (ONE-WAY)

ELEVATION PROFILE

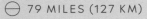

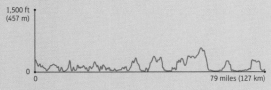

1,500 ft (457 m)

0

0 — 79 miles (127 km)

224

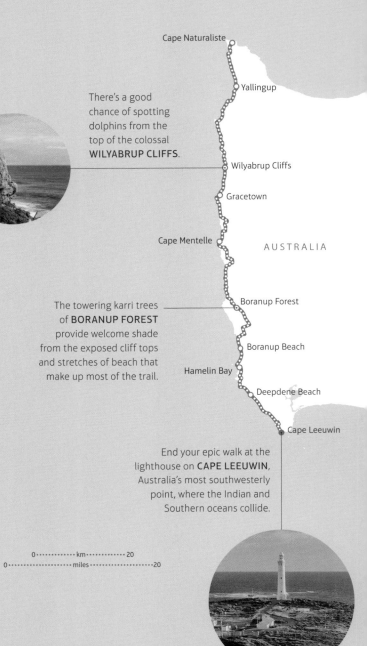

There's a good chance of spotting dolphins from the top of the colossal **WILYABRUP CLIFFS**.

Cape Naturaliste

Yallingup

Wilyabrup Cliffs

Gracetown

Cape Mentelle

AUSTRALIA

The towering karri trees of **BORANUP FOREST** provide welcome shade from the exposed cliff tops and stretches of beach that make up most of the trail.

Boranup Forest

Boranup Beach

Hamelin Bay

Deepdene Beach

Cape Leeuwin

End your epic walk at the lighthouse on **CAPE LEEUWIN**, Australia's most southwesterly point, where the Indian and Southern oceans collide.

0 — km — 20
0 — miles — 20

MAKE IT LONGER

Away from the Track

If you can bear to leave the coast, there are several worthwhile detours from the trail. The Margaret River Region's vineyards are never far away, and the area's permeable limestone has been hollowed out into more than 100 cave systems along the ridge; try Jewel Cave, Mammoth Cave, or Ngilgi Cave.

114

Barrk Sandstone Walk

KAKADU NATIONAL PARK, AUSTRALIA

Admire World Heritage-listed Aboriginal rock art on this challenging bushwalk, which passes through one of the most breathtaking corners of Kakadu National Park.

6 MILES (10 KM) · 925 FT (282 M) · 1 DAY (LOOP)

A standout day hike in a national park full of excellent trails, the Barrk Sandstone Walk takes its name from the Bininj people's word for the male black wallaroo, a member of the kangaroo family native to the area. Looping around Burrungkuy (Nourlangie), a sandstone outlier rising above the sun-baked scrubland, this crude bush trail—marked by orange triangles—can be tricky to follow, but your efforts will be well rewarded. The route is peppered with Aboriginal rock art, some of which dates back at least 12,000 years. As you hike through the outback, wallaroos bounding through the surrounding bush and peregrine falcons wheeling in the air above, you'll encounter Anbangbang and Nanguluwur, two rock art galleries. Here, painted on the rust-red sandstone, are an array of striking depictions, including ancient spirit beings, local wildlife, and even a European ship.

A highlight of the **NANGULUWUR GALLERY** is the depiction of early contact between Aboriginal people and Europeans in the form of a two-masted sailing ship.

ELEVATION PROFILE

1,500 ft (457 m) — 0

0 ——— 6 miles (10 km)

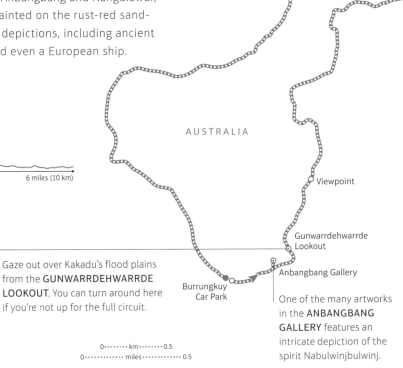

Nanguluwur Gallery

AUSTRALIA

Viewpoint

Gunwarrdehwarrde Lookout

Burrungkuy Car Park

Anbangbang Gallery

Gaze out over Kakadu's flood plains from the **GUNWARRDEHWARRDE LOOKOUT**. You can turn around here if you're not up for the full circuit.

One of the many artworks in the **ANBANGBANG GALLERY** features an intricate depiction of the spirit Nabulwinjbulwinj.

0 ···· km ···· 0.5
0 ···· miles ···· 0.5

AUSTRALASIA

A winding path through
the Ikara-Flinders
Ranges National Park

115

The Heysen Trail

CAPE JERVIS TO PARACHILNA
GORGE, AUSTRALIA

*The longest dedicated walking trail in Australia, the epic
Heysen Trail winds along dramatic sea cliffs, deserted
beaches, rolling hills, and craggy mountains before
reaching the red dust of the South Australian outback.*

693 MILES (1,116 KM)
68,094 FT (20,755 M)
2 MONTHS

To say the Heysen Trail is diverse just
doesn't do it justice. Every day brings something different: walking along a deserted
beach, scrambling through dense native
bushland, meandering through gently
undulating wine country, swimming in the
clear cascades of a waterfall, or joining the
laughter in a small-town country pub.

But don't think this all comes easy;
the trail is closed during Australia's steamy
summer months, opening most years
between April and November only. This
small window of time—plus the sheer
length of the hike and lack of water and
resources in some of the more remote
parts—means that thru-hiking the Heysen
Trail is rare. ▶

ELEVATION PROFILE

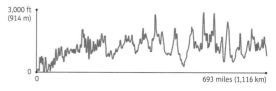

3,000 ft
(914 m)

0

0   693 miles (1,116 km)

226

Tip
The trail website
(heysentrail.asn.au) is
packed with useful trail
notes and interactive
maps of the route.

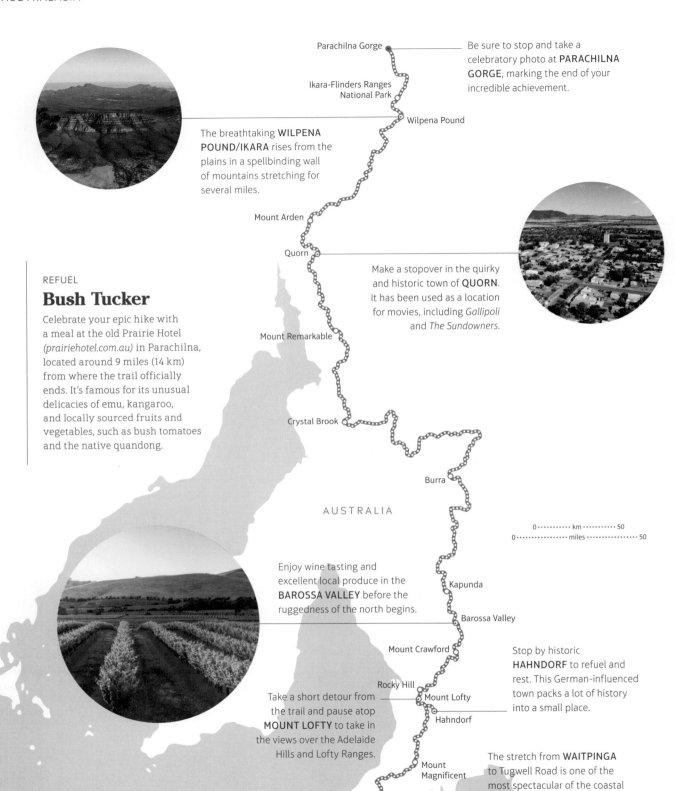

Parachilna Gorge

Be sure to stop and take a celebratory photo at **PARACHILNA GORGE**, marking the end of your incredible achievement.

Ikara-Flinders Ranges National Park

Wilpena Pound

The breathtaking **WILPENA POUND/IKARA** rises from the plains in a spellbinding wall of mountains stretching for several miles.

Mount Arden

Quorn

Make a stopover in the quirky and historic town of **QUORN**. It has been used as a location for movies, including *Gallipoli* and *The Sundowners*.

REFUEL
Bush Tucker

Celebrate your epic hike with a meal at the old Prairie Hotel *(prairiehotel.com.au)* in Parachilna, located around 9 miles (14 km) from where the trail officially ends. It's famous for its unusual delicacies of emu, kangaroo, and locally sourced fruits and vegetables, such as bush tomatoes and the native quandong.

Mount Remarkable

Crystal Brook

Burra

AUSTRALIA

0 ·········· km ·········· 50
0 ·········· miles ·········· 50

Enjoy wine tasting and excellent local produce in the **BAROSSA VALLEY** before the ruggedness of the north begins.

Kapunda

Barossa Valley

Mount Crawford

Stop by historic **HAHNDORF** to refuel and rest. This German-influenced town packs a lot of history into a small place.

Rocky Hill

Mount Lofty

Take a short detour from the trail and pause atop **MOUNT LOFTY** to take in the views over the Adelaide Hills and Lofty Ranges.

Hahndorf

Mount Magnificent

The stretch from **WAITPINGA** to Tugwell Road is one of the most spectacular of the coastal sections. Keep an eye out for whales, seals, and dolphins.

Cape Jervis

Waitpinga

228

It's an endeavor saved only for the hardiest of hikers. Those who do take on the challenge need to be fully self-sufficient and prepared to rough it. You'll need to plan ahead, ensuring you carry enough food and water and are equipped to spend your nights camping in back-to-basics bush campsites, or one of the small network of huts along the trail. (The huts are as basic as the campsites, with a sleeping platform, the odd fireplace, and—if you're lucky—a rare other hiker to keep you company.) If this all makes hiking the full 693 miles (1,116 km) sound a little daunting, rest assured that it's totally worth it. And there's always the comfort of the occasional town that provides the perfect place to refuel, stock up, and enjoy some good old small-town Aussie hospitality—and perhaps also the luxury of a shower and a comfy bed in a motel, bed-and-breakfast, or RV park.

Following the jagged spine of South Australia, most thru-hikers opt to walk south to north, from the azure ocean and golden sands of Cape Jervis to the spectacular Parachilna Gorge in the Ikara-Flinders Ranges National Park. This way around comes with an easier start on comparatively gentle terrain, before hitting the more challenging stretches of isolated semi-arid desert. Either way, you can expect the journey to take a grand total of around two months.

> When the trail eventually turns inland, the gold and turquoise hues of the coast make way for undulating green farmland and grazing pastures.

Colorful blooms in the Mount Lofty Botanic Gardens

Setting off from Cape Jervis, the well-marked trail follows sandy coastal tracks, juxtaposed with jade-green hillsides. Waves crash against the cliffs below, seals lounge on the rocks, and dolphins frolic in the waves. You can sometimes spot whales making their annual migration along the Australian coastline.

When the trail eventually turns inland, the gold and turquoise hues of the coast make way for undulating green farmland and grazing pastures, punctuated by tall forests and fields of native flowers and grass trees. Even when the trail makes its way through more urban sections, it somehow still manages to feel rural. Mount Lofty Botanic Gardens is a highlight, giving a preview of the flora you'll encounter as you continue northward. In fact, this is one of the most scenic parts of the southern section of the Heysen—standing 2,329 ft (710 m) tall, Mount Lofty is the crowning jewel of the rolling Adelaide Hills. There are some good detours to cute villages here, too, including the historic town of Hahndorf; founded by German settlers in 1838, it's now an artisan village with plenty of appealing spots to relax and refuel. ▶

The further north the trail goes, the more remote it begins to feel, but there's an opportunity for a treat or two in the iconic Barossa Valley wine region before things get too rugged. With the prospect of sipping its famous Shiraz after a long day on the trail, it's hard not to want to stay for longer. But say goodbye you must, leaving the lush vineyards of Barossa behind for scrubland and vast swathes of countryside.

Eventually—after over a month on the trail—the green landscapes slowly turn to red, a sure sign that you're about to enter the Heysen Trail's pièce de résistance: the Ikara-Flinders Ranges. With a landscape that's more than 800 million years old, walking here feels as though you're traversing the most ancient place on earth.

Days upon days are spent in this otherworldly, semi-arid landscape, a place that conjures up the barren, red-dusted

IN FOCUS
Out of this World

Comparing the Ikara-Flinders Ranges to Mars is no hyperbole. The region has been home to various Mars-related research projects thanks to its geological similarities, including fossils that are over 500 million years old. Testing was carried out here for the same technology used in NASA's Perseverance Rover, which landed on the Red Planet in early 2021.

surface of Mars. Here, you can go days without seeing anyone. Walking in solace, a familiar routine is established, with the sound of your footsteps crunching on the path bookended by the warm glow of stunning sunrises and sunsets. The rugged peaks and rocky gorges are breathtaking at every turn.

You'd be forgiven for thinking that a landscape such as the Flinders would be short of flora and fauna, but instead, it teems with native wildlife. Emus roam the plains, kangaroos and wallabies pause, silhouetted against the horizon, and eagles soar above. A fine haze of red covers the resilient scrubland, and rocky paths lead the way deeper and deeper into the mountains.

The star attraction of the range is no doubt Wilpena Pound, also known by its Adnyamathanha name of Ikara, meaning "meeting place." The towering mountains appear as if from nowhere, rising abruptly

An emu strutting through the arid foothills of the Flinders Range

Wilpena Pound/Ikara, a natural amphiteatre in Ikara-Flinders Ranges National Park

from the surface of the arid earth to form a natural amphitheater of peaks standing 11 miles (17 km) long and 5 miles (8 km) wide. The Heysen Trail's final section has been carefully devised to maximize views of this ancient and humbling site, providing a spectacular parting memory for an adventure that is all-too-soon coming to an end.

Walking the Heysen Trail is a truly once-in-a-lifetime experience and one that shows Australia's remoteness, diversity, and history in all its glory. When you finally make it to Parachilna—where the rocky peaks of the Ikara-Flinders Ranges give way to the dramatic vermillion of the outback—it is a moment that will stay with you forever.

ANOTHER WAY
Mawson Trail

If hiking the Heysen Trail sounds too time-consuming, you could always cycle the Mawson Trail instead. This 559-mile (900 km) mountain biking path follows a similar route to the walkers-only Heysen Trail but takes less than three weeks to complete.

116

Grampians Peak Trail

MOUNT ZERO PICNIC AREA TO DUNKELD, AUSTRALIA

Trace the backbone of a mountain range famed for its rugged scenery and rich Aboriginal heritage on this blockbuster multiday hike in central-western Victoria.

Fully opened in 2021, the Grampians Peak Trail is an epic journey from the tip to the tail of Grampians National Park. Supporting an abundance of traditional food sources—from wattleseed to wallaby—as well as water and shelter, the mountainous landscape here is central to the Dreaming (stories and beliefs of Creation) of the region's Aboriginal people. This area is particularly important to the local Djab Wurrung and Jardwadjali people, who know it as Gariwerd.

The craggy terrain does mean that the trail can be tough—expect plenty of steep sections. But thankfully there are state-of-the-art campgrounds to rest up in en route. There's plenty to distract from the burn in your legs, too—you'll have chance to visit at least one of the Grampians's five Aboriginal rock art sites open to the public, as well as spy some of the park's 975 plant species, many of which have long been used by Aboriginal people for their medicinal properties. Throw in lush waterfalls, spectacular lookouts, and plenty of wildlife-spotting, and it's easy to see why this is fast becoming one of Australia's most loved hikes.

- ⊖ 96 MILES (155 KM)
- ◎ 23,405 FT (7,134 M)
- ◷ 13 DAYS (ONE-WAY)

ELEVATION PROFILE

6,500 ft
(1,981 m)

0

0   96 miles (155 km)

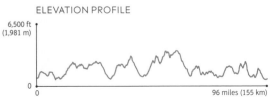

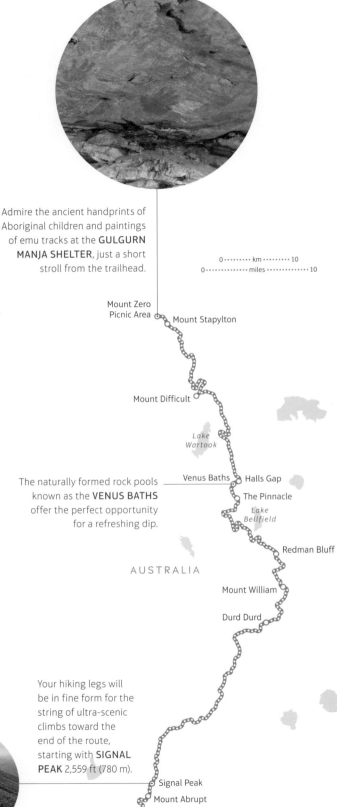

Admire the ancient handprints of Aboriginal children and paintings of emu tracks at the **GULGURN MANJA SHELTER**, just a short stroll from the trailhead.

0 ·········· km ·········· 10
0 ·········· miles ·········· 10

Mount Zero Picnic Area

Mount Stapylton

Mount Difficult

Lake Wartook

The naturally formed rock pools known as the **VENUS BATHS** offer the perfect opportunity for a refreshing dip.

Venus Baths — Halls Gap

The Pinnacle

Lake Bellfield

Redman Bluff

AUSTRALIA

Mount William

Durd Durd

Your hiking legs will be in fine form for the string of ultra-scenic climbs toward the end of the route, starting with **SIGNAL PEAK** 2,559 ft (780 m).

Signal Peak

Mount Abrupt

Dunkeld

Watch for wildlife near **RONNY CREEK**— you're likely to meet grazing wombats, Bennett's wallabies, and pademelons; if you're quiet, patient, and lucky, you might spot echidna or platypus.

Ronny Creek

Crater Falls

Lake Lilla

Crater Lake

Dove Lake

From **MARIONS LOOKOUT**, drink in panoramic views down to glistening Crater Lake and up to the shattered ridge of Cradle Mountain.

Marions Lookout

Hansons Peak

TASMANIA

117
Dove Lake-Cradle Mountain

RONNY CREEK, TASMANIA, AUSTRALIA

Conquer Tasmania's most iconic peak on a challenging but supremely scenic lake-littered hike.

9 MILES (15 KM)

2,750 FT (838 M)

1 DAY (LOOP)

With diverse landscapes and profuse wildlife, the "Apple Isle" is hikers' heaven. The heart of this paradise is Cradle Mountain-Lake St. Clair National Park, a slice of Australian wilderness laced with tempting trails. Combining a handful of these paths, this rewarding one-day circuit takes in a memorable array of glittering alpine lakes and craggy ridges.

Start out along boardwalks over button-grass moorland grazed by shambling wombats, then delve into a gully clad with lush temperate rainforest. Heading on, you'll pass by the sparkling waters of Crater Lake and Kathleens Pool, before reaching the foot of Cradle Mountain. At 5,069 ft (1,545 m), it's not the island's loftiest summit—but it is the most dramatic and photogenic. The ascent is a testing scramble over gargantuan boulders, rewarded with far-reaching vistas across the alpine wilderness. Return above the east shore of Dove Lake, home to prickly echidnas, and pause at the northern end to glimpse Cradle's scalloped peak reflected in Tasmania's most perfect tarn.

Cradle Mountain

Make the vertiginous ascent over the boulders lining the flanks of **CRADLE MOUNTAIN** to conquer the summit and enjoy far-reaching vistas across its namesake national park.

233

ELEVATION PROFILE

6,500 ft (1,981 m)

0

0   9 miles (15 km)

MAKE IT LONGER
Overland Track

This circuit includes part of the first leg of the Overland Track, a 40-mile (65 km), six-day trek from Cradle Valley to Lake St. Clair, traversing high alpine moorland.

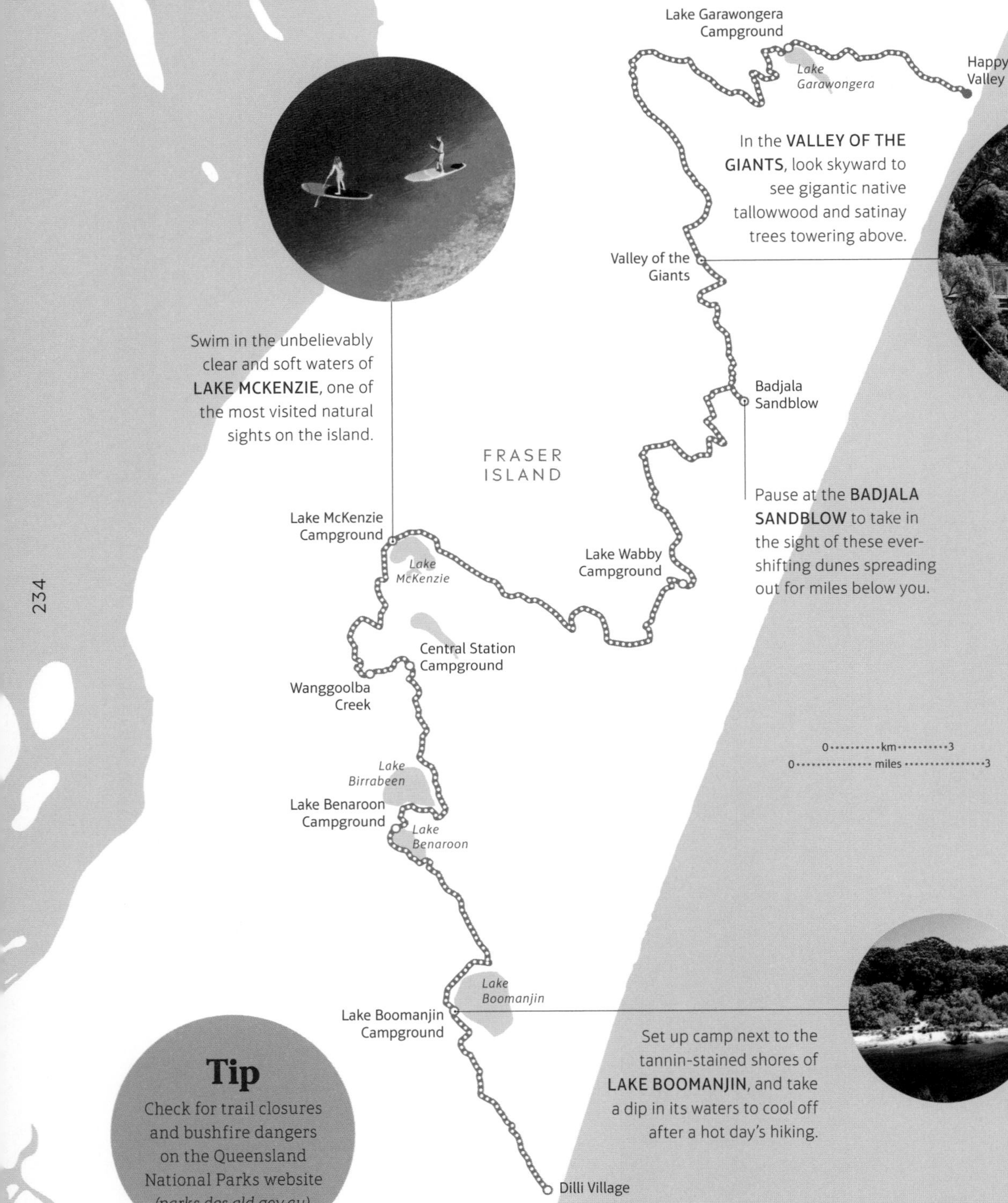

Lake Garawongera
Campground

*Lake
Garawongera*

Happy
Valley

In the **VALLEY OF THE
GIANTS**, look skyward to
see gigantic native
tallowwood and satinay
trees towering above.

Valley of the
Giants

Badjala
Sandblow

Swim in the unbelievably
clear and soft waters of
LAKE MCKENZIE, one of
the most visited natural
sights on the island.

FRASER
ISLAND

Pause at the **BADJALA
SANDBLOW** to take in
the sight of these ever-
shifting dunes spreading
out for miles below you.

Lake McKenzie
Campground

*Lake
McKenzie*

Lake Wabby
Campground

Central Station
Campground

Wanggoolba
Creek

*Lake
Birrabeen*

Lake Benaroon
Campground

*Lake
Benaroon*

0 ·········· km ·········· 3
0 ·········· miles ·········· 3

Lake Boomanjin
Campground

*Lake
Boomanjin*

Set up camp next to the
tannin-stained shores of
LAKE BOOMANJIN, and take
a dip in its waters to cool off
after a hot day's hiking.

234

Tip

Check for trail closures
and bushfire dangers
on the Queensland
National Parks website
(*parks.des.qld.gov.au*).

Dilli Village

118

K'gari (Fraser Island) Great Walk

DILLI VILLAGE TO HAPPY VALLEY,
FRASER ISLAND, AUSTRALIA

Discover the meaning of paradise as you explore 1,000-year-old rainforests, scale giant dunes, and swim in sparkling inland lakes on a remote hike across the world's largest sand island.

45 MILES (72 KM)

5,351 FT (1,631 M)

5–7 DAYS (ONE-WAY)

Stretching 76 miles (123 km) long and 14 miles (22 km) wide, Fraser Island is the world's largest sand island and part of the Great Sandy National Park in Queensland. It's known as K'gari (paradise) by the Indigenous Butchulla people, and—with its pristine beaches, clear freshwater lakes, vast dunes, and lush rainforests—it's little wonder.

Zigzagging through an eastern slice of this idyllic island is the multiday K'gari (Fraser Island) Great Walk. While the route itself isn't particularly difficult in terms of terrain and ascent, its remote nature means it can be challenging. There are no restaurants or hotels en route, so you'll need to be fully self-sufficient, carrying both a tent and supplies with you. It can be tough and you'll have to rough it—but the island's stunning, diverse scenery will more than make up for any hardship.

The walk starts near the 75 Mile Beach Highway, a seemingly never-ending stretch of golden sand; here, 4WD enthusiasts zoom along the sandy shore, while scenic flights glide above. The route doesn't linger here for long, however—you'll quickly leave the coast behind, heading deep into the interior, far away from where the tourists play.

From here, the route follows a mixture of traditional Butchulla pathways and old logging roads, winding through some truly diverse landscapes that are all the more surprising for an island made of sand. ▶

ELEVATION PROFILE

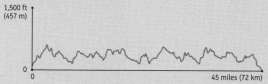

1,500 ft (457 m)

0

0   45 miles (72 km)

IN FOCUS

An Island of Many Names

The island's original name was K'gari, given to it by the Indigenous Butchulla people who occupied the land for over 5,500 years. Following the arrival of Europeans, it was briefly known as the Great Sandy Island (for obvious reasons) before being renamed Fraser Island in the 19th century, after Eliza Fraser, who was shipwrecked here in 1836.

Left Towering satinay trees in the rainforest on K'gari (Fraser Island)

One day you'll be ascending steep forested ridges, emerging from the trees to find astounding views across miles upon miles of desertlike dunes, wild waves crashing against them in the distance. The next, you'll tread softly along wooden board-walks beside fern-lined creeks, such as Wanggoolba, whose waters are so clear they're almost invisible. And to end, you'll pass through the Valley of the Giants, deep in the heart of the island, in the company of towering, 10 ft (6 m) wide, 1,000-year-old satinay trees.

All along the route, you'll encounter beautiful freshwater lakes that cry out for you to take a dip

All along the route, you'll encounter beautiful freshwater lakes that cry out for you to take a dip (the weather here can get hot, hot, hot). First comes the tannin-stained Lake Boomanjin, tinged a reddish-brown from the surrounding tea trees, and midway along the route lies the unspoiled white sand and turquoise waters of ever-popular Lake McKenzie and the emerald-green Lake Wabby, fringed by the golden Hammerstone Sandblow. At the latter lake, the dunes are slowly encroaching on the water—it's likely that a hundred years from now, the lake will have ceased to exist.

If you're lucky you may even meet some of K'gari's furry and feathered friends as you make your way north. The island is home to some iconic Australian wildlife, including kangaroos, wallabies, and hundreds of species of native birds.

But perhaps the most iconic of them all is the dingo—these beautiful yet unpredictable wild dogs roam across the island, foraging through the dunes and relaxing in the shade of the rainforest. Listen at dawn and dusk to hear their wolflike howls echoing across the island.

Each night, as evening descends, you'll pitch your tent in basic bush campsites (book in advance) with nothing but the clear, star-studded skies above you. And every morning, you'll wake to the sounds of native birdsong filling the air. Eventually, the hike wends its way back to the coast, finishing in the aptly named Happy Valley. This cheerful seaside village offers a quaint selection of hotels, restaurants, and retreats, as well as beautiful ocean views— making it the perfect place to put your feet up after your intrepid hike.

Center Lake Wabby, fringed by the golden Hammerstone Sandblow

Right One of the many wild dingos that inhabit the island

MAKE IT SHORTER
Lake Birrabeen Loop

If you don't fancy tackling the whole route, try the 8-mile (13-km) round-trip hike from Central Station, once the center of the island's forestry industry, to Lake Birrabeen. The trail winds through dense native forest and skirts around deep-blue Lake Jennings, before emerging onto the white-sand shore of Lake Birrabeen.

119

Solitary Islands Coastal Walk

RED ROCK TO SAWTELL, AUSTRALIA

Linking a string of golden beaches, wildlife-rich nature reserves, and historical and cultural sites on the east coast of New South Wales, this seaside trail also serves up superb coastal views aplenty.

35 MILES (57 KM)

1,647 FT (502 M)

3–4 DAYS (ONE-WAY)

238

The warm waters of the East Australian Current meet the cool, temperate waters of the Tasman Sea in Solitary Islands Marine Park, bringing together a cornucopia of marine life. Surfing dolphins, migrating whales, and dive-bombing seabirds are just some of the highlights on the Solitary Islands Coastal Walk, which traces a beautiful and culturally significant stretch of the New South Wales coast.

Located on the traditional lands of the Gumbaynggir Aboriginal people, this relatively easy 35-mile (57 km) trail can be comfortably navigated (usually north to south) over four days. There's natural beauty in abundance here, including gorgeous soft-sand beaches, windswept craggy headlands, and pockets of lush subtropical rainforest. Feel the sun on your back and the salty sea spray on your skin as you meander through these diverse coastal landscapes, pausing to admire native wildlife such as ospreys and eastern gray kangaroos. If you bring binoculars, you might even be able to spy white-bellied sea eagles swooping around the trail's namesake islands, found just off the coast.

But it's not just nature that astounds here—the trail also brims with rich Aboriginal history. Keep your eyes peeled for a variety of cultural artifacts, especially middens: these ancient piles of shell and bone are a reminder of great feasts once enjoyed by the Gumbaynggir people. At Corindi Beach, you can step off the trail to learn more about local Aboriginal history and culture at the Yarrawarra Aboriginal Cultural Centre, while on the route itself numerous information panels provide details about the area's Aboriginal connections. You'll also spy glimpses of the coast's storied European history, too. At Woolgoolga Beach, look out for the bones of the 128 ft (39 m) long wreck of the *Buster*, a vessel that washed up in 1893. And at Moonee Beach, learn about the pioneering Dammerel family, who operated the lighthouse on South Solitary Island for 40 years from 1884. By the time you reach Sawtell, at the trail's end, your own tale will be ready to add to the archives.

ELEVATION PROFILE

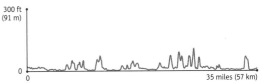

300 ft (91 m)

0

0

35 miles (57 km)

Aim to pass the village of **ARRAWARRA** at low tide, where Aboriginal fish traps used by the Gumbaynggir people can be seen on the northern side of the headland.

Make time to stop at the Yarrawarra Aboriginal Cultural Centre at **CORINDI BEACH** to learn about the history and culture of the Gumbaynggir people.

WOOLGOOLGA HEADLAND offers the best vantage point for spotting migrating humpback whales between May and October. Bring binoculars for a close-up view of the theatrics.

Admire eastern gray kangaroos grazing at **LOOK AT ME NOW HEADLAND** in Moonee Beach Nature Reserve as native raptors patrol the skies above.

Between August and April, thousands of wedge-tailed shearwaters (muttonbirds) can be seen nesting on **MUTTONBIRD ISLAND**, connected to Coffs Harbour by a breakwater.

REFUEL

The Hilltop Store

Top off your journey with a memorable lunch at The Hilltop Store in Sawtell (*thehilltopstore.com.au*). The culinary lovechild of top former Sydney chefs Carla Jones and Richie Dolan, the buzzing venue serves refined café fare in a beautifully restored general store.

Red Rock
Corindi Beach
Arrawarra
Woolgoolga Headland
Woolgoolga
Emerald Beach
Look at Me Now Headland

AUSTRALIA

Sapphire Beach
Coffs Harbour
Muttonbird Island
Boambee Beach
Sawtell

0 ·······km······· 5
0 ·······miles······· 5

239

120
Rakiura Track

LEE BAY TO FERN GULLY ROAD, RAKIURA/
STEWART ISLAND, NEW ZEALAND

*Catch a glimpse of the rare native kiwi, or the even more elusive
Southern Lights, on one of New Zealand's more remote outposts—
Rakiura/Stewart Island.*

The idyllic coastline of
Rakiura/Stewart Island
from the Rakiura Track

Looping around Rakiura/Stewart Island,
an untouched wilderness off the southern
coast of New Zealand, is the 17-mile (27 km)
Rakiura Track. On this trail, your days are
filled with easy walking along golden
beaches and through the dappled shadows
of native trees, surrounded by lilting
birdsong and little else.

Not all of the fun takes place during
the day, though—in fact, it's after sunset
that the track truly comes
alive. The island is an
International Dark Sky
Sanctuary, and at night the heavens
shimmer with millions of stars. You may
even glimpse the magical glow of the
Aurora Australis (Southern Lights) dancing
across the horizon.

Nighttime is also the best opportunity
for an encounter with the nocturnal kiwi,
one of the country's rarest birds. While
stargazing at each hut or campsite, make
sure to listen for its piercing cry from the
forest. Despite being nicknamed Kiwis,
many New Zealanders haven't glimpsed
this elusive bird—fingers crossed you
get lucky.

240

ELEVATION PROFILE

1,500 ft
(457 m)

0

0   17 miles (27 km)

⊖ 17 MILES (27 KM)

⊗ 2,930 FT (893 M)

🕐 3 DAYS (ONE-WAY)

Tip
To maximize your
chances of seeing a kiwi,
stay quiet, use a flash-
light with a red light,
and follow their ear-
piercing cry.

Head out searching for the
rare native kiwi in the bush
around **NORTH ARM HUT**
(or Port William)—after
dusk and before sunrise are
the best times to spot one.

If it's warm enough,
revive your tired limbs by
swimming in the ocean at
the beautiful white-sand
MĀORI BEACH, encircled
by regenerating forest.

Māori
Beach

Lee Bay

At **LEE BAY**, a chain-link sculpture
refers to the Māori myth of Rakiura/
Stewart Island being the anchor
stone for the *waka* (canoe)
of the demigod Māui.

RAKIURA/
STEWART
ISLAND

North
Arm Hut

Fern Gully
Road

0 ···········km··········· 1.5
0 ···········miles··········· 1.5

121

Hooker Valley Track

AORAKI/MOUNT COOK NATIONAL PARK, NEW ZEALAND

Take a stroll through some of New Zealand's most dramatic landscapes for views of the country's tallest peak, the mighty Aoraki/Mount Cook.

6 MILES (10 KM)
580 FT (177 M)
0.5 DAYS (RETURN)

The Hooker Valley Track is famed as one of New Zealand's most spectacular day hikes, and it's clear why—this flat, easy track leads you on a journey into the very heart of the Southern Alps. It can make even the youngest or most timid rambler feel like an intrepid adventurer, crossing swing bridges, tracing alpine streams, and staring up at the imposing peaks and creaking glaciers.

In late spring and early summer, the valley floor is peppered with impressive white buttercups, while in winter, snow and ice turn the landscape into a winter wonderland. Regardless of the season, aim to arrive at Hooker Lake for sunset (remember to pack a headlamp for the way back). Watching the last of the sun's light turn Aoraki/Mount Cook's southern face spectacular shades of gold and pink is about as picture perfect as New Zealand gets.

ELEVATION PROFILE

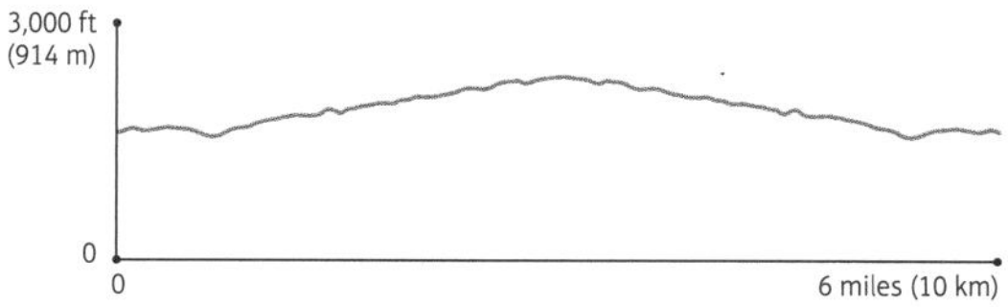

At the end of the track lies the beautiful **HOOKER LAKE**, nestled beneath the towering peak of Aoraki/Mount Cook.

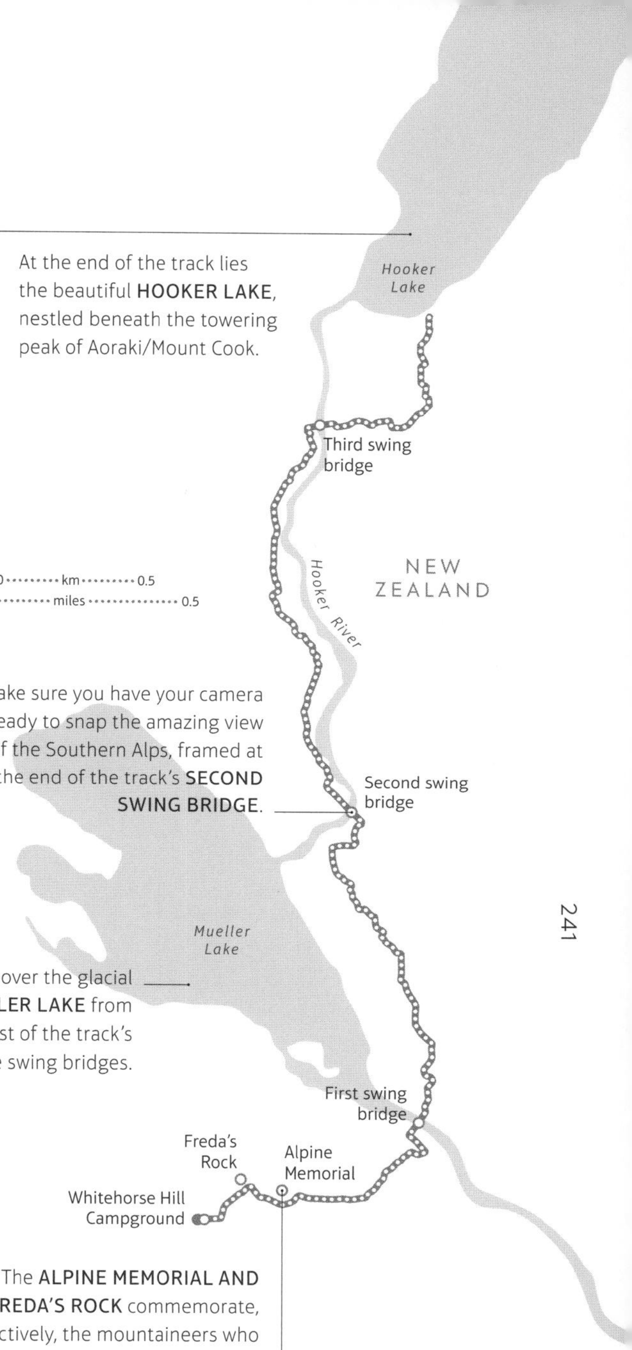

Make sure you have your camera ready to snap the amazing view of the Southern Alps, framed at the end of the track's **SECOND SWING BRIDGE**.

Gaze over the glacial **MUELLER LAKE** from the first of the track's three swing bridges.

The **ALPINE MEMORIAL AND FREDA'S ROCK** commemorate, respectively, the mountaineers who have lost their lives in the park, and the first woman to ever climb Aoraki/Mount Cook in 1910.

122

Milford Track

GLADE WHARF TO SANDFLY POINT, NEW ZEALAND

Taking in mist-shrouded mountains, glacier-carved fjords, and dense, emerald forests, this world-famous route offers up some of the South Island's most spectacular scenery.

Tip

Book early: facilities are open only from October to April and just 40 people per day may start the track.

33 MILES (54 KM)

4,718 FT (1,438 M)

4 DAYS (ONE-WAY)

242

The Milford Track was named as "the finest walk in the world" by *The Spectator* magazine back in 1908—a claim that still holds true today, over 100 years later. One of New Zealand's "Great Walks," this well-marked, multiday route serves up beautiful landscapes in spades as it takes you on a journey into the heart of the remote Fiordland National Park.

One thing to note before you head off: at some point, it'll probably rain, so make sure you pack your waterproofs. Fiordland is, after all, one of the wettest regions in the world. Luckily, the wet weather only adds to the dramatic scenery, shrouding the endless peaks in mist, giving life to the lush rainforests, and powering the waterfalls that engrave their way through the wild, imposing mountainscape. There's no need to worry about soggy tents, either— camping isn't allowed on the Milford Track, and so nights are spent in the warm and comfortable, if basic, huts that dot the route.

ELEVATION PROFILE

5,000 ft
(1,524 m)

0

0   33 miles (54 km)

Hiking through the verdant rainforest that surrounds the Milford Track

The journey begins with a boat trip across the clear waters of Lake Te Anau. From a simple wooden jetty, the track disappears into a damp, mossy forest rich in plantlife; here, red and silver beech trees stand tall over an understory of sturdy ferns. This first section follows gravel paths and wooden boardwalks across relatively flat ground, so the going isn't too tough. Eventually, though, the trail begins to ascend, becoming rockier, narrower, and steeper as you climb. The landscape changes, too, with dense forest giving way to an alpine carpet of wiry grass and bright mountain daisies and buttercups. Ascending toward MacKinnon

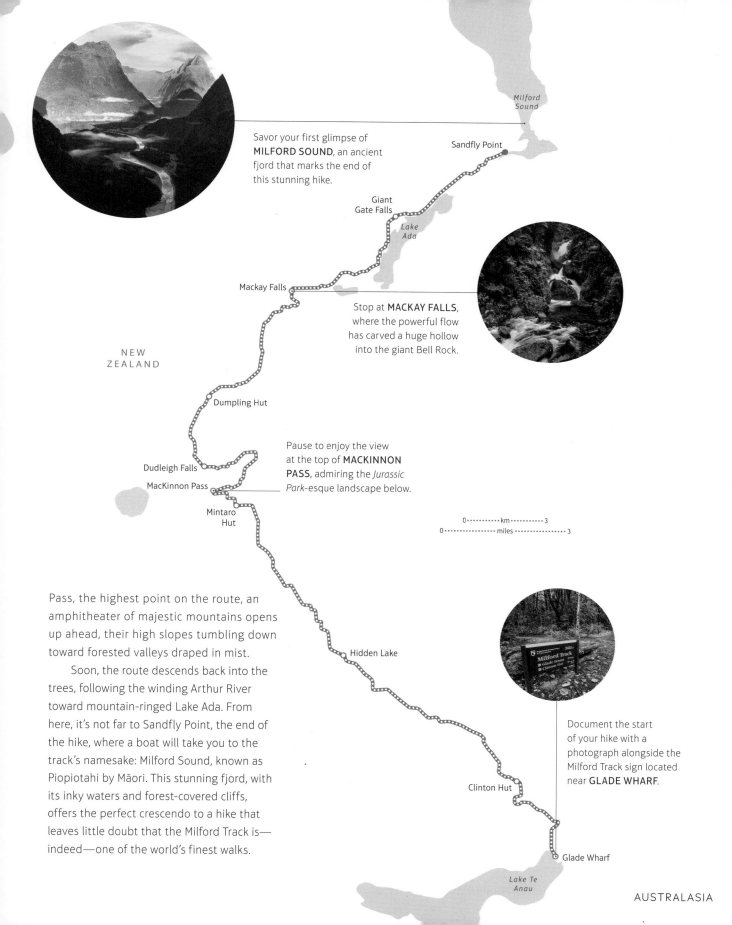

Savor your first glimpse of **MILFORD SOUND**, an ancient fjord that marks the end of this stunning hike.

Milford Sound

Sandfly Point

Giant Gate Falls

Lake Ada

Mackay Falls

Stop at **MACKAY FALLS**, where the powerful flow has carved a huge hollow into the giant Bell Rock.

NEW ZEALAND

Dumpling Hut

Dudleigh Falls

Pause to enjoy the view at the top of **MACKINNON PASS**, admiring the *Jurassic Park*-esque landscape below.

MacKinnon Pass

Mintaro Hut

0 ·········· km ·········· 3
0 ·········· miles ·········· 3

Pass, the highest point on the route, an amphitheater of majestic mountains opens up ahead, their high slopes tumbling down toward forested valleys draped in mist.

Soon, the route descends back into the trees, following the winding Arthur River toward mountain-ringed Lake Ada. From here, it's not far to Sandfly Point, the end of the hike, where a boat will take you to the track's namesake: Milford Sound, known as Piopiotahi by Māori. This stunning fjord, with its inky waters and forest-covered cliffs, offers the perfect crescendo to a hike that leaves little doubt that the Milford Track is—indeed—one of the world's finest walks.

Hidden Lake

Document the start of your hike with a photograph alongside the Milford Track sign located near **GLADE WHARF**.

Clinton Hut

Glade Wharf

Lake Te Anau

AUSTRALASIA

123

Queen Charlotte Track

MERETOTO/SHIP COVE TO ANAKIWA,
NEW ZEALAND

*Weave through lush coastal forest around the fractal shoreline of
the Marlborough Sounds, on a classic Kiwi trek blessed with rich
history and melodious birdlife.*

Tip

The nearest town to the
trek's start and end
points is Picton;
prebook boat transfers
at qctrack.co.nz.

43 MILES (69 KM)

9,633 FT (2,936 M)

3–4 DAYS (ONE-WAY)

244

In this epic land of fire and ice, the
Marlborough Sounds region has neither
volcanoes nor glaciers—instead, its natural
wonder is an impossibly labyrinthine coast.
The gnarled fingers of South Island's
northeasternmost extremity claw the
waters of the Cook Strait with a grasp
that's almost fractal: peninsulas shrink to
promontories to points, extending into
sounds that encompass arms, inlets, bays,
and even tinier coves. Suffice it to say that
trails don't run in straight lines here.

That's the nub of the Queen Charlotte
Track's appeal. It's not an A to B route—
more ahhh to bay, created by linking
historic bridle trails between ridge-top
lookouts and alluring little anchorages.
The fact that the start is accessible only
by boat simply adds to the charm, as does
its relative obscurity. Unlike the big-name
Great Walks dominating trekkers' bucket
lists—Milford, Routeburn, Kepler—hiker

numbers are scant, and advance booking
mostly unnecessary. That said, the route
is well endowed with places to stay and
eat; sure, you can camp, but with comely
lodges at key stops, why would you?

The track aptly starts with a boat
drop-off at Meretoto, dubbed Ship Cove
by English explorer Captain James Cook;
he anchored here during his first visit to
South Island in 1770 while HMS *Endeavour*
was overhauled and supplies replenished.
Cook's repeated visits to Meretoto over
the following years witnessed the first
sustained contact between Europeans

ELEVATION PROFILE

3,000 ft
(914 m)

0

0   43 miles (69 km)

The turquoise waters and forested edges of
Queen Charlotte Sound, viewed from the track

Pause at **PUNGA COVE**, one of the prettiest patches of shore on the trail, for a picnic or a cooling dip at the end of a day's hike.

Detour to **ONAHAU LOOKOUT**, arguably the most spectacular viewpoint on the trail, affording panoramic 360-degree vistas east and south across Queen Charlotte Sound, and west over Kenepuru Sound.

Admire the Māori *pouwhenua* (carved wooden posts) at **MERETOTO/SHIP COVE**, then delve into podocarp and broadleaved forest.

Enjoy a relaxing end to the hike through beech forest to **ANAKIWA**, before catching a water taxi to Picton—watch for playful dolphins en route.

Meretoto/
Ship Cove

Resolution
Bay

Endeavour
Inlet

Punga Cove

NEW
ZEALAND

Kenepuru
Sound

Bay of
Many
Coves

Onahau
Lookout

Torea
Bay

Blackwood
Bay

Queen
Charlotte Sound

Onahau
Bay

Anakiwa

0 ········· km ········· 3
0 ········· miles ········· 3

245

ANOTHER WAY
Nydia Track

For a shorter introduction to the beauty of the Marlborough Sounds, try the Nydia Track. This 17-mile (27 km), two-day hike between Shag Point and Duncan Bay traverses virgin forest laced with waterfalls and bustling with birds.

and Māori, mostly of the Ngāti Kuia and Rangitāne *iwi* (tribes), who had fished the bountiful waters of Tōtaranui, as they called Queen Charlotte Sound, for centuries.

The trail follows a serpentine meander west to Anakiwa via a succession of saddles and panoramic lookouts, skirting evocatively named bays: Resolution, Endeavour, Bay of Many Coves, and more. Watch (and listen) for wildlife above and below. Dusky and Hector's dolphins are among the cetaceans gliding through the sounds, while flightless weka, korimako (bellbirds), and tui scuttle and flit among trees that were already venerable when Cook arrived.

The track ends on the shore of the sound, which takes its English name from George III's wife. And certainly, this trail tracing its northern edge provides trekking fit for a queen.

124
Tongariro Alpine Crossing

TONGARIRO NATIONAL PARK,
NEW ZEALAND

Embark on a challenging day tramp through the otherworldly volcanic landscapes of New Zealand's oldest national park.

Steaming vents, ancient lava flows, and craters the color of crimson—there are times on this epic hike through Tongariro National Park when you'd be forgiven for thinking you were setting foot on Mars rather than tramping across New Zealand's North Island. This dramatic landscape was formed by a series of volcanic eruptions over 275,000 years ago—it's little wonder that Tongariro means "fire carried away" in Māori.

The area is still very much active, with the whiff of sulfur hanging in the thin air—stay on the marked track and check the latest volcanic activity before you set off. Sudden splashes of intense color bring life to the barren backdrop, including the streaked brown-and-burgundy cavity of Red Crater, the shimmering waters of Emerald Lakes, and the turquoise hue of the acidic Blue Lake. There are magnificent views to be had over Kaimanawa Forest Park, too, and, on a clear day, as far west as Mount Taranaki.

- ⊖ 12 MILES (20 KM)
- ⊘ 2,631 FT (802 M)
- ◷ 1 DAY (ONE-WAY)

ELEVATION PROFILE

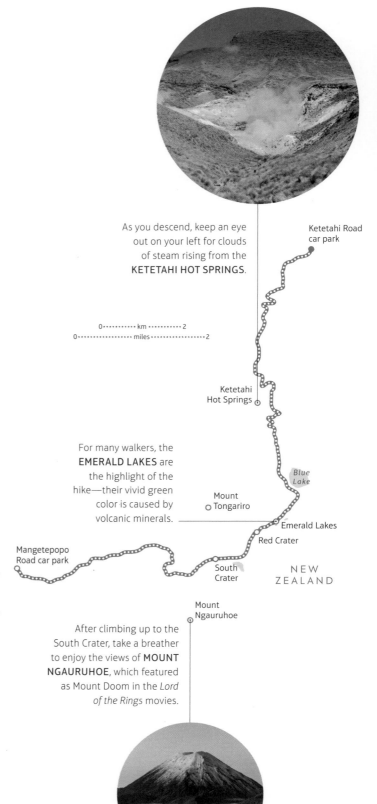

As you descend, keep an eye out on your left for clouds of steam rising from the **KETETAHI HOT SPRINGS**.

Ketetahi Road car park

0 ·········· km ·········· 2
0 ·········· miles ·········· 2

Ketetahi Hot Springs

Blue Lake

For many walkers, the **EMERALD LAKES** are the highlight of the hike—their vivid green color is caused by volcanic minerals.

Mount Tongariro

Emerald Lakes

Red Crater

Mangetepopo Road car park

South Crater

NEW ZEALAND

Mount Ngauruhoe

After climbing up to the South Crater, take a breather to enjoy the views of **MOUNT NGAURUHOE**, which featured as Mount Doom in the *Lord of the Rings* movies.

125

Lake Waikaremoana Track

ONEPOTO BAY TO HOPURUAHINE LANDING,
NEW ZEALAND

Explore the splendid shores of Lake Waikaremoana and
the unique history of the Te Urewera region and the Tūhoe
on the quietest of New Zealand's Great Walks.

29 MILES (46 KM)

5,636 FT (1,718 M)

3–4 DAYS (ONE-WAY)

The Lake Waikaremoana Track, in the Te Urewera region, is not only the most isolated of New Zealand's nine Great Walks but it is also the only one to be managed by the local *iwi* (Māori tribe)—the Tūhoe. In 2014, New Zealand made history by elevating Te Urewera to the status of personhood and giving it the legal rights of a human being. Management of the area was restored to the Tūhoe, who are recognized as the guardians of its unique fauna and flora.

Today, visitors are invited to explore this pristine region, walking along undulating ridgelines, tracing the edge of the rippling Lake Waikaremoana, and voyaging through lush rainforest full of birdsong. These wanderings become even more special come evening, when the hut wardens share stories and myths about their enchanting spiritual homeland.

The steep climb to the top of **PANEKIRE BLUFF** rewards with an unparalleled panorama of picture-perfect Lake Waikaremoana.

ELEVATION PROFILE

6,500 ft (1,981 m)

0

0

29 miles (46 km)

Hopuruahine Landing

Whanganui Hut

Waiharuru Hut

Marauti Hut

NEW ZEALAND

Lake Waikaremoana

Korokoko Falls

Panekire Bluff

Onepoto Bay

Waiopaoa Hut

Panekire Hut

Meander through the rainforest and rock-hop over streams to the beautiful **KOROKOKO FALLS**; it's a one-hour side trip that shouldn't be missed.

0 ·········· km ·········· 3
0 ·············· miles ·············· 3

The Tūhoe believe the lake has a *taniwha* (water monster), but don't let that stop you from swimming—**WAIOPAOA HUT** is perfectly located to end your day with a dip.

AUSTRALASIA

Index

Acknowledgments

Dorling Kindersley would like to thank the following authors for their words:

Julianna Barnaby is a London-based travel writer and founder of the award-winning sites The Discoveries Of and London x London. When she's not searching out London's most unusual spots, she can often be found road-tripping around remote locations—recent favorites include the Lofoten Islands and the Atacama Desert.

Pashmina Binwani is an off-beat adventurer and solo traveler, who is drawn to barren landscapes and distant communities that have relatively little contact with the modern world. Having found hiking and cycling the best way to discover them, she writes about her adventures on thegonegoat.com to inspire people to embark on experiences they might never have thought they could be part of.

Paul Bloomfield is a writer specializing in active adventures, wildlife, conservation, and history. He's hiked, cycled, kayaked, and run thousands of miles on six continents, penning travel features for newspapers, magazines, websites, and books including *The Telegraph*, *The Times*, *National Geographic Traveller*, *Wanderlust*, and *BBC Wildlife*.

Ann Marie Brown is the author of 14 travel guidebooks plus hundreds of articles that have appeared in *Sunset*, *VIA*, *Travel + Leisure*, *Islands*, *Backpacker*, *Hemispheres*, *AFAR*, *San Francisco Chronicle*, and *Los Angeles Times*. When she's not traipsing along a trail, she can be found at her home in California's Sierra Nevada Mountains.

Keith Drew, a former Managing Editor at Rough Guides, has hiked in all four corners of the globe and writes about his adventures for *The Telegraph* and *BBC Travel* among others. He is the cofounder of family-travel website Lijoma.com, a curated selection of inspirational itineraries—most including a good walk or two—to exciting destinations like California, Iceland, Morocco, and Japan.

Gabrielle Innes is a travel writer and editor. She lives in Berlin with her family but dreams always of her Melbourne home.

Anita Isalska is a freelance writer and editor based in San Francisco. Anita writes about travel, technology, and outdoor adventures, especially hiking, cycling, and winter sports. Anita specializes in France, Eastern Europe, and her adopted home, California. Read her stuff on anitaisalska.com or find her on Twitter @lunarsynthesis.

David LaHuta is a Bermuda-based travel journalist who regularly writes for *Condé Nast Traveler*, *Travel + Leisure*, and *The New York Times*, among others. When not on assignment, he enjoys boating and beachcombing near his home in Warwick, where he lives with his wife and two sons.

Jessica McKenzie is a journalist living in Brooklyn, New York. Her work has been printed in *The New York Times*, *National Geographic*, *Backpacker*, and *Grist*, among other publications. She loves backpacking, and has thru-hiked Vermont's Long Trail, the Northville-Placid Trail in New York and the Cohos Trail in New Hampshire.

Shafik Meghji is an award-winning travel writer, journalist, and author. Specializing in Latin America and South Asia, he writes for publications such as *BBC Travel* and *Wanderlust*, has coauthored more than 40 guidebooks, and talks about travel on TV, radio, and podcasts. He can be found at shafikmeghji.com and on Twitter and Instagram @ShafikMeghji.

Alice Milne is a Kiwi whose true loves are hiking and chocolate. By day, she works as a Speech Language Therapist, while on the weekends, you'll find her soaking up New Zealand's wilderness. Alice runs a hiking blog, aliceadventuring.com, to inspire others to plan and achieve their own adventures.

Roger Naylor is an Arizona-based travel writer who hikes hundreds of miles on Southwestern trails every year. He is the author of several books, including *Arizona's Scenic Roads & Hikes* and *Death Valley: Hottest Place on Earth*. He is a member of the Arizona Tourism Hall of Fame. For more information, visit rogernaylor.com.

Jabulile Ngwenya is a travel writer based in South Africa. She has traveled to 18 African countries and contributed to various international publications. Jabulile is passionate about changing the Africa travel narrative and telling unique stories about the continent's landscapes, history, and, more importantly, its people.

Brooke Nolan discovered a love of the outdoors after hiking the Inca Trail in Peru for her 30th birthday. She's been chasing adventure across the world ever since, and when she's not outdoors exploring, you'll find her putting pen to paper in her day job as a writer.

Stefanie Payne is a communications strategist supporting NASA human spaceflight at the agency's headquarters in Washington, DC. When not telling the story of human exploration in space, she writes about adventures on earth—with articles appearing in many notable digital and print publications. She has also authored multiple books about the US National Parks.

Sarah Reid is an Australian travel writer, editor, and sustainable travel expert with a passion for positive-impact global travel. A keen hiker, Sarah was named 2020 Travel Writer of the Year by the Australian Society of Travel Writers and 2020 Specialist Travel Writer of the Year at the UK's Travel Media Awards.

Chris Scaife lives on the edge of the English Lake District and spends most of his time walking, cycling, and exploring caves. He is a member of the Outdoor Writers and Photographers Guild and has a real fondness for the wild and remote parts of the world.

Regis St. Louis was born in the flatlands of the American Midwest and developed an early fascination with mountainous horizons. He's hiked countless high-elevation trails across the globe, from the Peruvian Andes to the Kamchatka Peninsula. He's also contributed to more than 100 travel guides, covering destinations on six continents. He currently lives in New Orleans.

Dan Stables is a travel writer and journalist based in Manchester. He writes for a variety of print and online publications and has authored or contributed to more than 30 travel books on destinations across Europe, Asia, and the Americas. Find his work at danielstables.co.uk, or on Twitter @DanStables.

Emma Thomson writes for the UK national newspapers and magazines and contributes to radio, podcasts, and panel events. In 2019, she was named BGTW Travel Writer of the Year. Her hikes have led her all over the world: from the Sierra Nevada de Santa Marta mountains in Colombia to a world-first expedition along Namibia's Skeleton Coast.

Peter Watson is a travel writer and founder of outdoor travel blog Atlas & Boots. A keen trekker and climber, he can usually be found on the trails of the Greater Ranges of Asia. He's visited over 80 countries and is currently focused on climbing the seven summits—the highest mountain on every continent.

Christian Williams has been a freelance travel writer since 1998, and written or co-written some 20 guidebooks, a good few travel apps, and a host of related articles for magazines, websites, and UK newspapers. He specializes in Canada, Scotland, and Germany. Even when not working, he likes to explore—usually on one of his 10 bicycles.

The publisher would like to thank the following for their kind permission to reproduce their photographs:

(Key: a-above; b-below/bottom; c-centre; f-far; l-left; r-right; t-top)

123RF.com: Galyna Andrushko 36-37, Freda Bouskoutas 189tr, Iwona Grzywaczewska 163tr

4Corners: Onlyfrance / Robert Palomba 143cl, Massimo Ripani 91br

Afil-CC BY-SA: 154tl

Alamy Stock Photo: A Room With Views 115br, AfriPics.com 176tl, AGB Photo Library 89tl, / Horst Lieber 125bc, agefotostock / James Carroll Richardson 59cb, / Javier Larrea 77crb, Alizada Studios 159bc, All Canada Photos / Barrett & MacKay 31tr, All Canada Photos / Ron Erwin 27tl, Sally Anderson 209clb, Galyna Andrushko 161bl, Dr. Wilfried Bahnmüller / imageBROKER 166clb, Andrew Bain 92br, 93cr, 93bc, Tom Bean 42cra, Holly Bickerton 121cl, Gerry Bishop 243cra, Pat & Chuck Blackley 54cla, Andriy Blokhin 60b, Ian Bottle 106-07, Kevin Britland 108bl, Jean Brooks 105cr, Chris Bull 197bl, Cavan Images 59cra, Cavan Images / Menno Boermans 135cr, Mike Cavaroc 44cla, Bonita Cheshier 53ca, CHROMORANGE / Beate Tuerk 9tr, Corbin17 182tl, Curved Light Australia 232tr, Luis Dafos 163crb, Danita Delimont 51cr, Danita Delimont Creative / Yuri Choufour 15br, DanitaDelimont / Martin Zwick 69crb, Barry Davis 62tc, DGB 119cl, Joshuah Dowell 215clb, dpa picture alliance / Britta Pedersen 127br, DPK-Photo 47cra, eFesenko 197br, Effi 176br, Michele Falzone 62cra, Lincoln Fowler 228cra, Zachary Frank 40bl, Eddie Gerald 74tc, Oliver Gerhard 236t, GFC Collection 201tr, Gil Giuglio / Hemis.fr 64cr, gotravel 111tl, 171tl, Andrew Greaves 185crb, Christopher Heil 29bl, 30-31t, Hemis.fr / Bertrand Rieger 139tr, Hemis.fr / Julien Garcia 99br, Hemis.fr / Philippe Renault 24bl, Adrian Hepworth 76tc, Louise Heusinkveld 139cla, Lukas Hodon 172bl, Holmes Garden Photos / Neil Holmes 112cla, Graham Hunt 109ca, Image Leaks 198tc, Image Professionals GmbH / Lengler, Gregor 183crb, Image Professionals GmbH / TravelCollection 127ca, imageBROKER / Marc Rasmus 129bl, imageBROKER / Martin Siepmann 160tl, imageBROKER / Matthias Graben 174tl, imageBROKER / Moritz Wolf 241tc, Jam World Images 148bl, Carolyn Jenkins 109tl, Don Johnston_EC 29crb, Jon Arnold Images Ltd / Walter Bibikow 154cra, JSK 193cr, 211cra, Kaedeenari 219bl, Wolfgang Kaehler 245cr, Joseph Khoury 190cra, Christian Kober 1 8bl, Chris LaBasco 43cr, Samer Lahoud / EyeEm 171crb, LatitudeStock / Patrick Ford 181clb, Ben Lewis 245cb, Yan Liao 210bl, Stephen Lioy 189crb, Ilene MacDonald 35cr, mauritius images GmbH / Bernd Ritschel 130bc, Gareth McCormack 97cra, 132tr, Jon Mclean 33tl, Mieneke Andeweg-van Rijn 105bl, Hugh Mitton 246tr, Raquel Mogado 80tr, Dawn Monrose 112tr, Martin Mwaura 180br, Joe Ng 21cl, Ingo Oeland 228tl, 230bl, 232bc, Edson Oliveira 85cra, Oneworld Picture / Stefan Oberhauser 184cr, Only France / Onlyfrance.fr / Robert Palomba 143tc, Only France / Onlyworld.net / David Ducoin 74crb, George Ostertag / agefotostock 43crb, Robert Palomba / Onlyfrance.fr 143cra, Panoramic Images 44crb, Panther Media GmbH 150cr, Panther Media GmbH / Ursula Perreten 199ca, Sean Pavone 221b, Marieke Peche 185tr, photocay 124br, Solveig Placier / Photononstop 220tl, 220br, Christopher Price 18cr, Prisma by Dukas Presseagentur GmbH / CCOphotostock_KMN 38cra, Prisma by Dukas Presseagentur GmbH / Frischknecht Patrick 133tr, Andreas Prott 202br, Pulsar Imagens 86bl, Random Lights Photography 224tc, Philippe Renault / hemis.fr 24tc, Lee Rentz 41cla, Robertharding / Christian Kober 72br, Robertharding / George Robertson 192b, Robertharding / Jochen Schlenker 199tr, Robertharding / Julian Elliott 140t, Robertharding / Loraine Wilson 157cb, Robertharding / Matthew Williams-Ellis 155cra, Robertharding / Rolf Richardson 211tl, David Robertson 153clb, William Robinson 229tr, Jon Rosenthal 185cla, Ellie Rothnie 134tc, Micah Rubin 55cr, Arkadij Schell 88br, Tillman Schlageter 225bl, Bernd Schunack / mauritius images GmbH 126br, Alex Segre 84clb, Igor Shtygashev 21tc, 21br, Dennis Stone / LatitudeStock 201cb, Olena Suvorova 32br, tahoelight.com / scott sady 39br, Steven Scott Taylor 119br, Alireza Teimoury 193tr, Markus Thomenius 38bl, TMI 34br, Alex Treadway / robertharding 142br, Thiago Trevisan 189cla, Anders Tukler 103b, Universal Images Group North America LLC / Jumping Rocks 247cra, Visions from Earth 76cr, Stefan Wackerhagen / imageBROKER 16br, Sebastian Wasek 114cl, 114br, Andrew Watson 233crb, 234cra, Jim West 51cb, Westend61 GmbH 144ca, 156tl, Westend61 GmbH / Markus Kapferer 129cb, Michael Wheatley 19tl, Chris Wildblood 183tl, wildnerdpix 48cr, Janusz Wrobel 73cr, Ben Young 203bc, Tomas Zavadil 67

AWL Images: Marco Bottigelli 228bl, ClickAlps 30tl, Danita Delimont Stock 231t, Niels van Gijn 180clb, ImageBROKER 27cr, Jason Langley 123cra, 166tl, 167cr, 168tl, 168cr, 168br, Richard Stanley 226-27

Anna Cochrane: 240tr

Depositphotos Inc: ericlaudonien93 63tr

Dreamstime.com: Debra Reschoff Ahearn 33br, Barmalini 121br, Tomislav Birtic 148t, Bubutu 153br, Diego Vito Cervo 148br, Rafał Cichawa 80cl, Francisco Crusat 146tl, Igor Dolgov 213tl, Cristian Duminecioiu 154crb, Andriy Dykun 128bc, Erastef 53crb, Ggw1962 29cl, Gestur Gislason 104br, Giuseppemasci 139cb, Diego Grandi 83tr, Hatzenbichler 14bl, Kristýna Henkeová 97bc, Laszlo Konya 147tc, Viktor Kovtun 159tr, Makaule 150bl, Matyas Rehak 79cl, 83cr, Saiko3p 138bl, Florian Schuetz 130cla, Jacek Sopotnicki 151tl, Ilona Titova 163c, Marc Witte 225tr

Keith Drew: 116crb, 116br

Druk Memoirs: Tshering 201tc

Frostavallen © Apelöga.: 100cra

Getty Images: Chris Bennett 61cr, Cavan Images 22, 28br, Matteo Colombo 246br, Sebastian Condrea 156cr, DigitalVision / Abstract Aerial Art 224crb, EyeEm / Igor Kondler 245tr, Feng Wei Photography 191bl, Francesco Vaninetti Photo 137, Roy Goldsberry 19cr, Manfred Gottschalk 141, Chris Griffiths 114tr, Marc Guitard 175tl, Gary Holpin / EyeEm 111tr, I love Photo and Apple. 219cla, Richard I'Anson 201cl, Markus Keller / imageBROKER 26tr, Veeravong Komalamena / EyeEm 91tc, Reimo Luck / EyeEm 98tl, Matthijs Borghgraef 122, MB Photography / Moment 237t, Moment / by Marc Guitard 179, Moment / Emad aljumah 205cr, Moment / Jamie Lamb - elusive-images.co.uk 233tl, Dmitry Naumov 244br, Nico De Pasquale Photography 42clb, Michael Nolan 69tl, NurPhoto 146br, James O'Neil / Photodisc 127tl, James Osmond / The Image Bank 2-3, Praveen P.N 196tl, Joe Daniel Price 113tr, Ketkarn sakultap 98br, Raphael Schneider 102clb, Schon 100tl, Sidney / The Image Bank 14tl, Solveig Placier / Photononstop 218br, Stone / John W Banagan 203cra, Stone / Peter Unger 236-37t, Westend61 123br, 243tl, Art Wolfe 18bl, David Woolley / Photodisc 110bl, Bruce Yuanyue Bi / The Image Bank 68cl, Tomas Zrna 68br, 97tl

iStockphoto.com: 8vFanl 125cla, a_Taiga 132clb, Alina555 84br, benedek 20br, bjdlzx / E+ 209br, DenisTangneyJr / E+ 54tr, DonFord1 65cr, Jordan Gagne 234crb, Derek Galon 65cl, gcosoveanu 47tl, George-Standen 109bc, gionnixxx 206bl, GoranQ / E+ 214tl, GordonBellPhotography 161, guenterguni / E+ 178bl, gyro 216-17, htrnr 48tc, Joel Carillet / E+ 58bl, LeManna 152tc, lightphoto 54cr, Lokibaho 38cla, Kateryna Mashkevych 200cra, PatricioHidalgoP 79tl,

Project Editors Elspeth Beidas, Rachel Laidler
Senior Designers Ben Hinks, Stuti Tiwari
Project Art Editor Bharti Karakoti
Designer Jordan Lambley
Illustrator Ben Spurrier
US Editor Jennette ElNaggar
Proofreader Kathryn Glendenning
Indexer Hilary Bird
Picture Researchers Adam Goff, Myriam Megharbi, Martin Copeland, Taiyaba Khatoon, Vagisha Pushp
Senior Cartographic Editor Casper Morris
Cartographer Ashif
Cartography Manager Suresh Kumar
Jacket Designer Ben Hinks
Jacket Picture Research Adam Goff, Ben Hinks
Senior Production Editor Jason Little
DTP Designer Rohit Rojal
Technical Prepress Manager Tom Morse
Senior Production Controller Samantha Cross
Managing Editor Hollie Teague
Managing Art Editor Bess Daly
Art Director Maxine Pedliham
Publishing Director Georgina Dee

First American Edition, 2022
Published in the United States by DK Publishing
1450 Broadway, Suite 801, New York, NY 10018

For the curious
www.dk.com

FSC MIX
Paper from responsible sources
www.fsc.org FSC™ C018179

The rapid rate at which the world is changing is constantly keeping the DK Eyewitness team on our toes. While we've worked hard to ensure that this edition of *Hike* is accurate and up-to-date, we know that trails are altered, routes can become impassable, places close, and new ones pop up in their stead. So if you notice we've got something wrong or left something out, we want to hear about it. Please get in touch at travelguides@dk.co.uk

Safety Considerations
Hikes are by their very nature potentially hazardous. All participants in such activities must assume responsibility for their own actions and safety. If you have any health problems or medical conditions, consult with your physician before starting your walk. The information contained in this book cannot replace sound judgment and good decision making, which can help reduce risk exposure, nor does the scope of this book allow for disclosure of all the potential hazards and risks involved in such activities. Neither the authors nor the publisher shall be liable or responsible for any loss or damage allegedly arising from any information or suggestion in this book. Learn as much as possible about the routes you are hiking, prepare for the unexpected, and be cautious. The reward will be a safer and more enjoyable experience.

GREENLAND

30

ICELAND
45

FAROE
ISLANDS
46

NORWAY
47

SWEDE

CANADA

3

1

4

5

2

12

22

7

9

10

8

56

57

53 U.K.
55   52
50   54
51

DENMARK
48
62   49
58
GERMANY   61
59   60

P

17

20

6

25

14

26

UNITED
STATES

24

68
FRANCE
70

66   64
67   63
65

69   ITALY

15   16

19

13

18   21

31

27
BERMUDA

23

CUBA

PORTUGAL
SPAIN

72

74

MEXICO

HAWAII

11

MADEIRA 73

MOROCCO
85

TUNISIA

CANARY
ISLANDS

71

WESTERN
SAHARA

ALGERIA

L

32

GUATEMALA

28
JAMAICA

29   DOMINICA

MAURITANIA

MALI

NIGER

NICARAGUA

COSTA RICA   33
34   PANAMA

VENEZUELA

GUYANA

SENEGAL

BURKINA
FASO

GUINEA

NIGERIA

35

COLOMBIA

SURINAM

SIERRA LEONE
86

CÔTE
D'IVOIRE

36
ECUADOR

LIBERIA

GHANA

CAMEROON

CON

PERU

BRAZIL

GABON

37

38   39

BOLIVIA

AN

40

PARAGUAY

41

43
EASTER
ISLAND

NAM

CHILE

URUGUAY

ARGENTINA

42

44